SPELL CHECKERS™

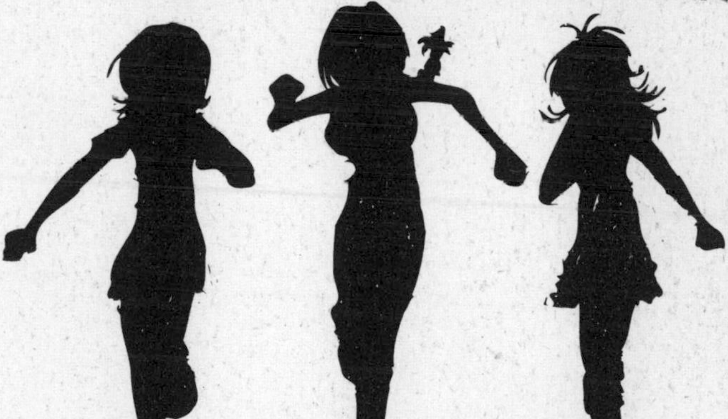

An Oni Press Publication

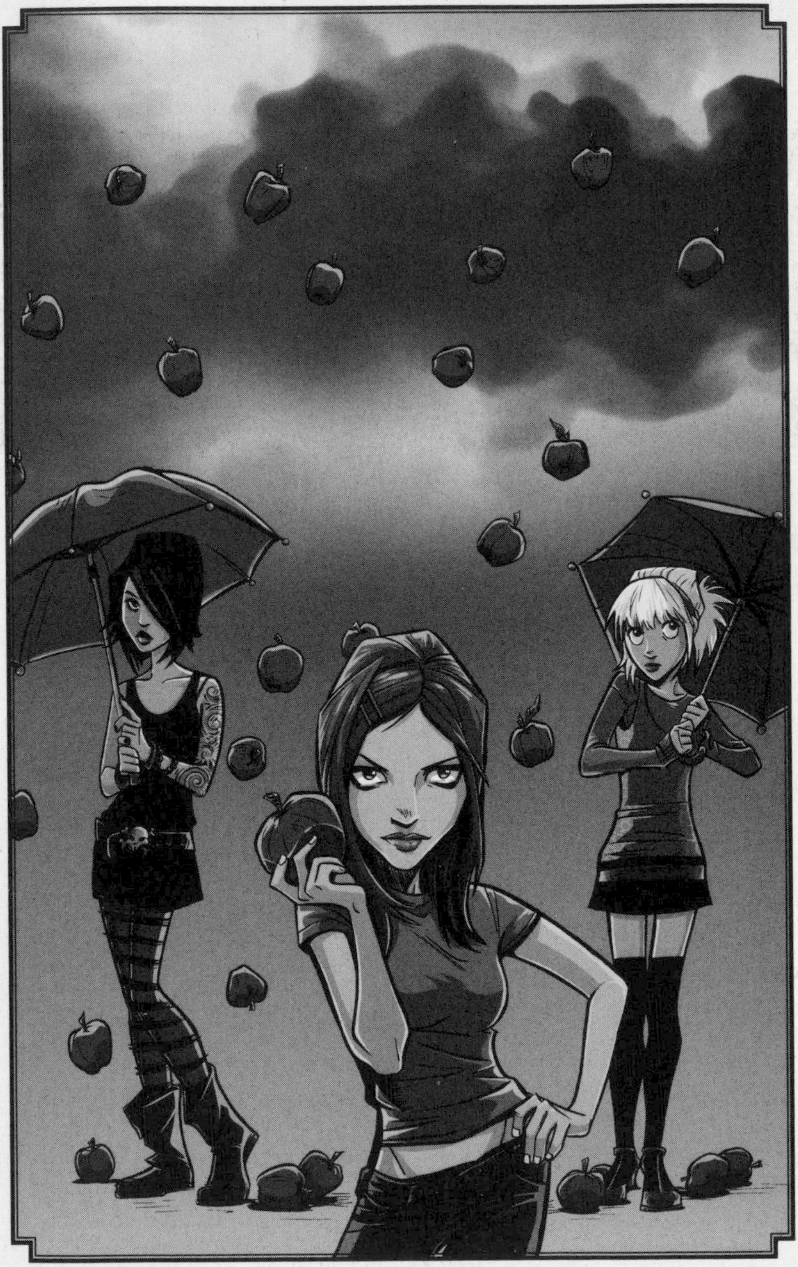

SPELL CHECKERS™

written by
JAMIE S. RICH

illustrated by
NICOLAS HITORI DE

flashbacks and cover
illustrated by
JOËLLE JONES

cover colored by
KIMBALL DAVIS

lettered by
DOUGLAS E. SHERWOOD

design by
KEITH WOOD

edited by
JILL BEATON

Oni Press, Inc.

publisher Joe Nozemack

editor in chief James Lucas Jones

marketing director Cory Casoni

art director Keith Wood

operations director George Rohac

associate editor Jill Beaton

associate editor Charlie Chu

production assistant Douglas E. Sherwood

Spell Checkers is created by Joëlle Jones and Jamie S. Rich.

Oni Press Inc.
1305 SE Martin Luther King Jr. Blvd.
Suite A
Portland, OR 97214

www.onipress.com

First Edition: April 2010
ISBN 978-1-934964-32-3

10 9 8 7 6 5 4 3 2 1

Printed in the U.S.A.

Chapter I
"Because of My Poor Education"

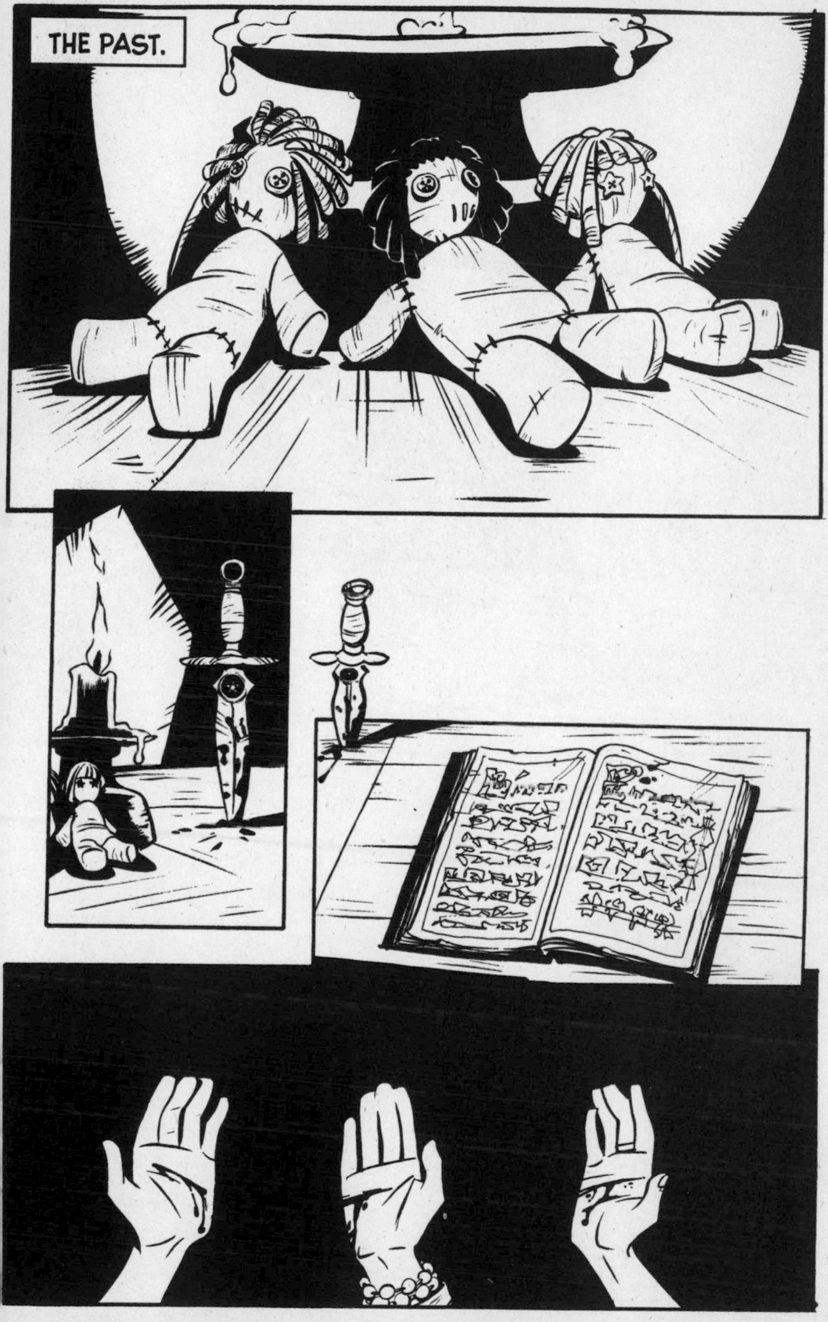
THE PAST.

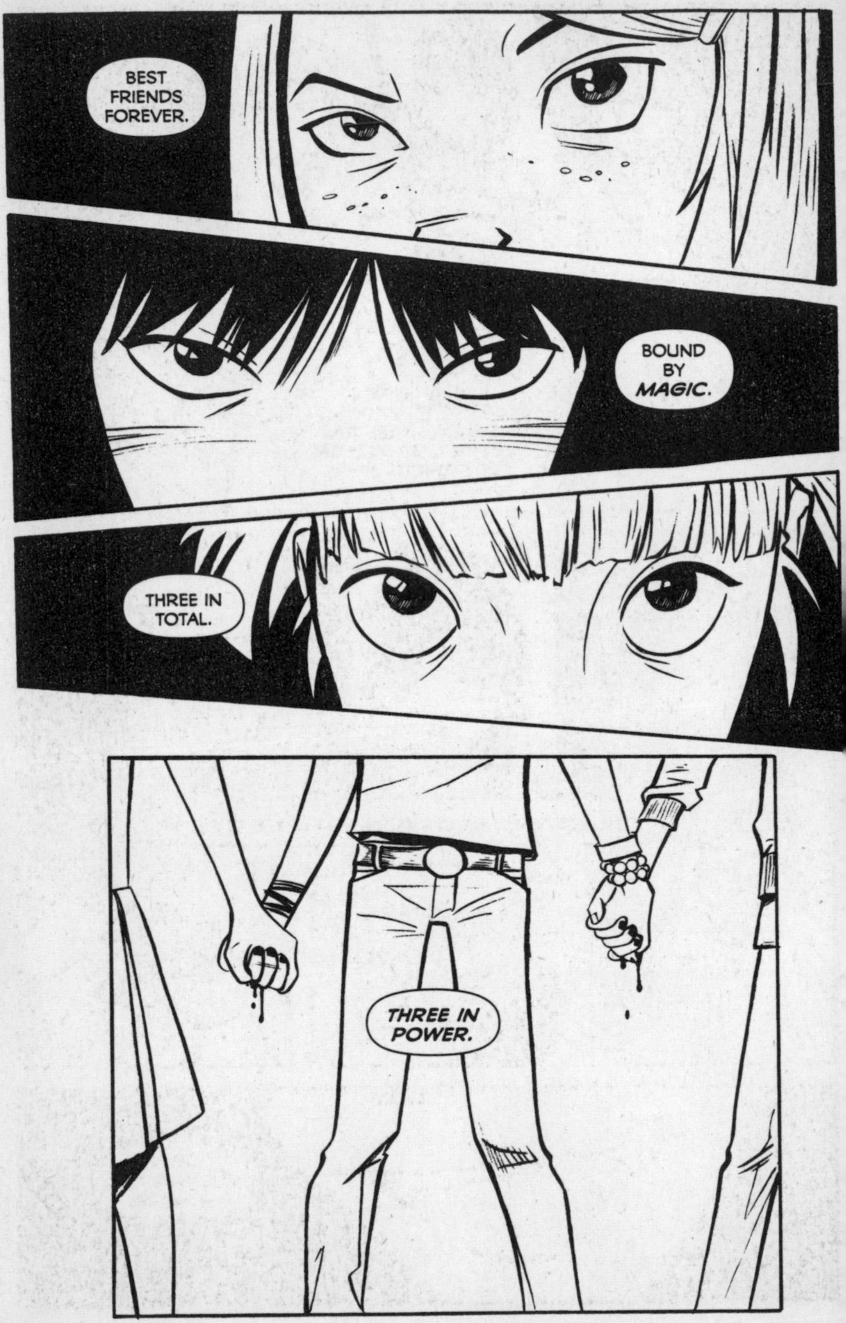
BEST FRIENDS FOREVER.
BOUND BY *MAGIC.*
THREE IN TOTAL.
THREE IN POWER.

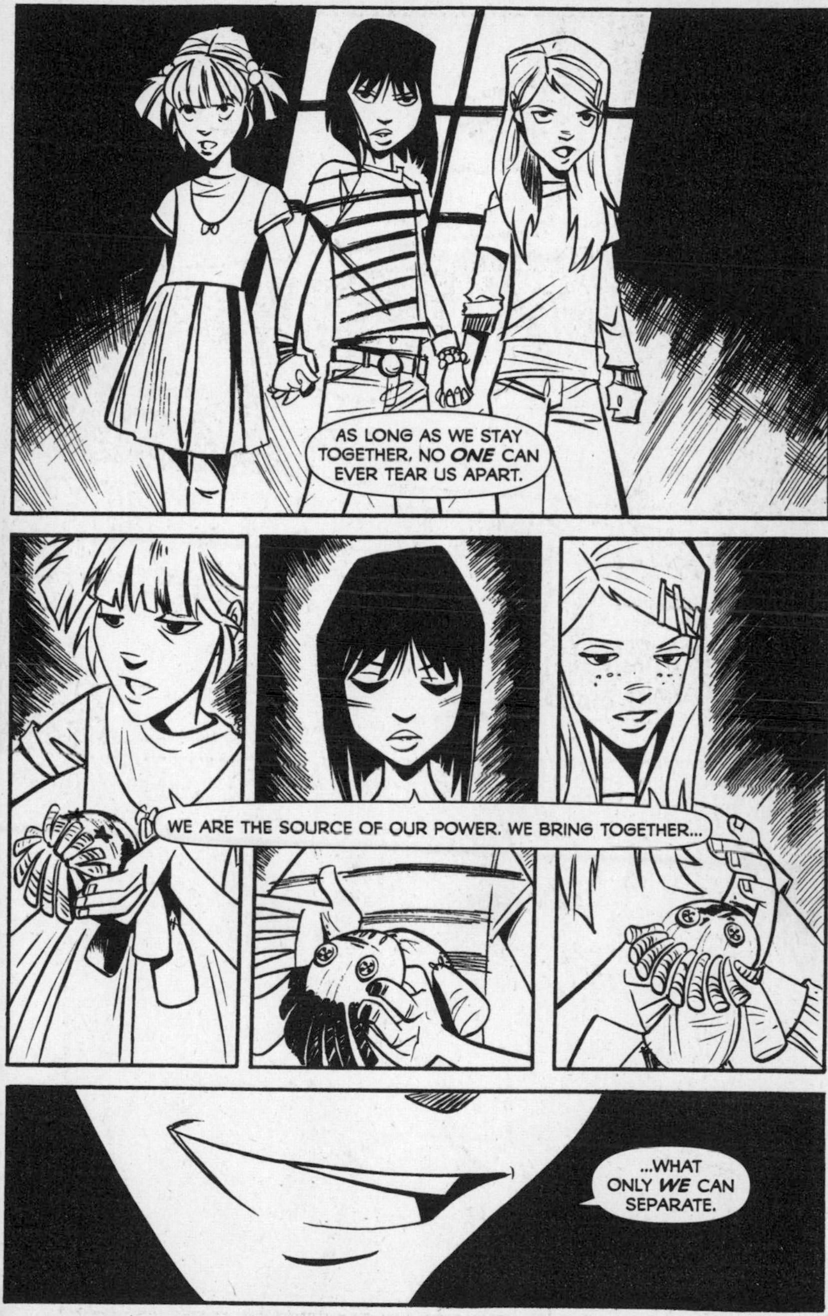
AS LONG AS WE STAY TOGETHER, NO ONE CAN EVER TEAR US APART.
WE ARE THE SOURCE OF OUR POWER. WE BRING TOGETHER...
...WHAT ONLY WE CAN SEPARATE.

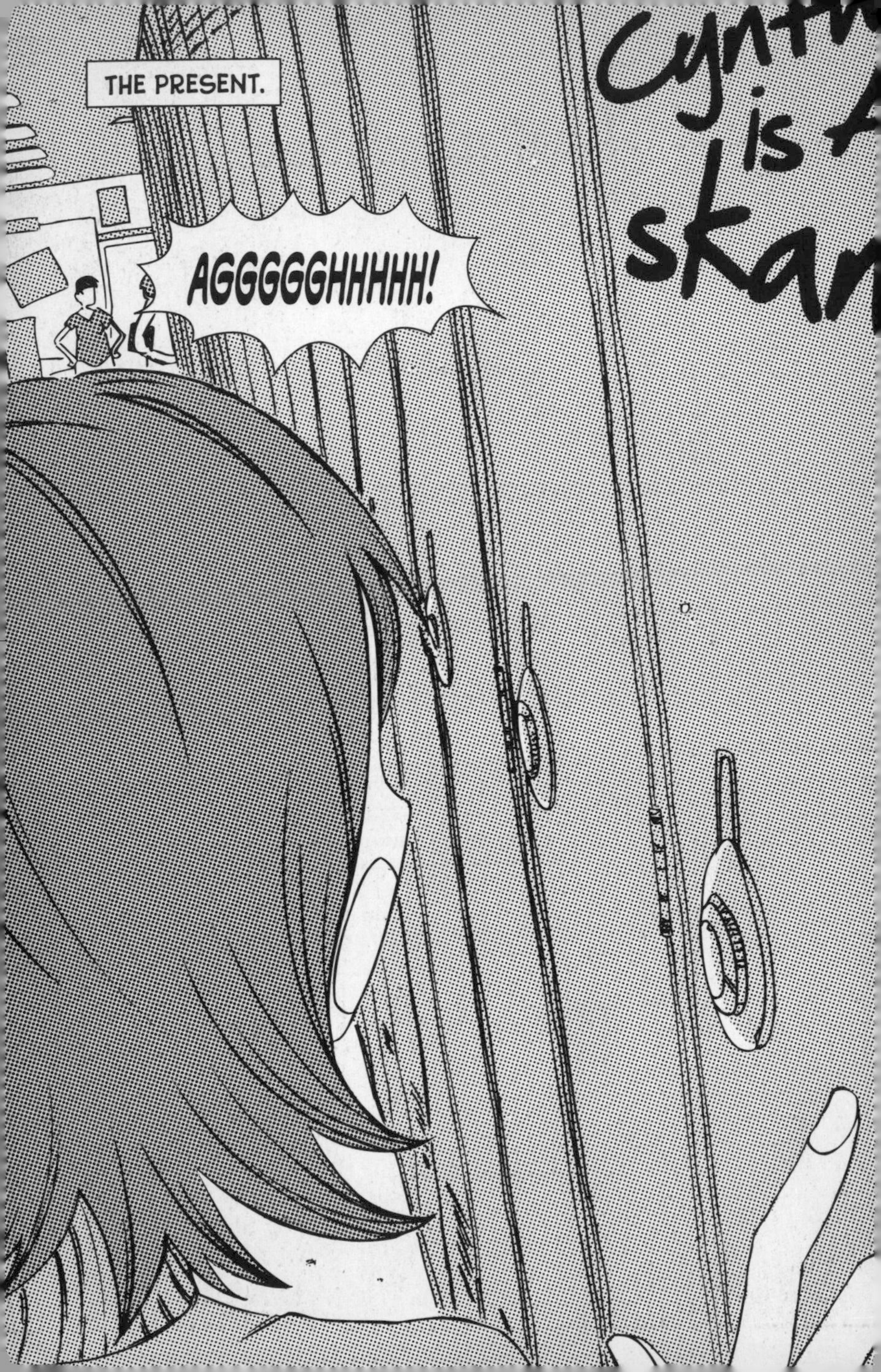
THE PRESENT.
AGGGGGHHHHH!
is

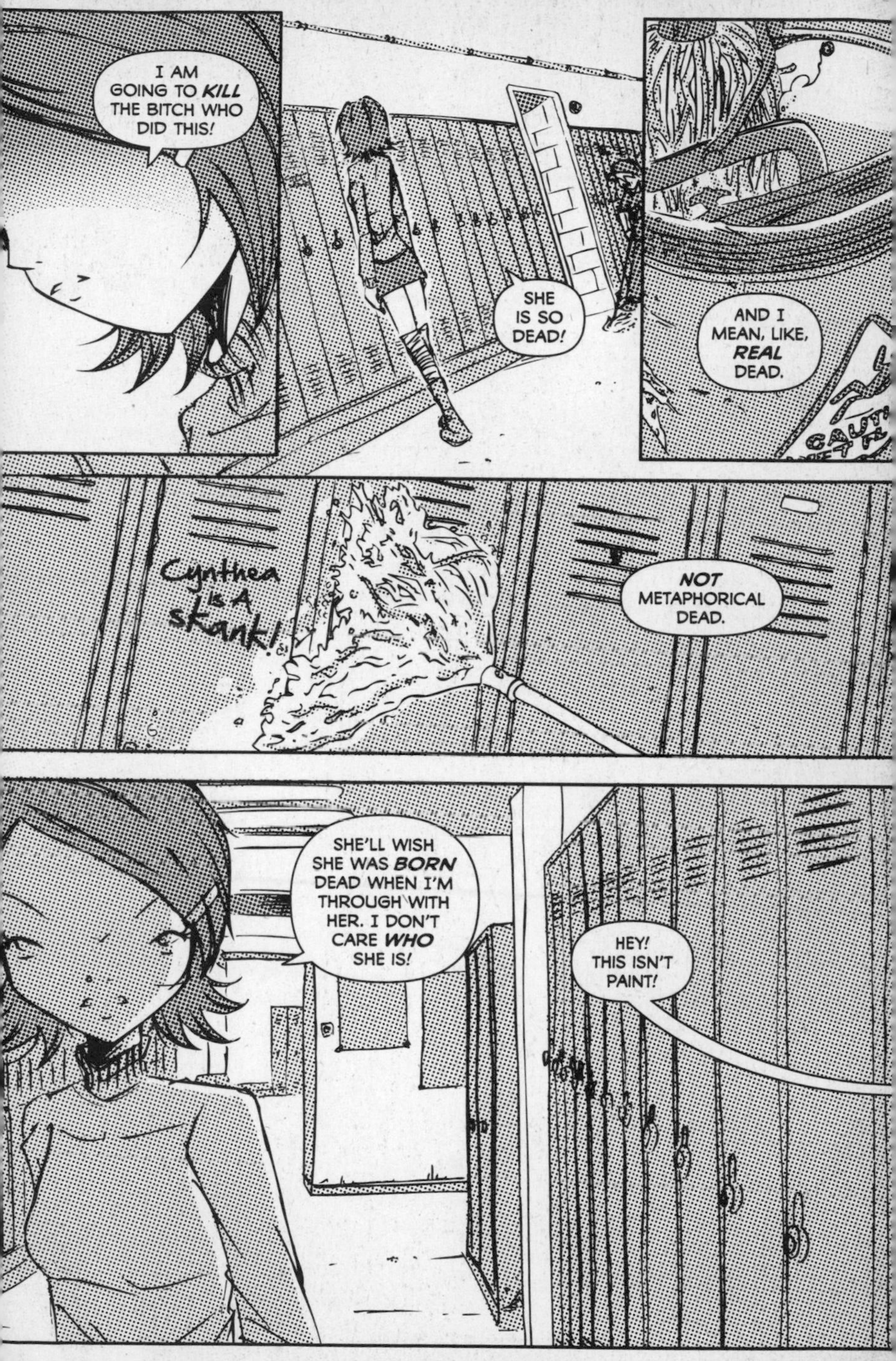
I AM GOING TO KILL THE BITCH WHO DID THIS!
SHE IS SO DEAD!
AND I MEAN, LIKE, REAL DEAD.
CAUT
Cynthea is A skank!
NOT METAPHORICAL DEAD.
SHE'LL WISH SHE WAS BORN DEAD WHEN I'M THROUGH WITH HER. I DON'T CARE WHO SHE IS!
HEY! THIS ISN'T PAINT!

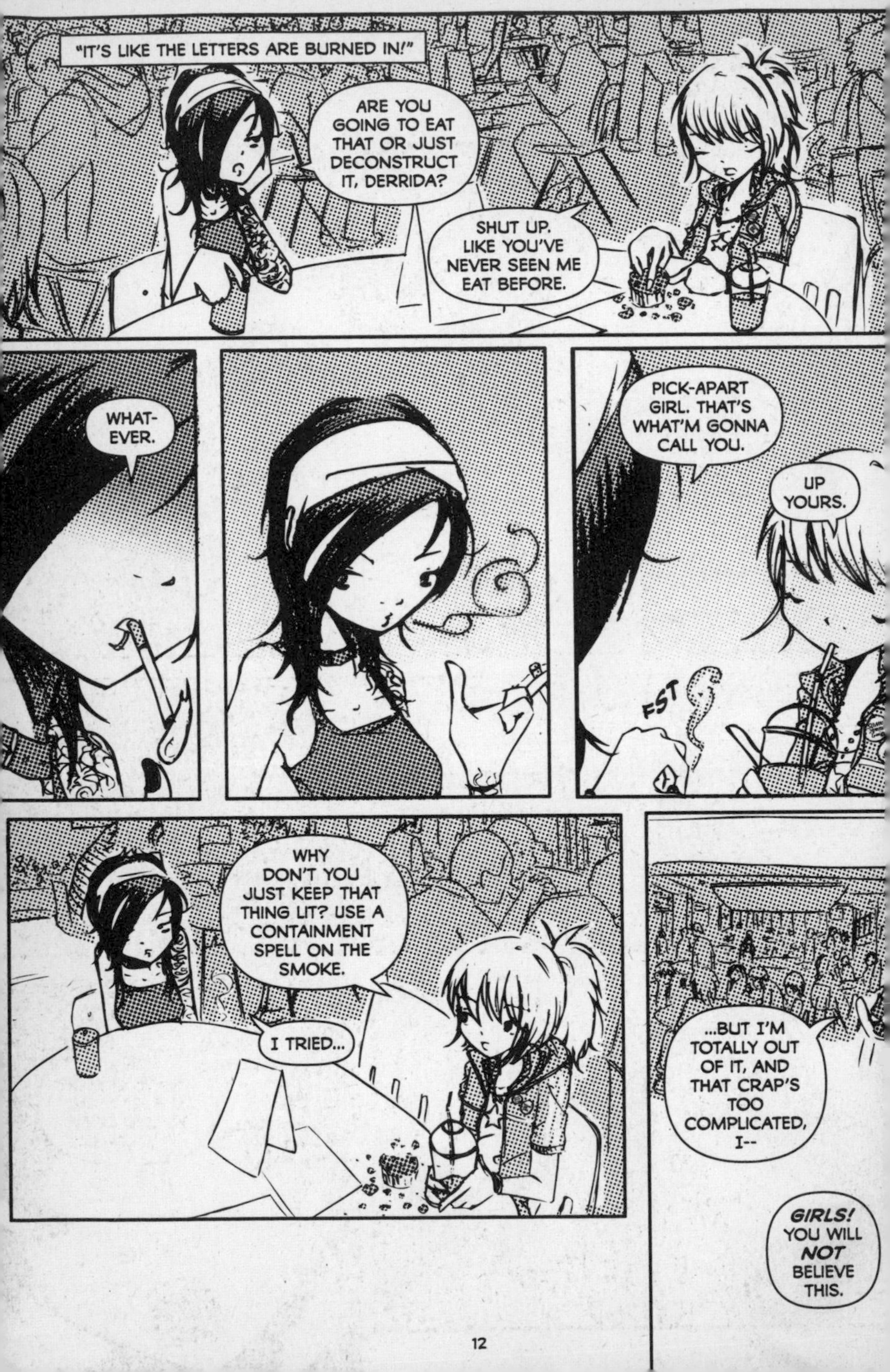
"IT'S LIKE THE LETTERS ARE BURNED IN!"
ARE YOU GOING TO EAT THAT OR JUST DECONSTRUCT IT, DERRIDA?
SHUT UP. LIKE YOU'VE NEVER SEEN ME EAT BEFORE.
WHAT-EVER.
PICK-APART GIRL. THAT'S WHAT'M GONNA CALL YOU.
UP YOURS.
FST
WHY DON'T YOU JUST KEEP THAT THING LIT? USE A CONTAINMENT SPELL ON THE SMOKE.
I TRIED...
...BUT I'M TOTALLY OUT OF IT, AND THAT CRAP'S TOO COMPLICATED, I--
GIRLS! YOU WILL NOT BELIEVE THIS.

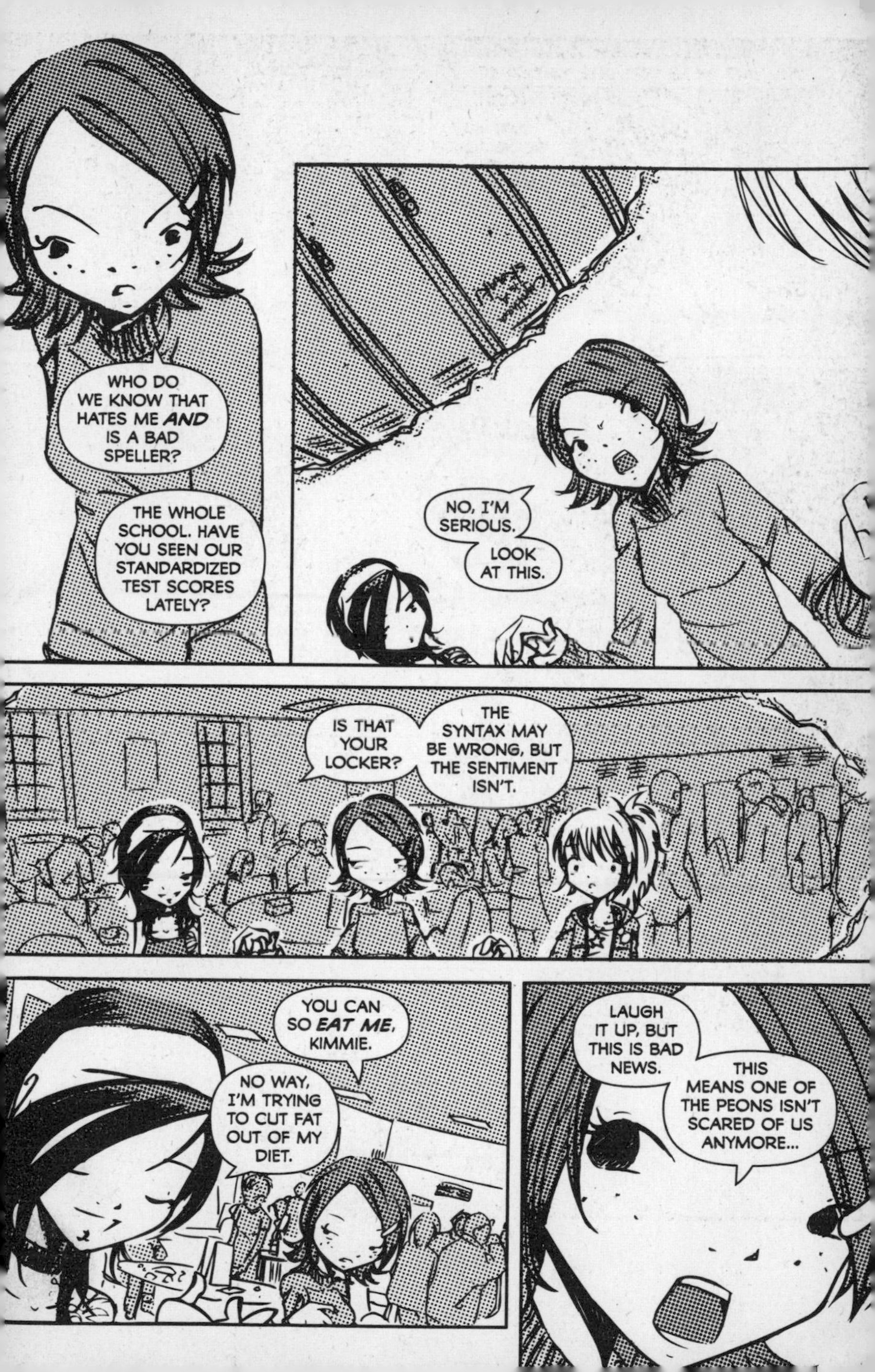
WHO DO WE KNOW THAT HATES ME *AND* IS A BAD SPELLER?
THE WHOLE SCHOOL. HAVE YOU SEEN OUR STANDARDIZED TEST SCORES LATELY?
NO, I'M SERIOUS.
LOOK AT THIS.
IS THAT YOUR LOCKER?
THE SYNTAX MAY BE WRONG, BUT THE SENTIMENT ISN'T.
YOU CAN SO *EAT ME*, KIMMIE.
NO WAY, I'M TRYING TO CUT FAT OUT OF MY DIET.
LAUGH IT UP, BUT THIS IS BAD NEWS.
THIS MEANS ONE OF THE PEONS ISN'T SCARED OF US ANYMORE...

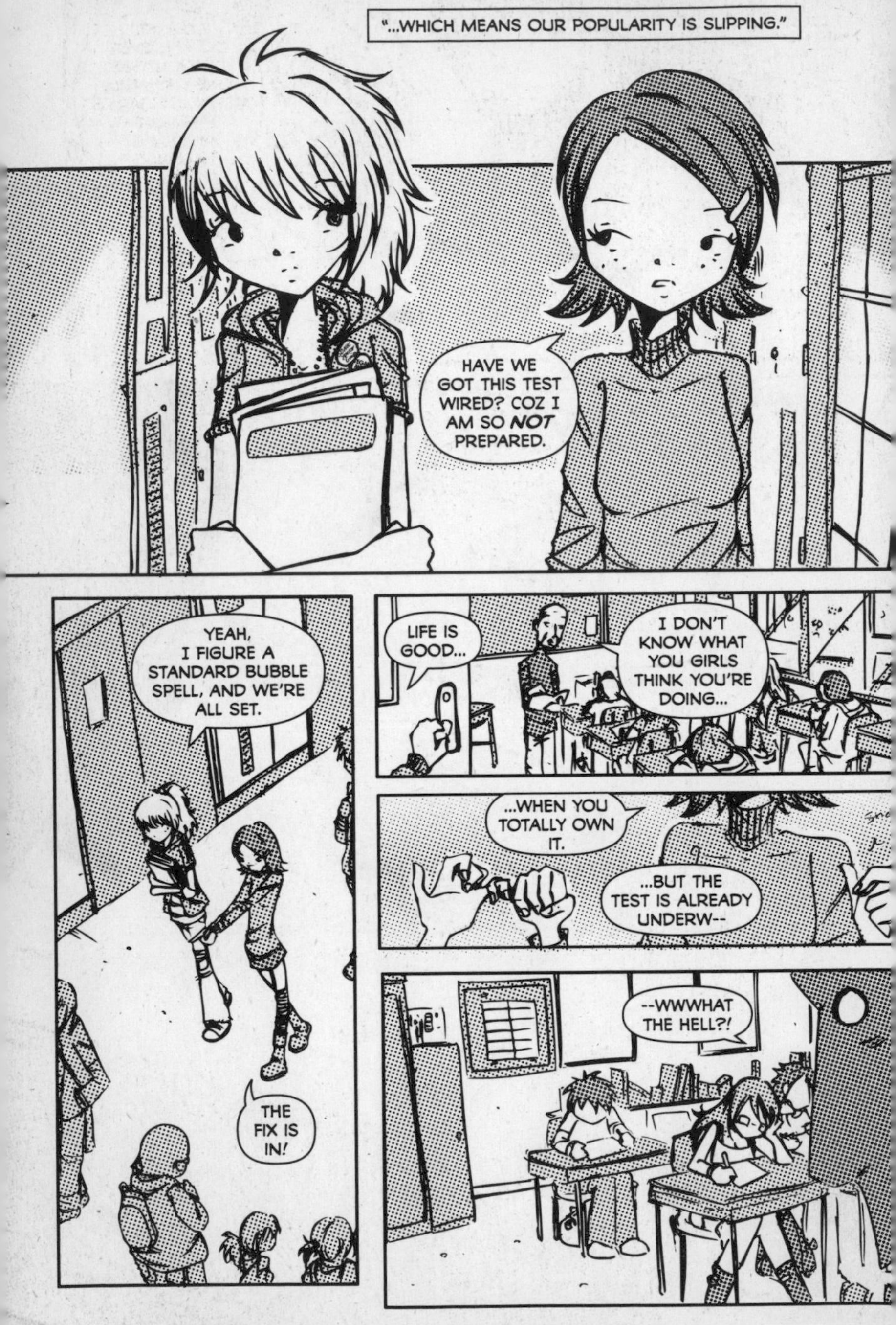
"...WHICH MEANS OUR POPULARITY IS SLIPPING."
HAVE WE GOT THIS TEST WIRED? COZ I AM SO *NOT* PREPARED.
YEAH, I FIGURE A STANDARD BUBBLE SPELL, AND WE'RE ALL SET.
THE FIX IS IN!
LIFE IS GOOD...
I DON'T KNOW WHAT YOU GIRLS THINK YOU'RE DOING...
...WHEN YOU TOTALLY OWN IT.
...BUT THE TEST IS ALREADY UNDERW--
--WWWHAT THE HELL?!

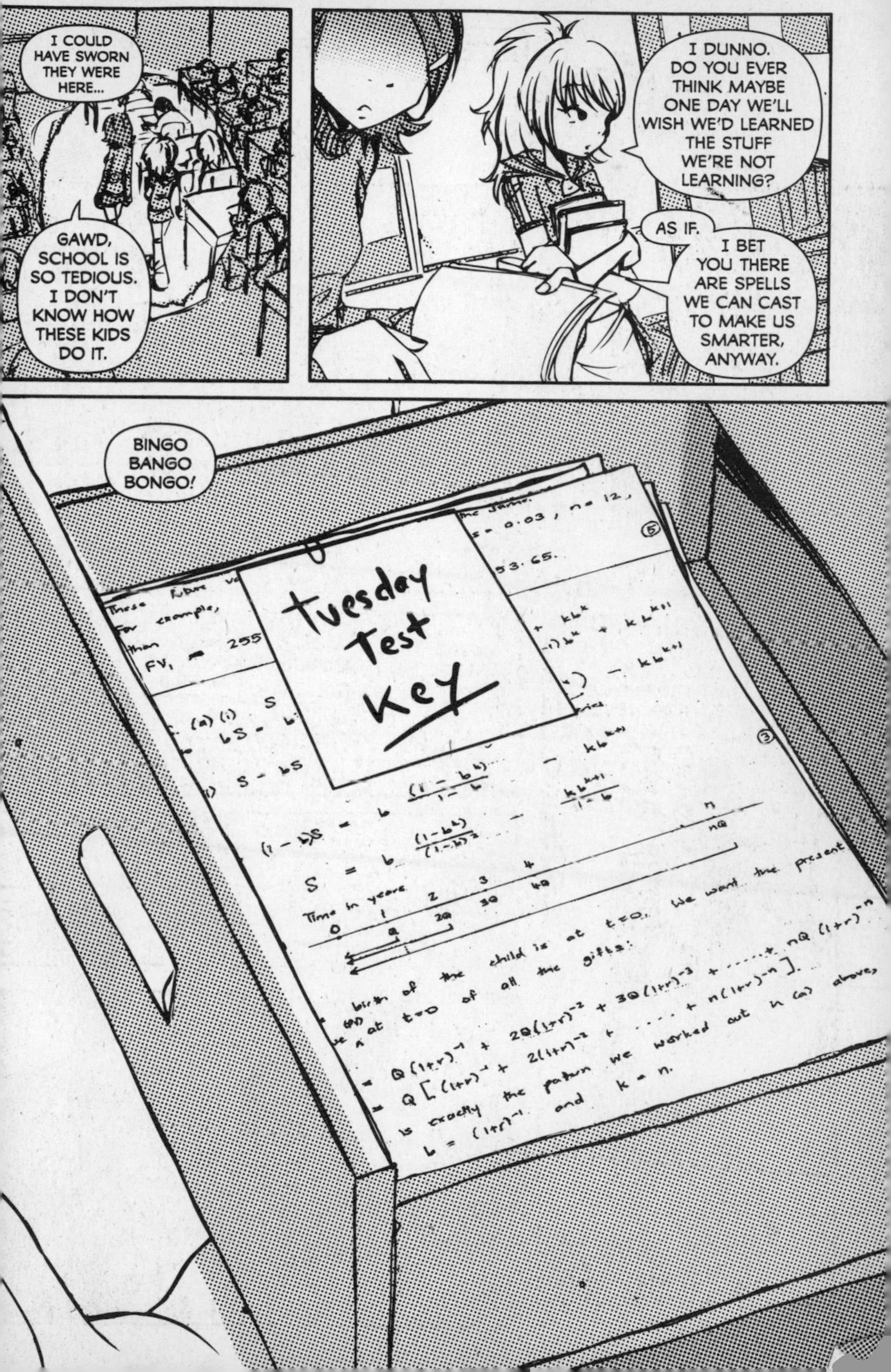
I COULD HAVE SWORN THEY WERE HERE...
GAWD, SCHOOL IS SO TEDIOUS. I DON'T KNOW HOW THESE KIDS DO IT.
I DUNNO. DO YOU EVER THINK MAYBE ONE DAY WE'LL WISH WE'D LEARNED THE STUFF WE'RE NOT LEARNING?
AS IF.
I BET YOU THERE ARE SPELLS WE CAN CAST TO MAKE US SMARTER, ANYWAY.
BINGO BANGO BONGO!
Tuesday Test Key

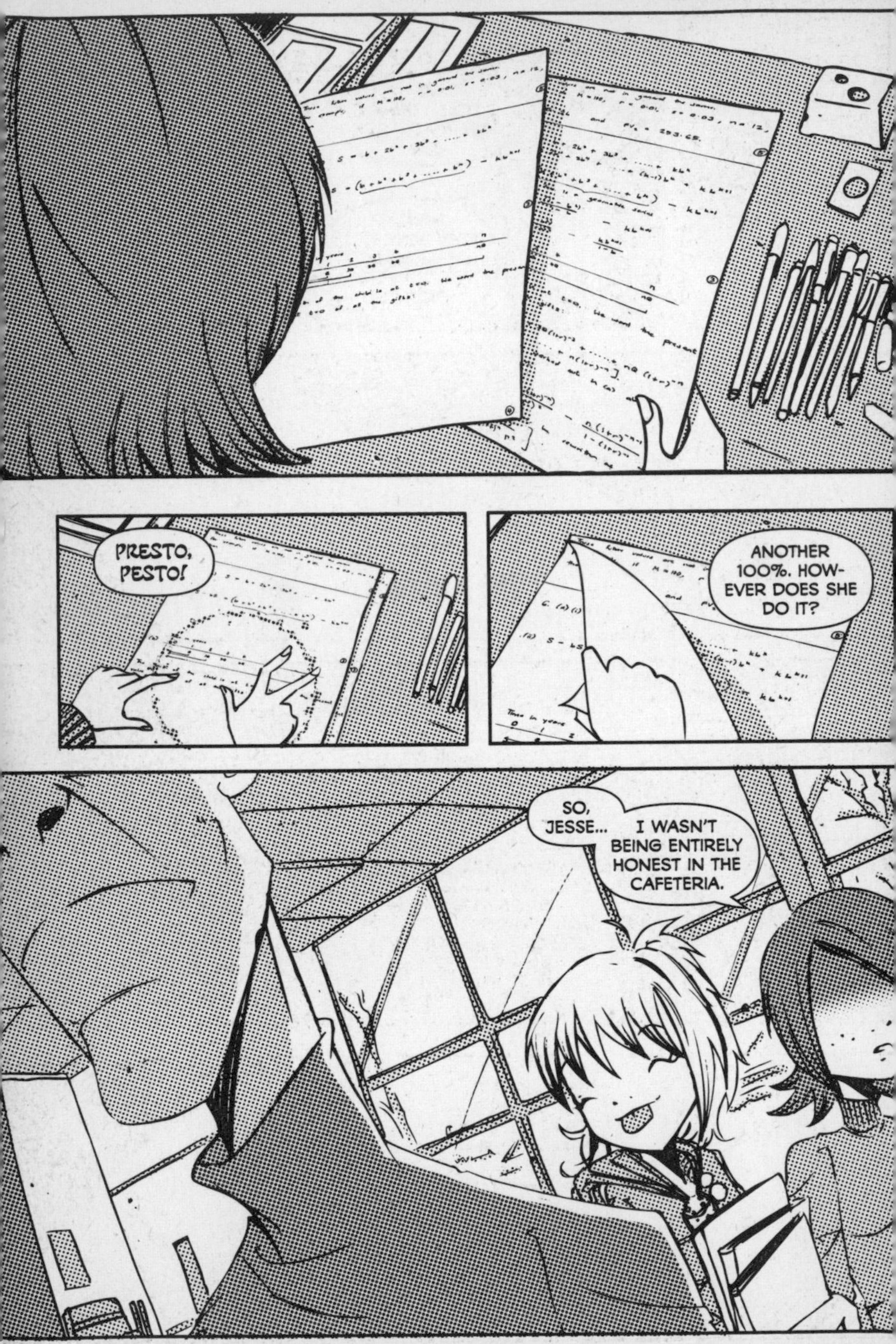
PRESTO, PESTO!
ANOTHER 100%. HOWEVER DOES SHE DO IT?
SO, JESSE...
I WASN'T BEING ENTIRELY HONEST IN THE CAFETERIA.

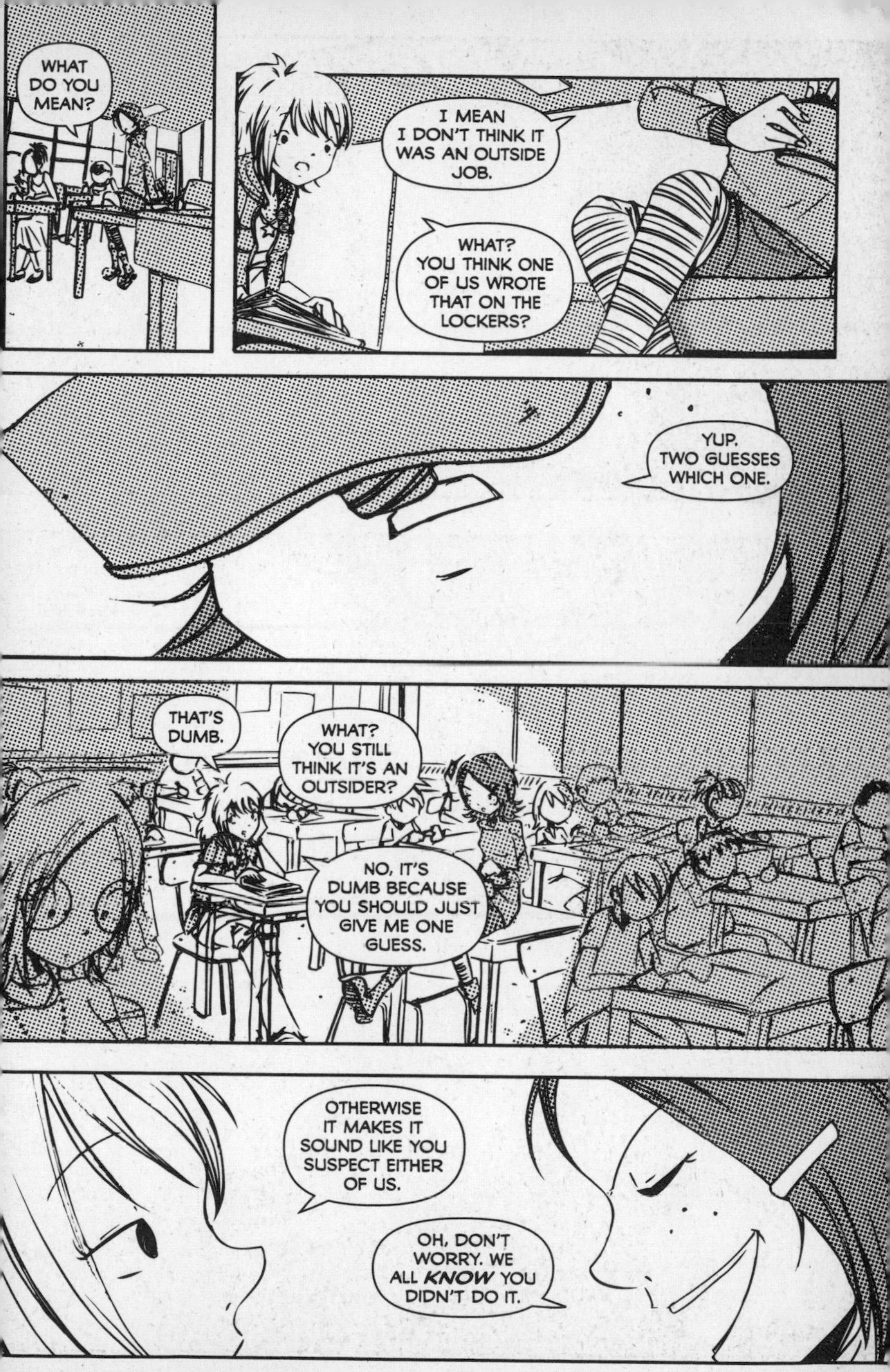
WHAT DO YOU MEAN?
I MEAN I DON'T THINK IT WAS AN OUTSIDE JOB.
WHAT? YOU THINK ONE OF US WROTE THAT ON THE LOCKERS?
YUP. TWO GUESSES WHICH ONE.
THAT'S DUMB.
WHAT? YOU STILL THINK IT'S AN OUTSIDER?
NO, IT'S DUMB BECAUSE YOU SHOULD JUST GIVE ME ONE GUESS.
OTHERWISE IT MAKES IT SOUND LIKE YOU SUSPECT EITHER OF US.
OH, DON'T WORRY. WE ALL *KNOW* YOU DIDN'T DO IT.

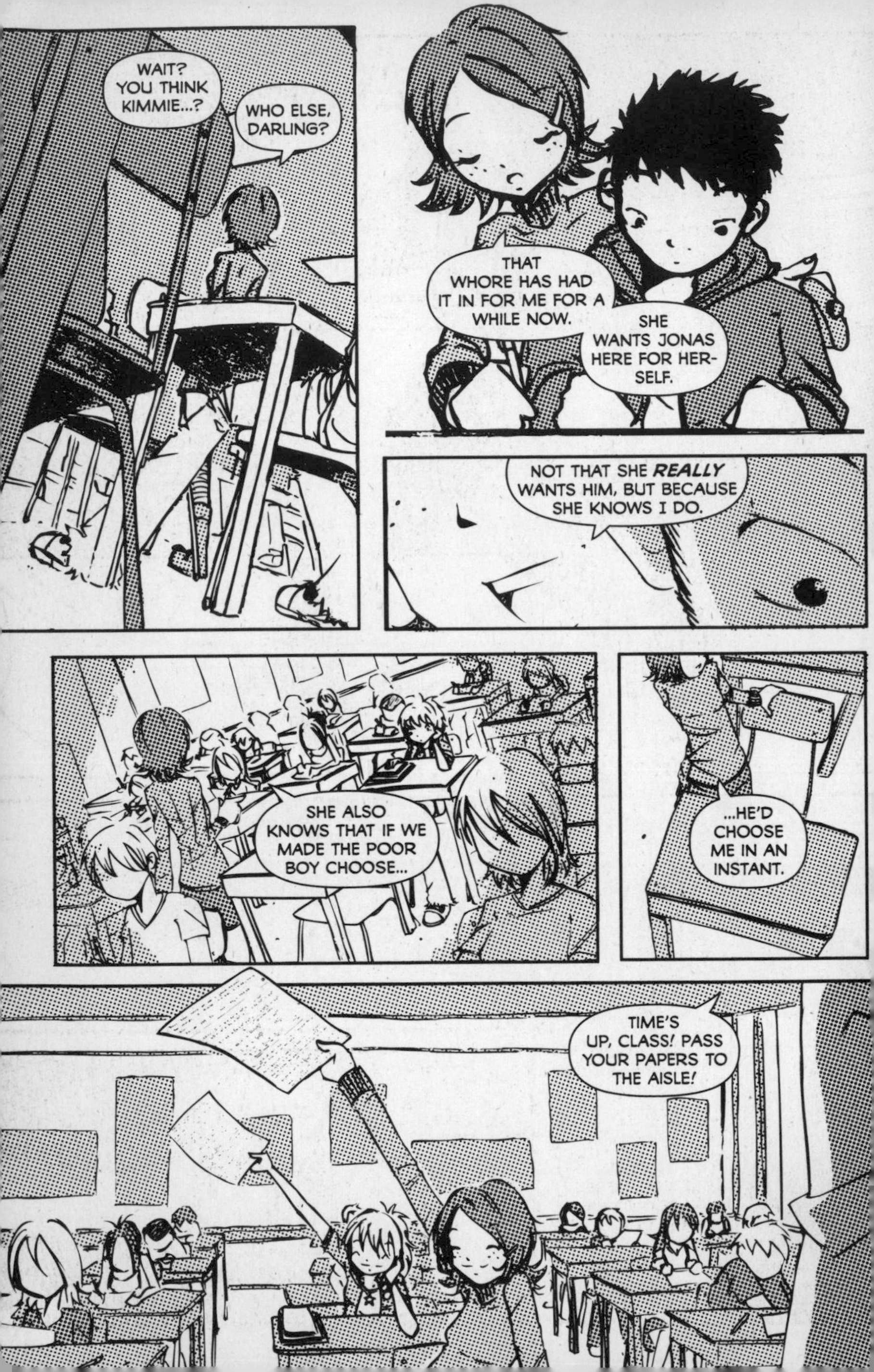
WAIT? YOU THINK KIMMIE...?
WHO ELSE, DARLING?
THAT WHORE HAS HAD IT IN FOR ME FOR A WHILE NOW.
SHE WANTS JONAS HERE FOR HER-SELF.
NOT THAT SHE *REALLY* WANTS HIM, BUT BECAUSE SHE KNOWS I DO.
SHE ALSO KNOWS THAT IF WE MADE THE POOR BOY CHOOSE...
...HE'D CHOOSE ME IN AN INSTANT.
TIME'S UP, CLASS! PASS YOUR PAPERS TO THE AISLE!

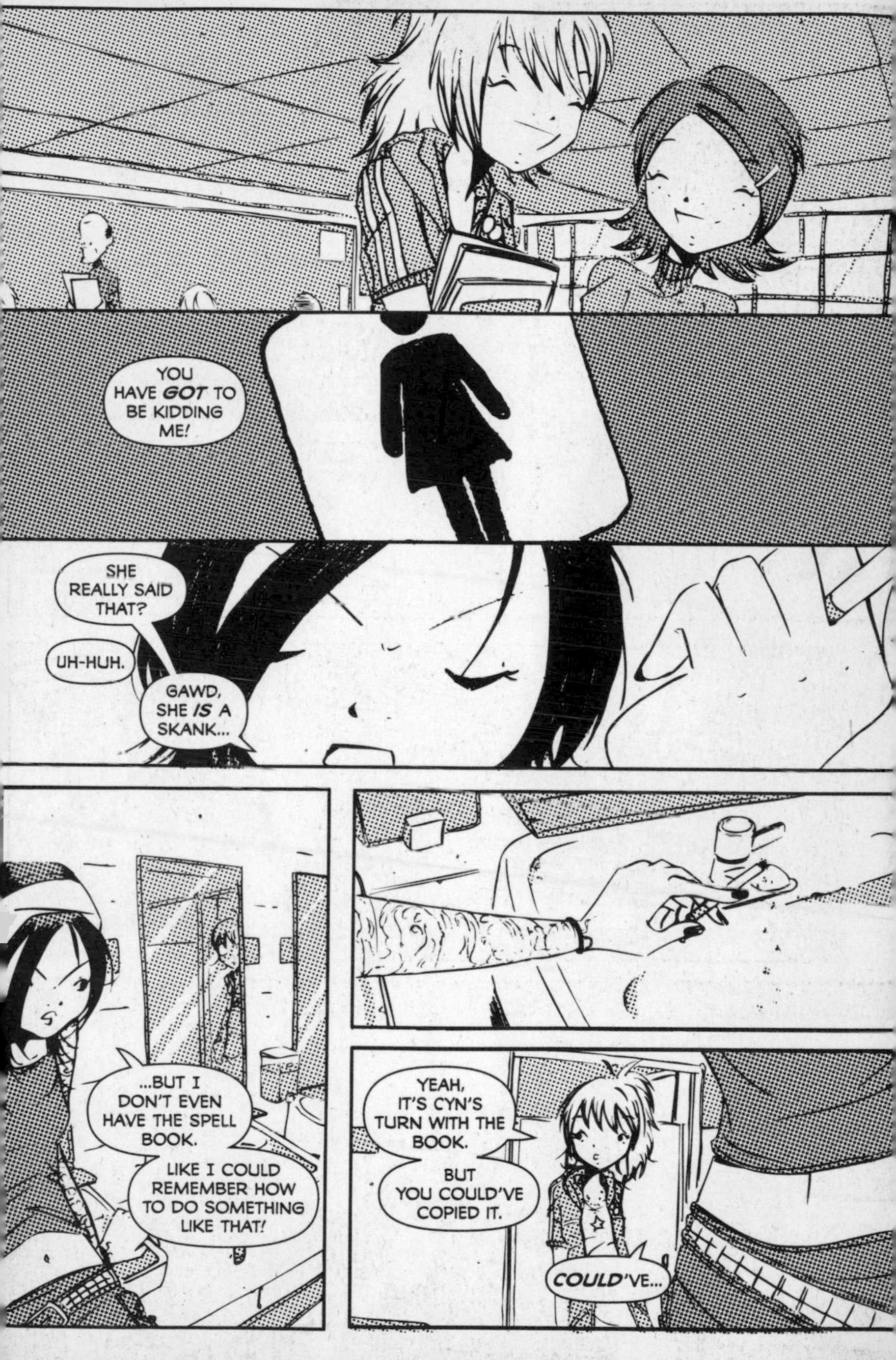
YOU HAVE GOT TO BE KIDDING ME!
SHE REALLY SAID THAT?
UH-HUH.
GAWD, SHE IS A SKANK...
...BUT I DON'T EVEN HAVE THE SPELL BOOK.
LIKE I COULD REMEMBER HOW TO DO SOMETHING LIKE THAT!
YEAH, IT'S CYN'S TURN WITH THE BOOK.
BUT YOU COULD'VE COPIED IT.
COULD'VE...

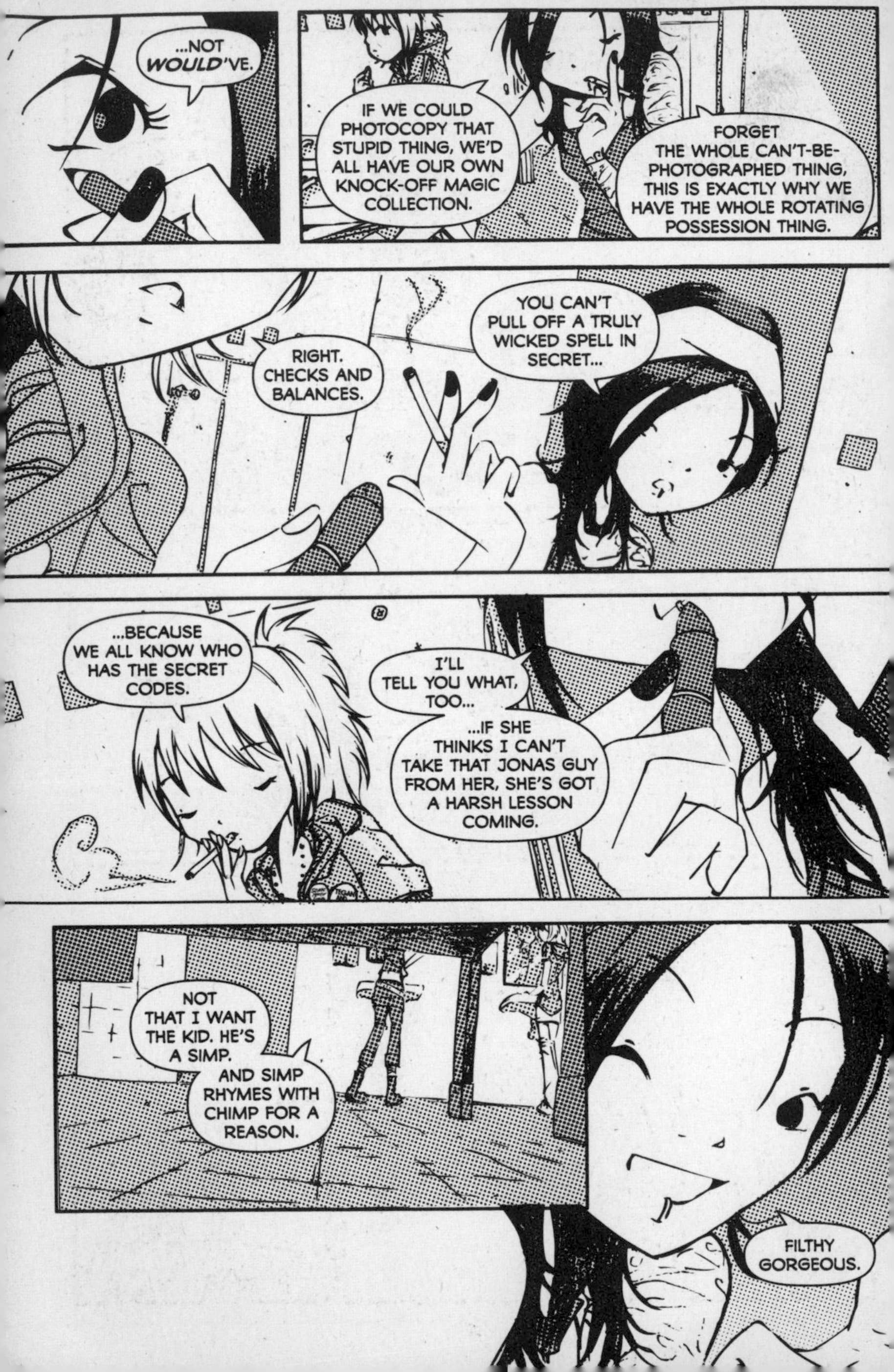
...NOT WOULD'VE.
IF WE COULD PHOTOCOPY THAT STUPID THING, WE'D ALL HAVE OUR OWN KNOCK-OFF MAGIC COLLECTION.
FORGET THE WHOLE CAN'T-BE-PHOTOGRAPHED THING, THIS IS EXACTLY WHY WE HAVE THE WHOLE ROTATING POSSESSION THING.
RIGHT. CHECKS AND BALANCES.
YOU CAN'T PULL OFF A TRULY WICKED SPELL IN SECRET...
...BECAUSE WE ALL KNOW WHO HAS THE SECRET CODES.
I'LL TELL YOU WHAT, TOO...
...IF SHE THINKS I CAN'T TAKE THAT JONAS GUY FROM HER, SHE'S GOT A HARSH LESSON COMING.
NOT THAT I WANT THE KID. HE'S A SIMP.
AND SIMP RHYMES WITH CHIMP FOR A REASON.
FILTHY GORGEOUS.

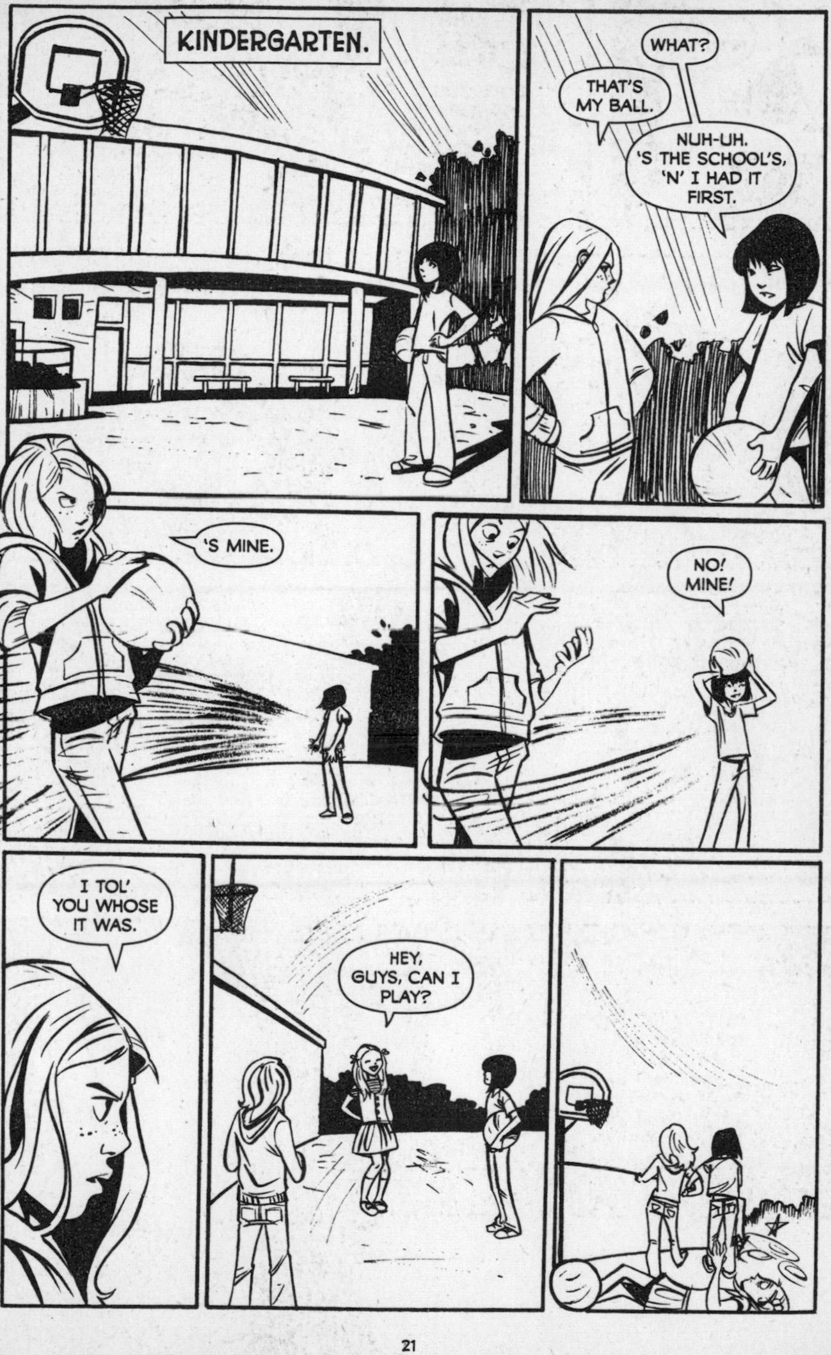
KINDERGARTEN.
WHAT?
THAT'S MY BALL.
NUH-UH. 'S THE SCHOOL'S, 'N' I HAD IT FIRST.
'S MINE.
NO! MINE!
I TOL' YOU WHOSE IT WAS.
HEY, GUYS, CAN I PLAY?

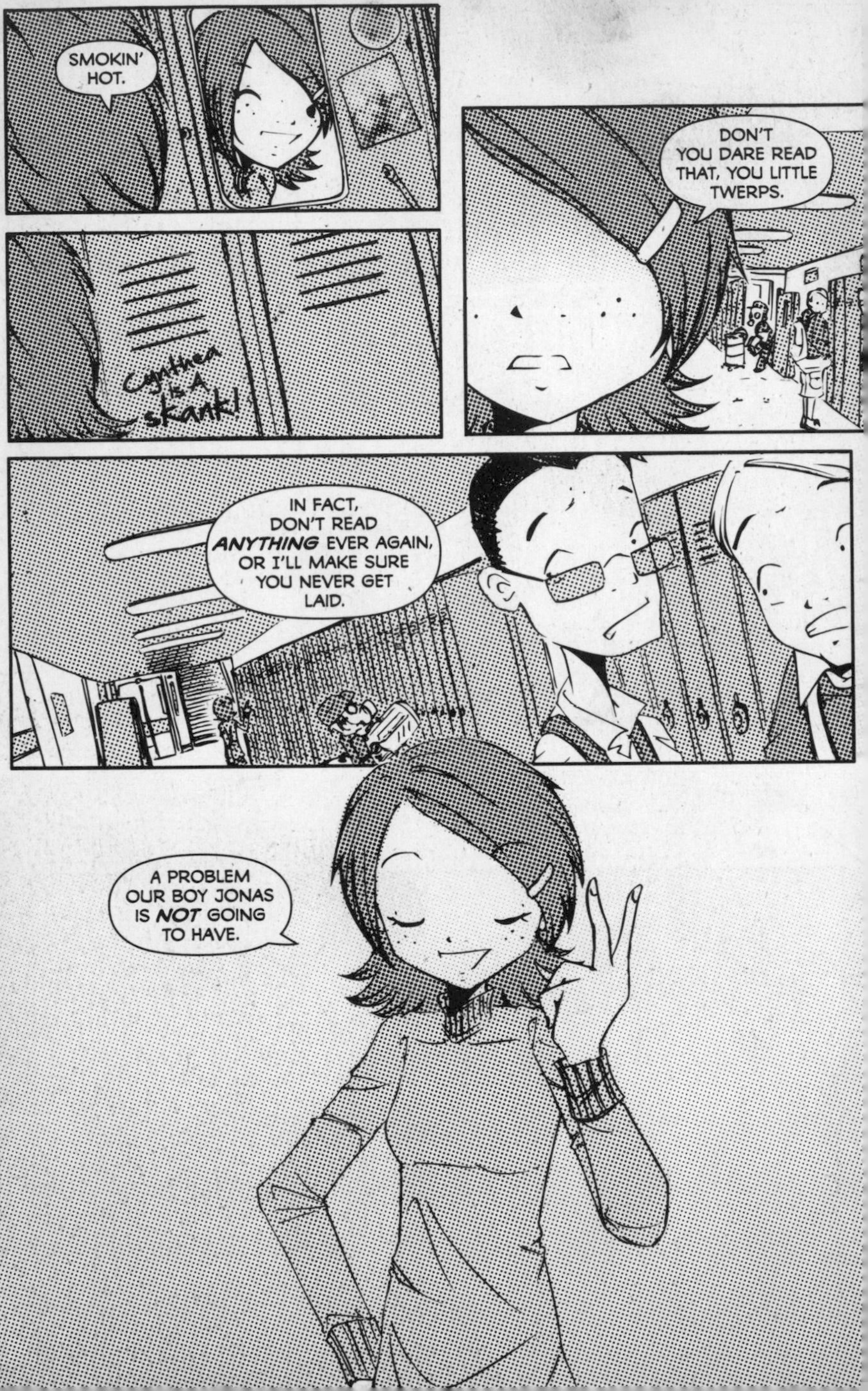
SMOKIN' HOT.
Cynthea is a skank!
DON'T YOU DARE READ THAT, YOU LITTLE TWERPS.
IN FACT, DON'T READ *ANTHING* EVER AGAIN, OR I'LL MAKE SURE YOU NEVER GET LAID.
A PROBLEM OUR BOY JONAS IS *NOT* GOING TO HAVE.

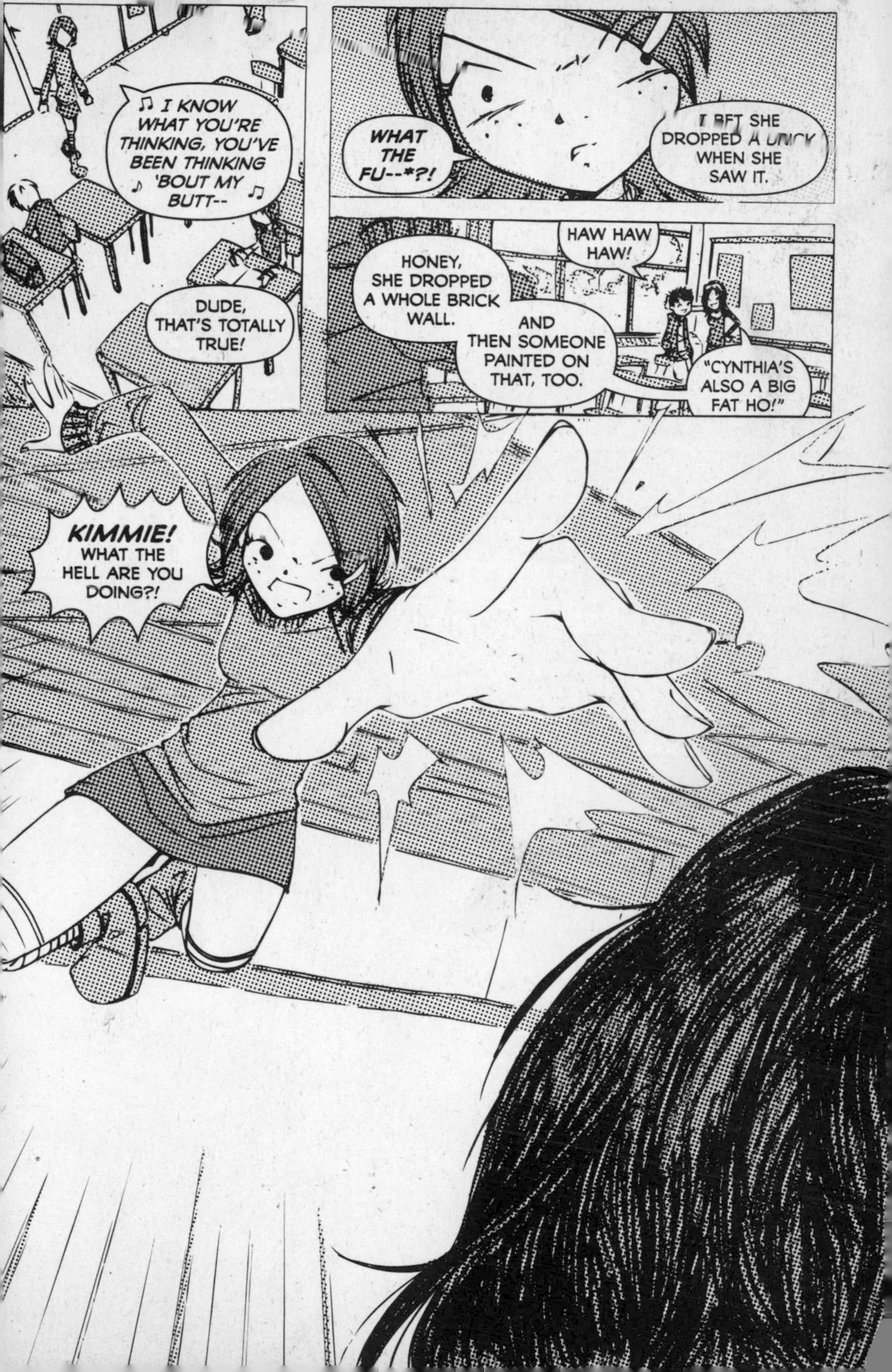
♫ I KNOW WHAT YOU'RE THINKING, YOU'VE BEEN THINKING ♪ 'BOUT MY BUTT-- ♫
DUDE, THAT'S TOTALLY TRUE!
WHAT THE FU--*?!
I BET SHE DROPPED A BRICK WHEN SHE SAW IT.
HONEY, SHE DROPPED A WHOLE BRICK WALL.
HAW HAW HAW!
AND THEN SOMEONE PAINTED ON THAT, TOO.
"CYNTHIA'S ALSO A BIG FAT HO!"
KIMMIE! WHAT THE HELL ARE YOU DOING?!

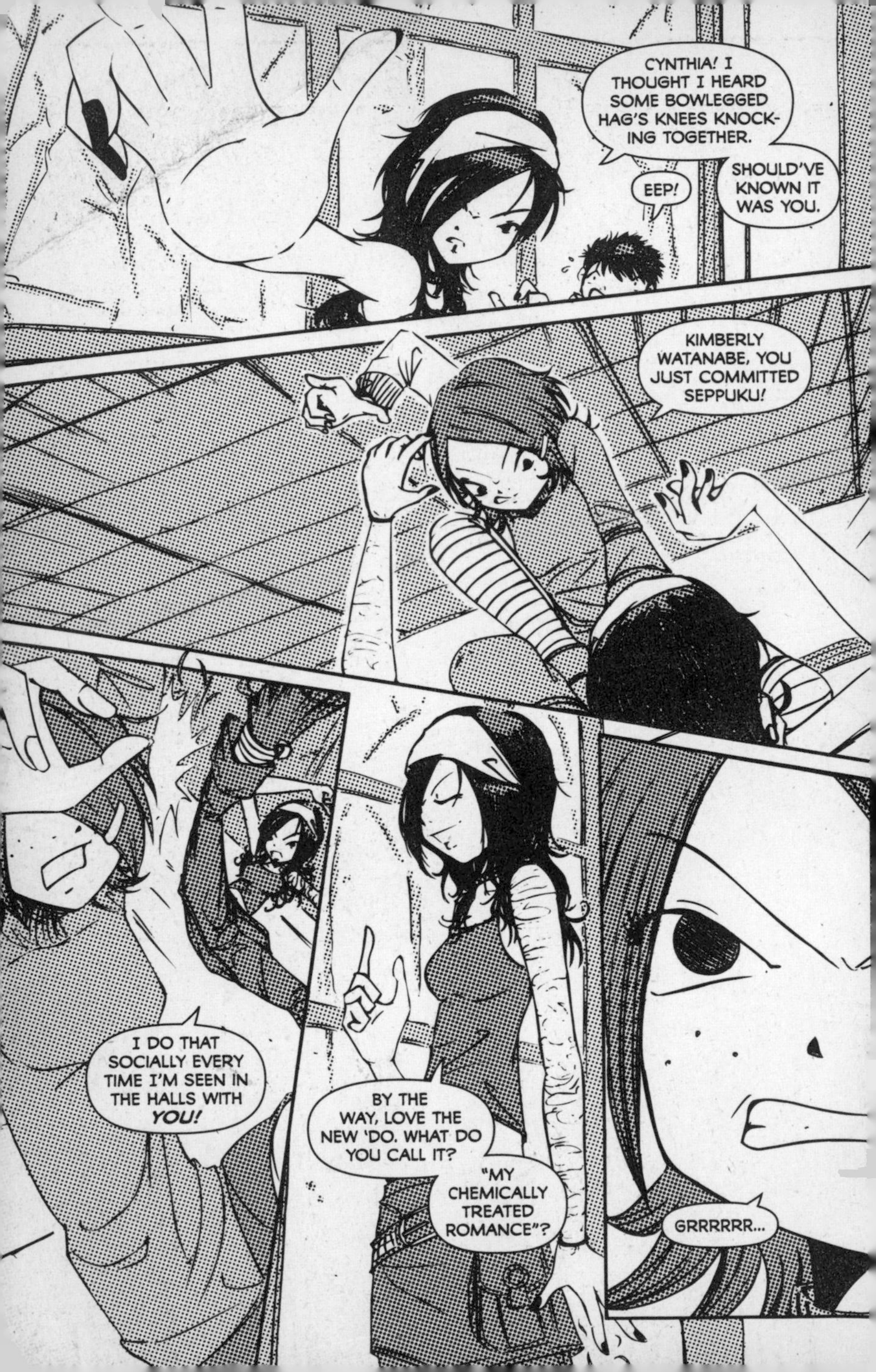
CYNTHIA! I THOUGHT I HEARD SOME BOWLEGGED HAG'S KNEES KNOCKING TOGETHER.
SHOULD'VE KNOWN IT WAS YOU.
EEP!
KIMBERLY WATANABE, YOU JUST COMMITTED SEPPUKU!
I DO THAT SOCIALLY EVERY TIME I'M SEEN IN THE HALLS WITH *YOU!*
BY THE WAY, LOVE THE NEW 'DO. WHAT DO YOU CALL IT?
"MY CHEMICALLY TREATED ROMANCE"?
GRRRRRR...

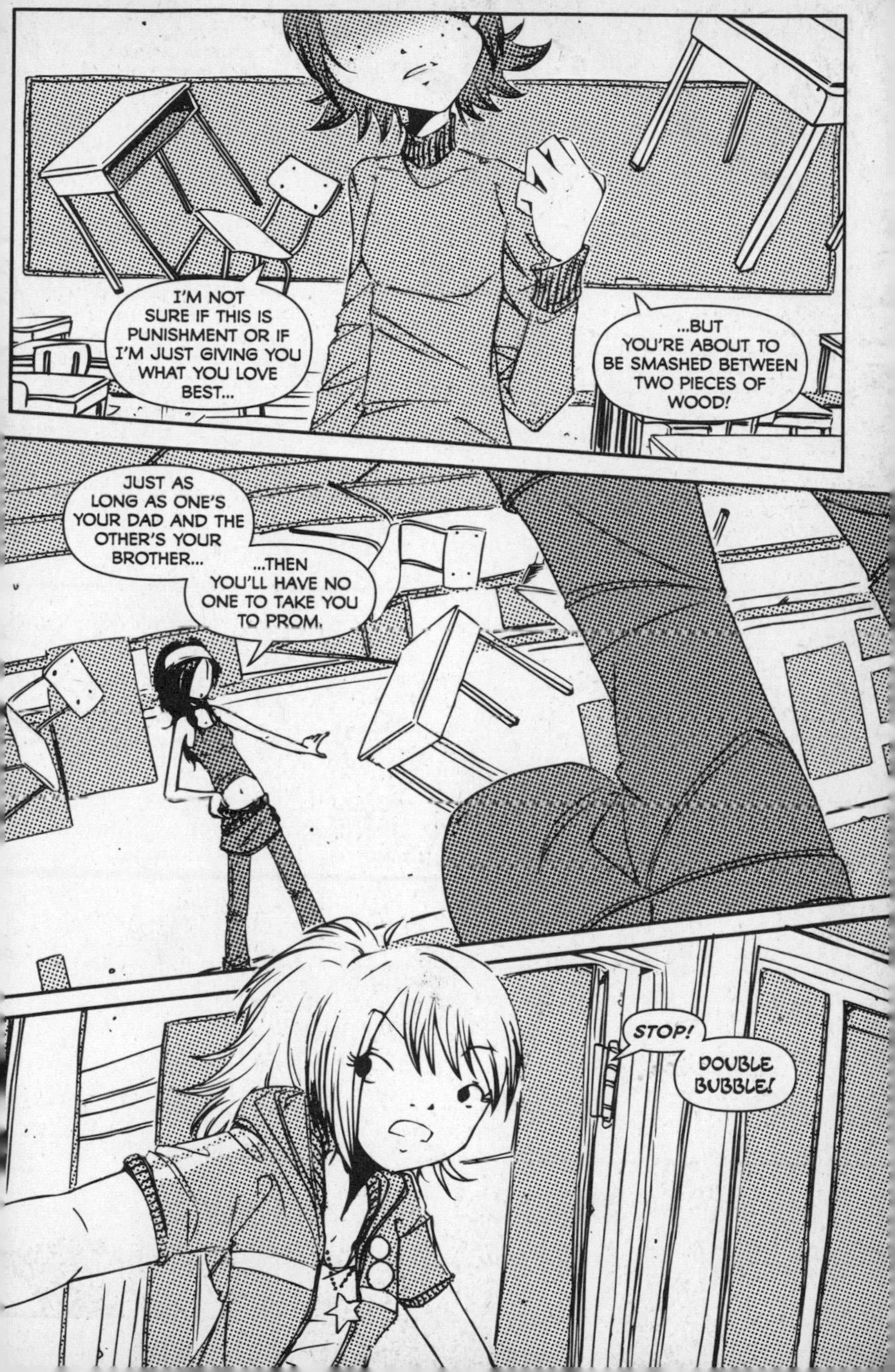
I'M NOT SURE IF THIS IS PUNISHMENT OR IF I'M JUST GIVING YOU WHAT YOU LOVE BEST...
...BUT YOU'RE ABOUT TO BE SMASHED BETWEEN TWO PIECES OF WOOD!
JUST AS LONG AS ONE'S YOUR DAD AND THE OTHER'S YOUR BROTHER...
...THEN YOU'LL HAVE NO ONE TO TAKE YOU TO PROM.
STOP!
DOUBLE BUBBLE!

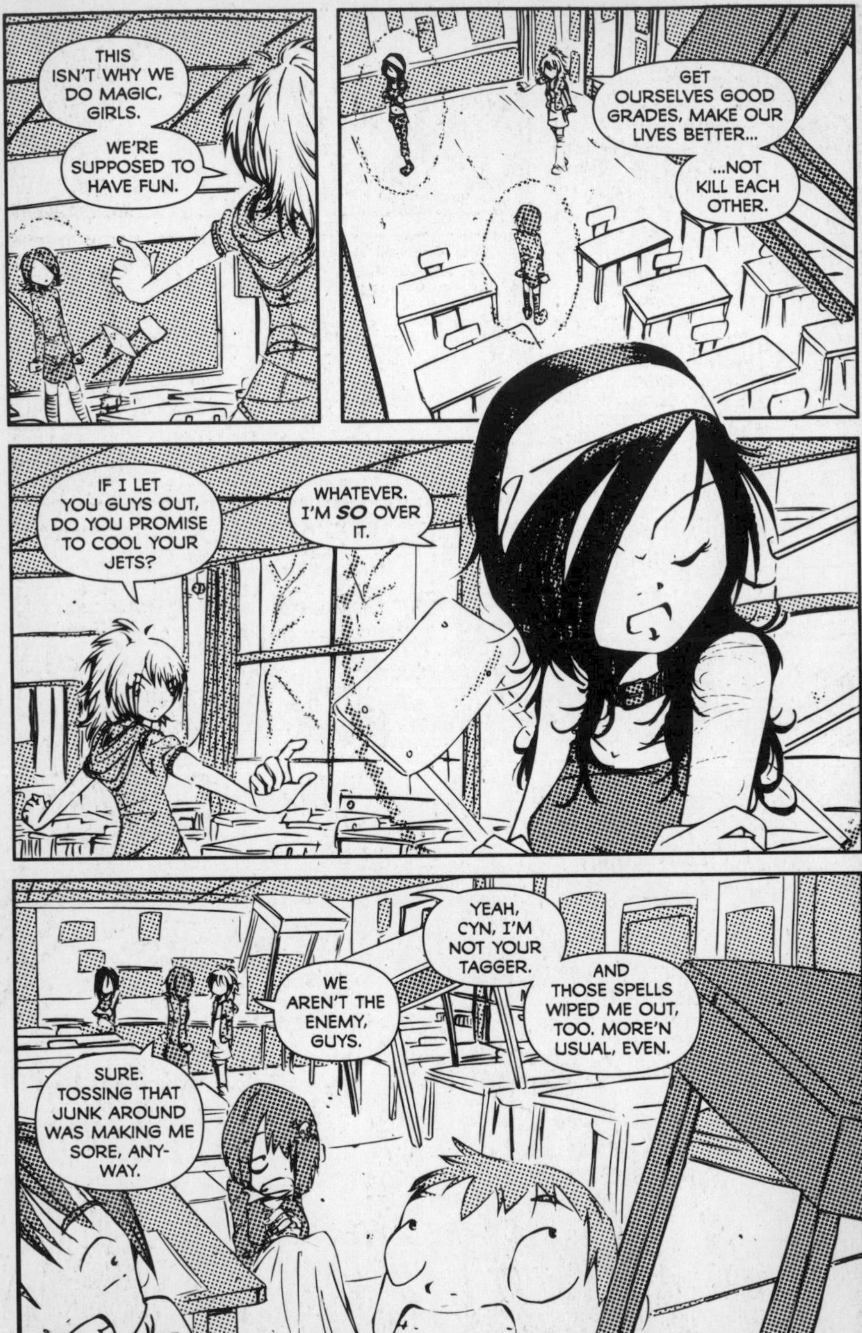
THIS ISN'T WHY WE DO MAGIC, GIRLS.
WE'RE SUPPOSED TO HAVE FUN.
GET OURSELVES GOOD GRADES, MAKE OUR LIVES BETTER...
...NOT KILL EACH OTHER.
IF I LET YOU GUYS OUT, DO YOU PROMISE TO COOL YOUR JETS?
WHATEVER. I'M *SO* OVER IT.
SURE. TOSSING THAT JUNK AROUND WAS MAKING ME SORE, ANY-WAY.
WE AREN'T THE ENEMY, GUYS.
YEAH, CYN, I'M NOT YOUR TAGGER.
AND THOSE SPELLS WIPED ME OUT, TOO. MORE'N USUAL, EVEN.

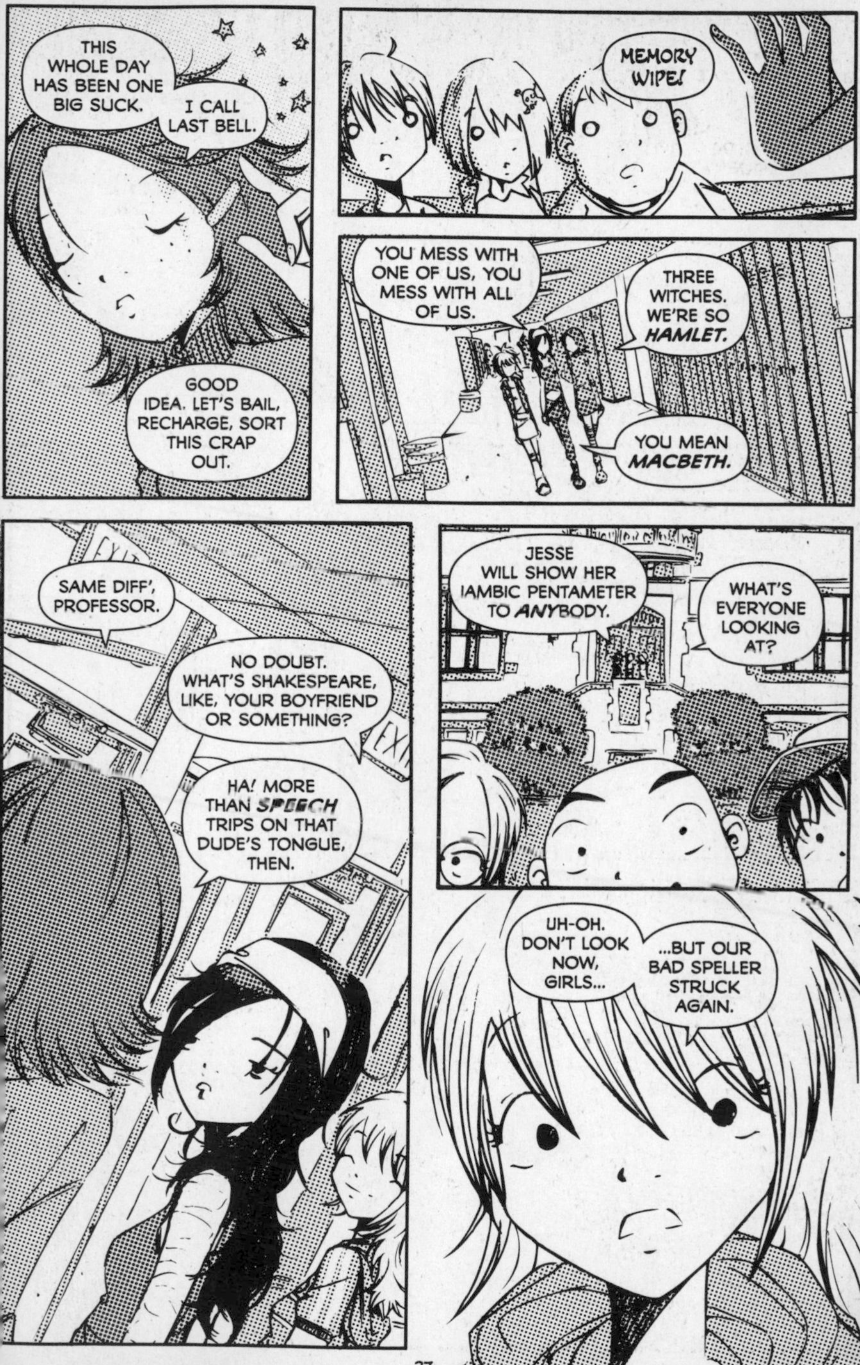
THIS WHOLE DAY HAS BEEN ONE BIG SUCK.
I CALL LAST BELL.
GOOD IDEA. LET'S BAIL, RECHARGE, SORT THIS CRAP OUT.
MEMORY WIPE!
YOU MESS WITH ONE OF US, YOU MESS WITH ALL OF US.
THREE WITCHES. WE'RE SO HAMLET.
YOU MEAN MACBETH.
SAME DIFF', PROFESSOR.
NO DOUBT. WHAT'S SHAKESPEARE, LIKE, YOUR BOYFRIEND OR SOMETHING?
HA! MORE THAN SPEECH TRIPS ON THAT DUDE'S TONGUE, THEN.
JESSE WILL SHOW HER IAMBIC PENTAMETER TO ANYBODY.
WHAT'S EVERYONE LOOKING AT?
UH-OH. DON'T LOOK NOW, GIRLS...
...BUT OUR BAD SPELLER STRUCK AGAIN.

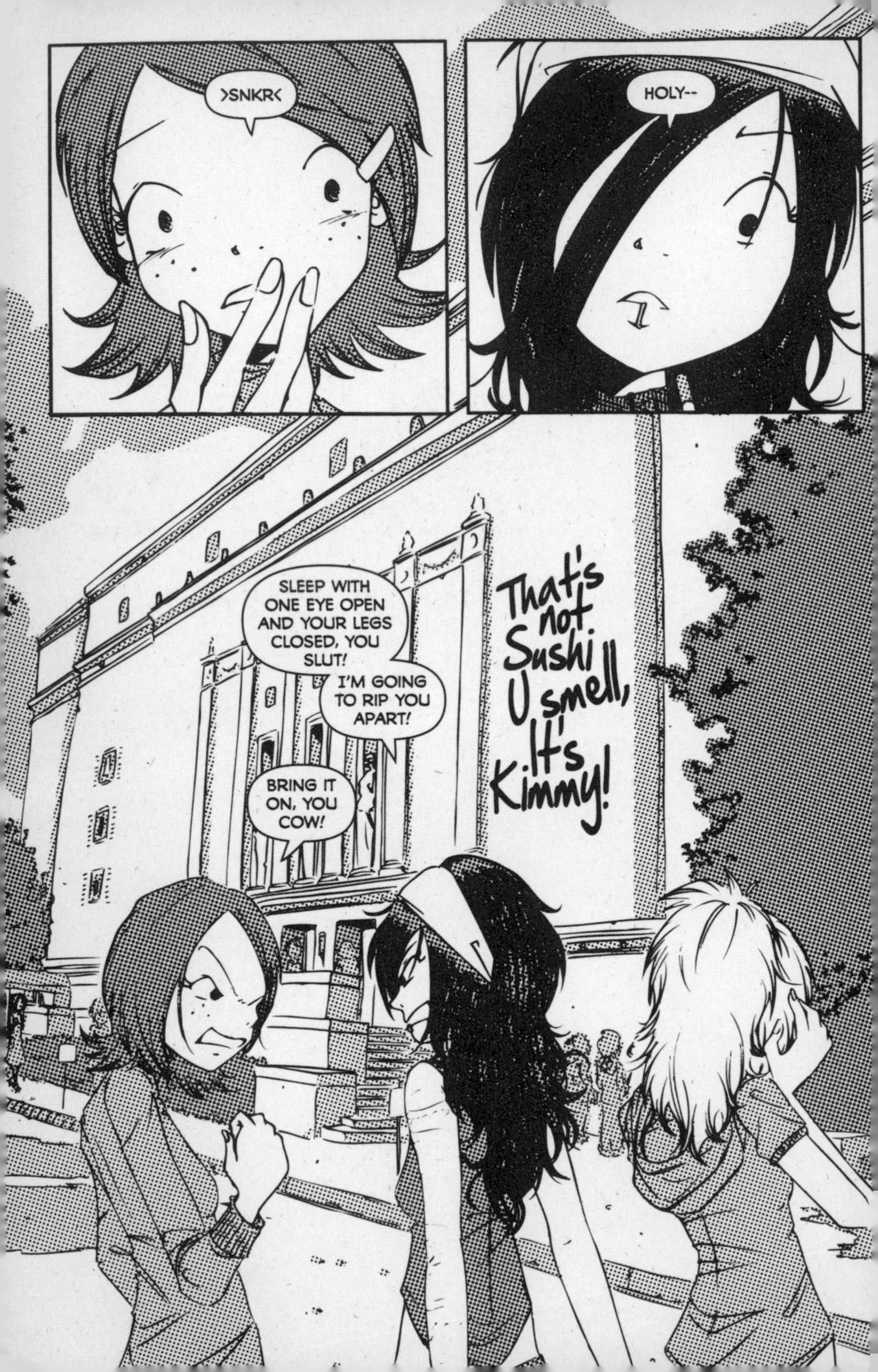

>SNKR<
HOLY--
SLEEP WITH ONE EYE OPEN AND YOUR LEGS CLOSED, YOU SLUT!
I'M GOING TO RIP YOU APART!
BRING IT ON, YOU COW!
That's not Sushi U smell, It's Kimmy!

Chapter 2
"No You Girls"

2

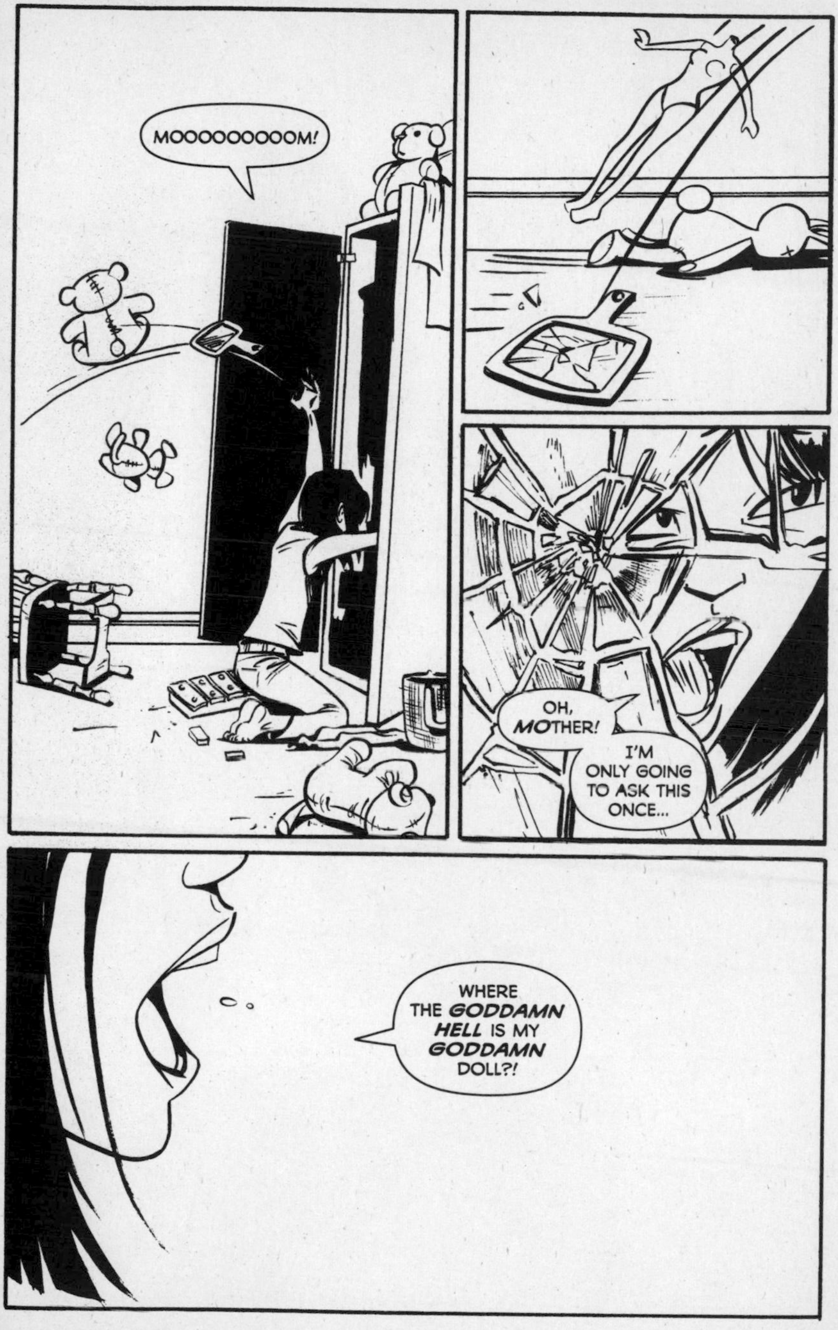
MOOOOOOOOOM!
OH, MOTHER!
I'M ONLY GOING TO ASK THIS ONCE...
WHERE THE GODDAMN HELL IS MY GODDAMN DOLL?!

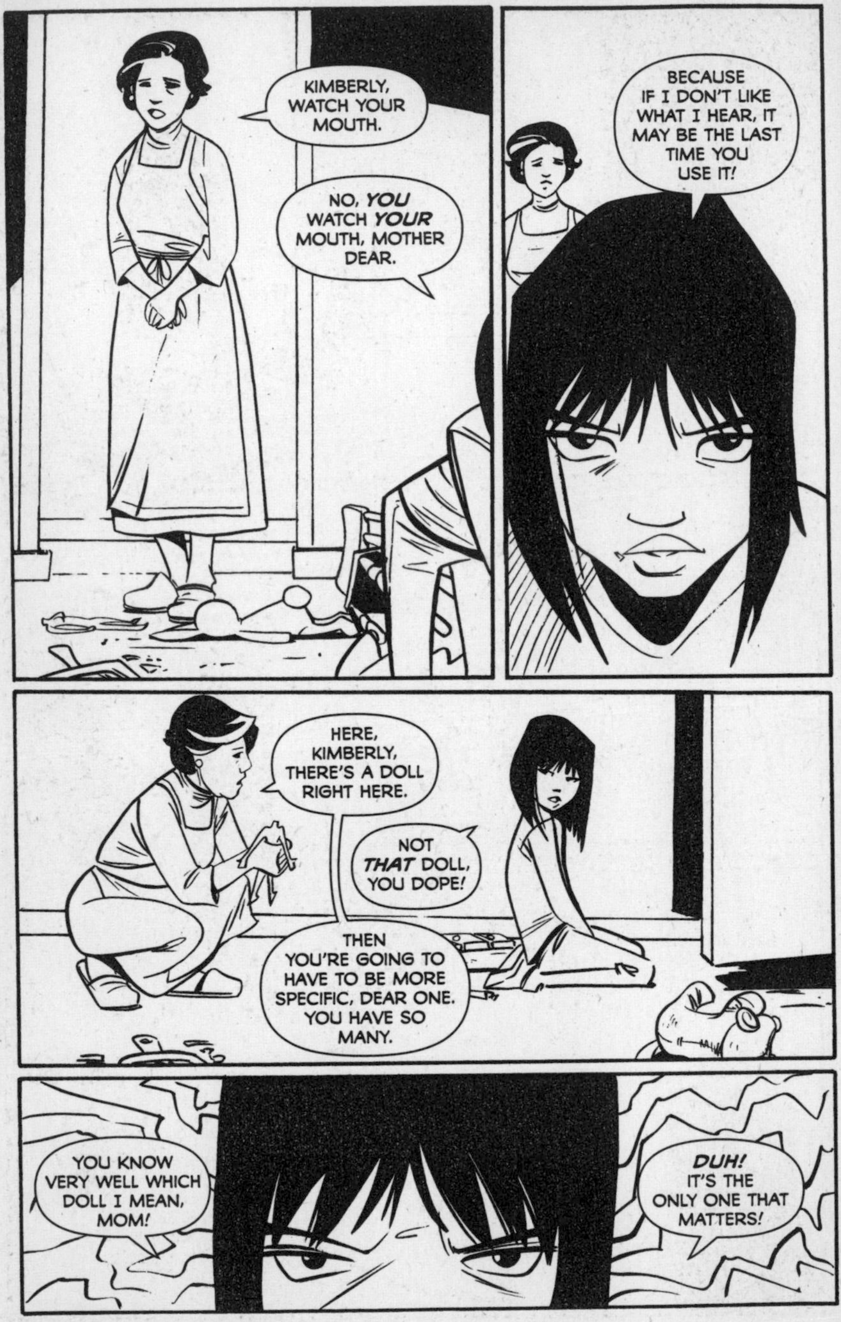
KIMBERLY, WATCH YOUR MOUTH.
NO, *YOU* WATCH *YOUR* MOUTH, MOTHER DEAR.
BECAUSE IF I DON'T LIKE WHAT I HEAR, IT MAY BE THE LAST TIME YOU USE IT!
HERE, KIMBERLY, THERE'S A DOLL RIGHT HERE.
NOT *THAT* DOLL, YOU DOPE!
THEN YOU'RE GOING TO HAVE TO BE MORE SPECIFIC, DEAR ONE. YOU HAVE SO MANY.
YOU KNOW VERY WELL WHICH DOLL I MEAN, MOM!
DUH! IT'S THE ONLY ONE THAT MATTERS!

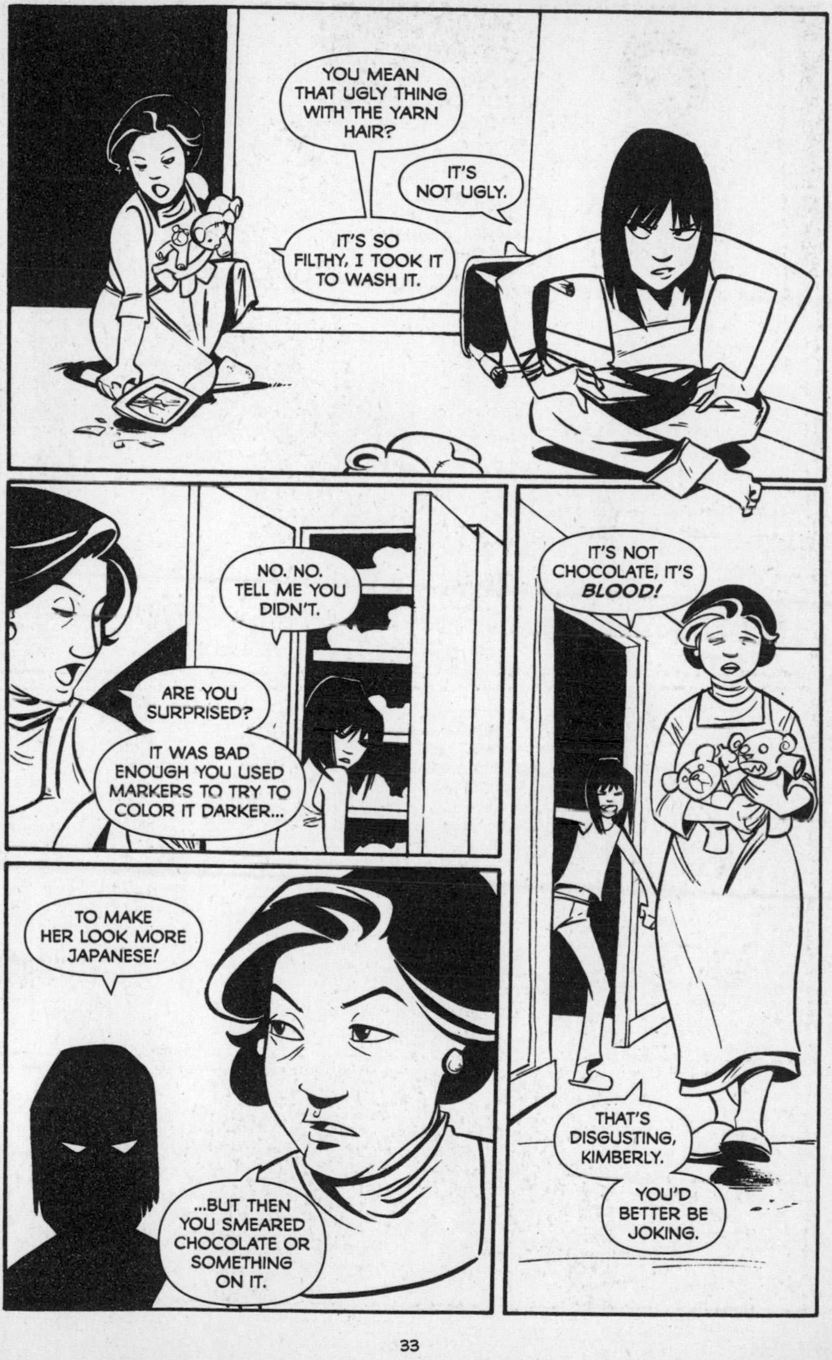

YOU MEAN THAT UGLY THING WITH THE YARN HAIR?
IT'S NOT UGLY.
IT'S SO FILTHY, I TOOK IT TO WASH IT.
NO. NO. TELL ME YOU DIDN'T.
ARE YOU SURPRISED?
IT WAS BAD ENOUGH YOU USED MARKERS TO TRY TO COLOR IT DARKER...
TO MAKE HER LOOK MORE JAPANESE!
...BUT THEN YOU SMEARED CHOCOLATE OR SOMETHING ON IT.
IT'S NOT CHOCOLATE, IT'S *BLOOD!*
THAT'S DISGUSTING, KIMBERLY.
YOU'D BETTER BE JOKING.

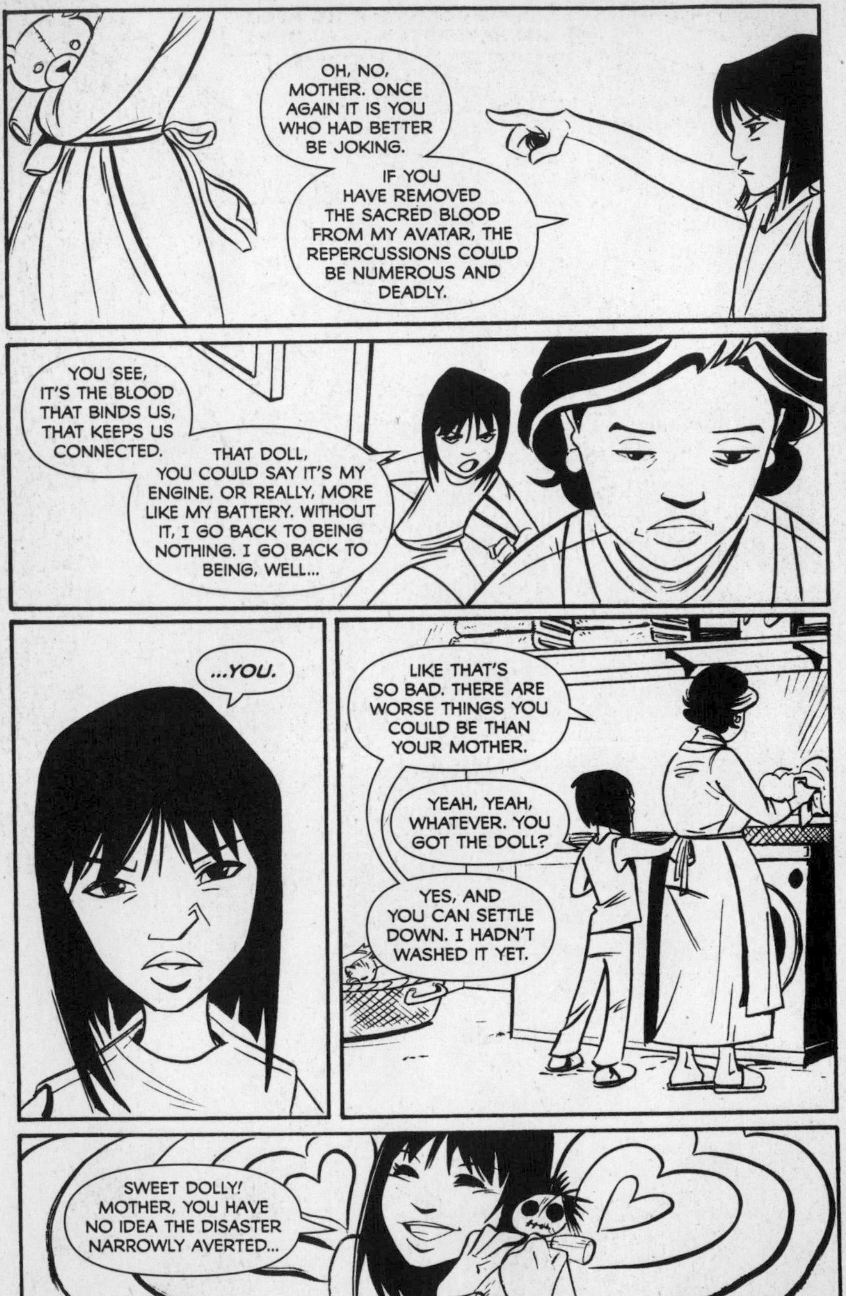
OH, NO, MOTHER. ONCE AGAIN IT IS YOU WHO HAD BETTER BE JOKING.
IF YOU HAVE REMOVED THE SACRED BLOOD FROM MY AVATAR, THE REPERCUSSIONS COULD BE NUMEROUS AND DEADLY.
YOU SEE, IT'S THE BLOOD THAT BINDS US, THAT KEEPS US CONNECTED.
THAT DOLL, YOU COULD SAY IT'S MY ENGINE. OR REALLY, MORE LIKE MY BATTERY. WITHOUT IT, I GO BACK TO BEING NOTHING. I GO BACK TO BEING, WELL...
...YOU.
LIKE THAT'S SO BAD. THERE ARE WORSE THINGS YOU COULD BE THAN YOUR MOTHER.
YEAH, YEAH, WHATEVER. YOU GOT THE DOLL?
YES, AND YOU CAN SETTLE DOWN. I HADN'T WASHED IT YET.
SWEET DOLLY! MOTHER, YOU HAVE NO IDEA THE DISASTER NARROWLY AVERTED...

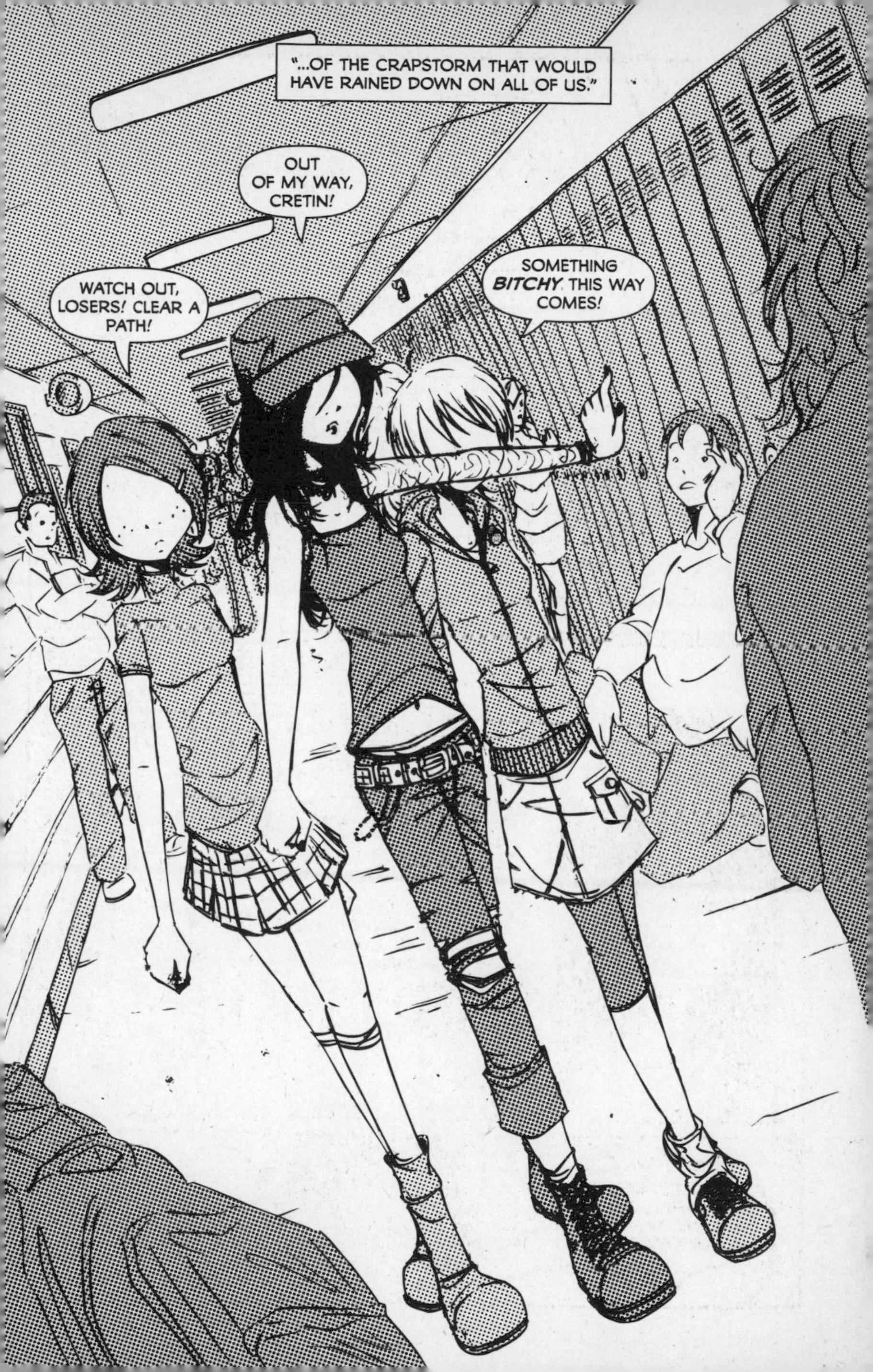
"...OF THE CRAPSTORM THAT WOULD HAVE RAINED DOWN ON ALL OF US."
OUT OF MY WAY, CRETIN!
WATCH OUT, LOSERS! CLEAR A PATH!
SOMETHING *BITCHY* THIS WAY COMES!

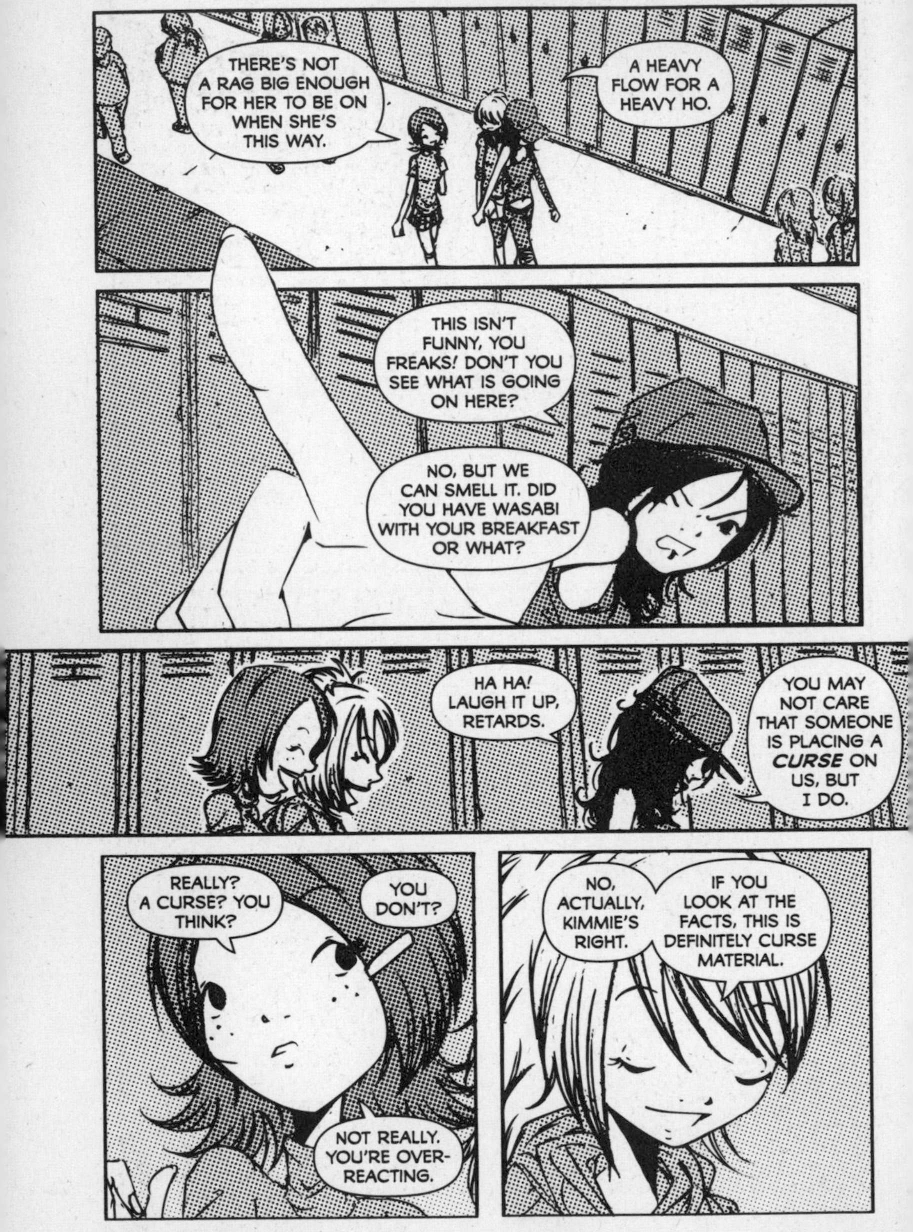
THERE'S NOT A RAG BIG ENOUGH FOR HER TO BE ON WHEN SHE'S THIS WAY.
A HEAVY FLOW FOR A HEAVY HO.
THIS ISN'T FUNNY, YOU FREAKS! DON'T YOU SEE WHAT IS GOING ON HERE?
NO, BUT WE CAN SMELL IT. DID YOU HAVE WASABI WITH YOUR BREAKFAST OR WHAT?
HA HA! LAUGH IT UP, RETARDS.
YOU MAY NOT CARE THAT SOMEONE IS PLACING A *CURSE* ON US, BUT I DO.
REALLY? A CURSE? YOU THINK?
YOU DON'T?
NOT REALLY. YOU'RE OVER-REACTING.
NO, ACTUALLY, KIMMIE'S RIGHT.
IF YOU LOOK AT THE FACTS, THIS IS DEFINITELY CURSE MATERIAL.

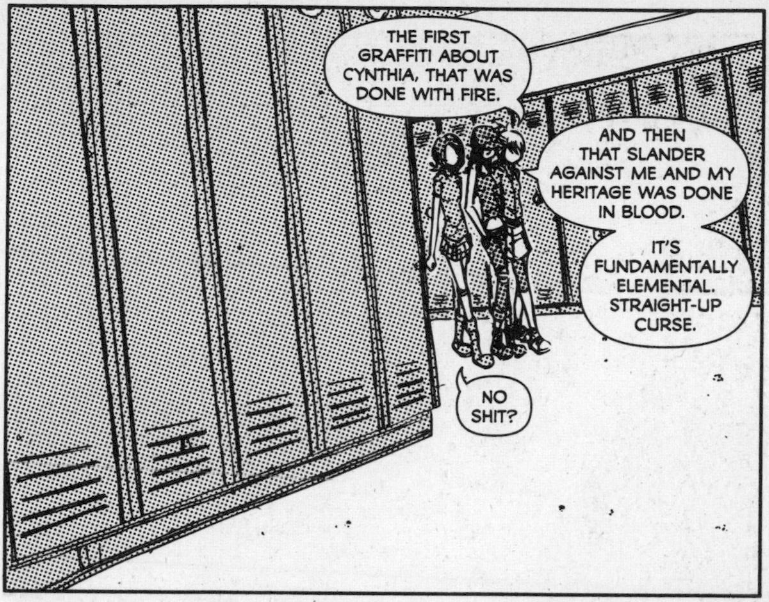
THE FIRST GRAFFITI ABOUT CYNTHIA, THAT WAS DONE WITH FIRE.
AND THEN THAT SLANDER AGAINST ME AND MY HERITAGE WAS DONE IN BLOOD.
IT'S FUNDAMENTALLY ELEMENTAL. STRAIGHT-UP CURSE.
NO SHIT?

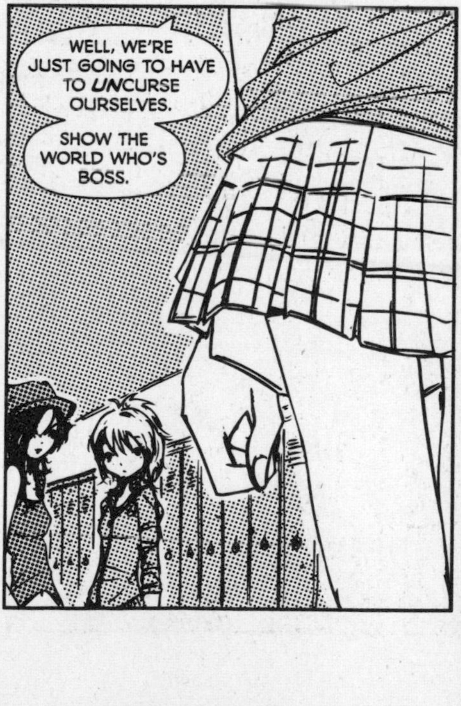
WELL, WE'RE JUST GOING TO HAVE TO *UN*CURSE OURSELVES.
SHOW THE WORLD WHO'S BOSS.

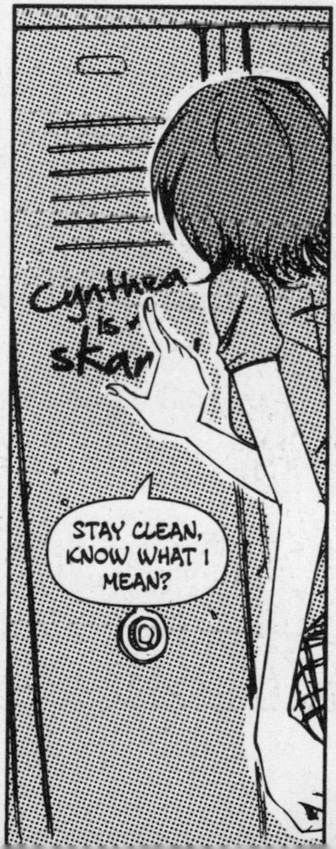
Cynthia is
STAY CLEAN, KNOW WHAT I MEAN?

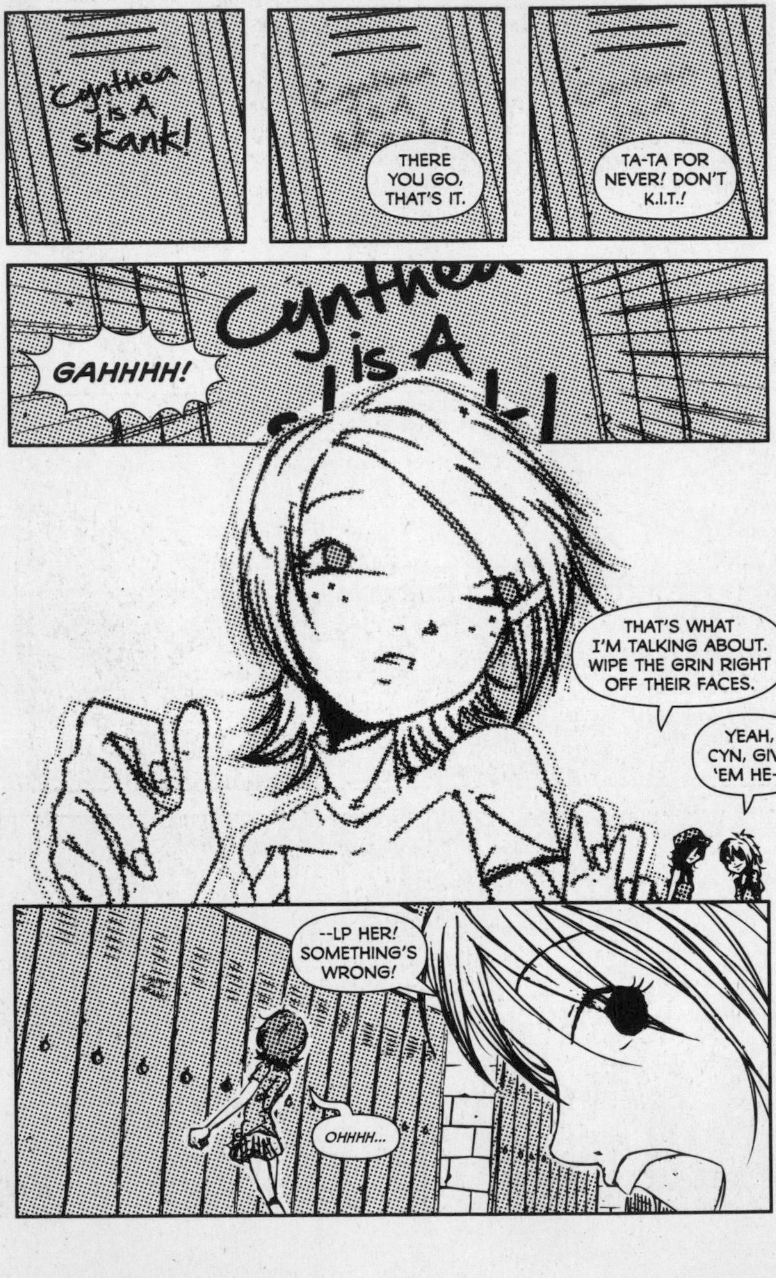
Cynthea is A skank!
THERE YOU GO, THAT'S IT.
TA-TA FOR NEVER! DON'T K.I.T.!
GAHHHH!
Cynthea is A
THAT'S WHAT I'M TALKING ABOUT. WIPE THE GRIN RIGHT OFF THEIR FACES.
YEAH, CYN, GIVE 'EM HE--
--LP HER! SOMETHING'S WRONG!
OHHHH...

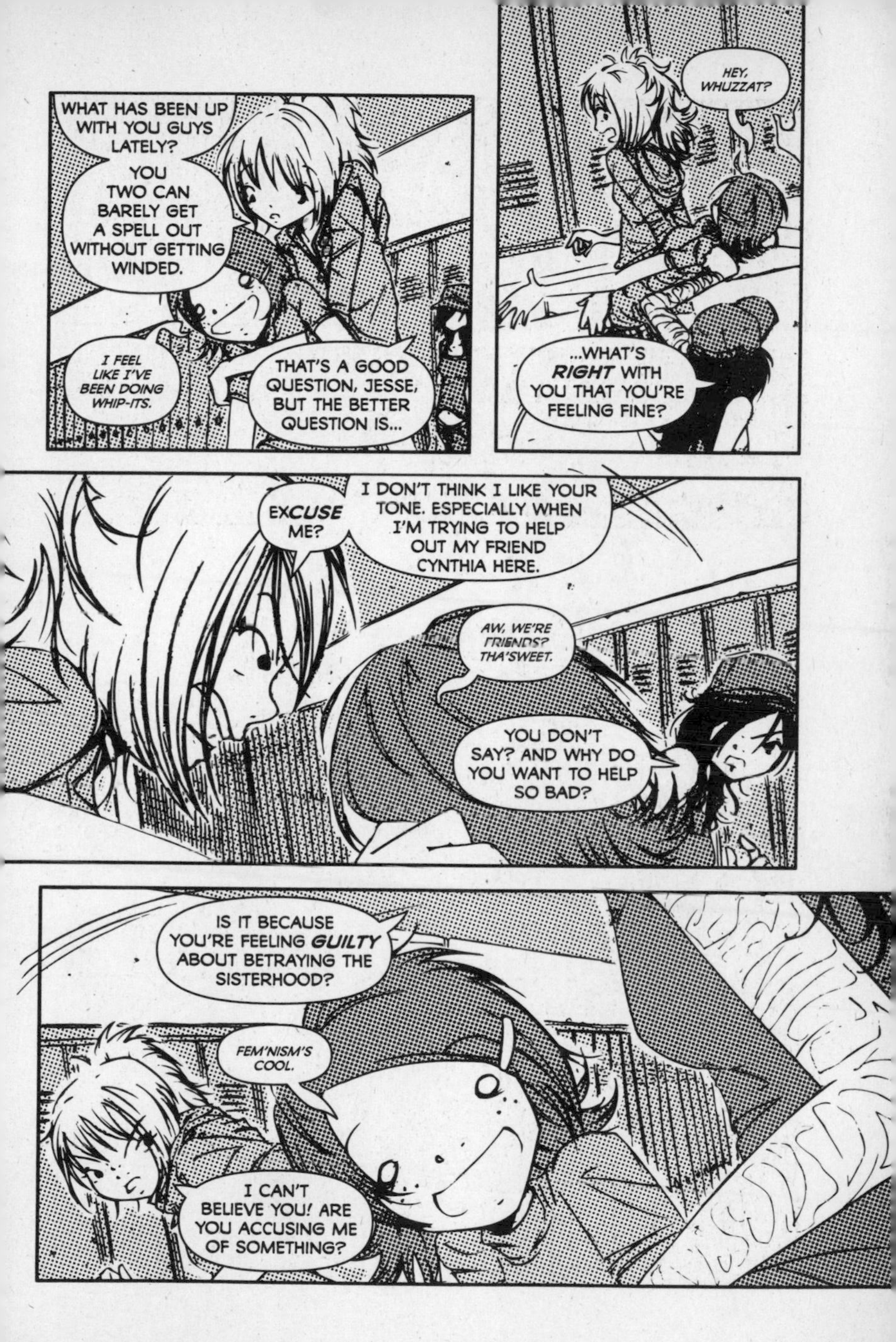
WHAT HAS BEEN UP WITH YOU GUYS LATELY?
YOU TWO CAN BARELY GET A SPELL OUT WITHOUT GETTING WINDED.
I FEEL LIKE I'VE BEEN DOING WHIP-ITS.
THAT'S A GOOD QUESTION, JESSE, BUT THE BETTER QUESTION IS...
HEY, WHUZZAT?
...WHAT'S *RIGHT* WITH YOU THAT YOU'RE FEELING FINE?
EX*CUSE* ME?
I DON'T THINK I LIKE YOUR TONE. ESPECIALLY WHEN I'M TRYING TO HELP OUT MY FRIEND CYNTHIA HERE.
AW, WE'RE FRIENDS? THA'SWEET.
YOU DON'T SAY? AND WHY DO YOU WANT TO HELP SO BAD?
IS IT BECAUSE YOU'RE FEELING *GUILTY* ABOUT BETRAYING THE SISTERHOOD?
FEM'NISM'S COOL.
I CAN'T BELIEVE YOU! ARE YOU ACCUSING ME OF SOMETHING?

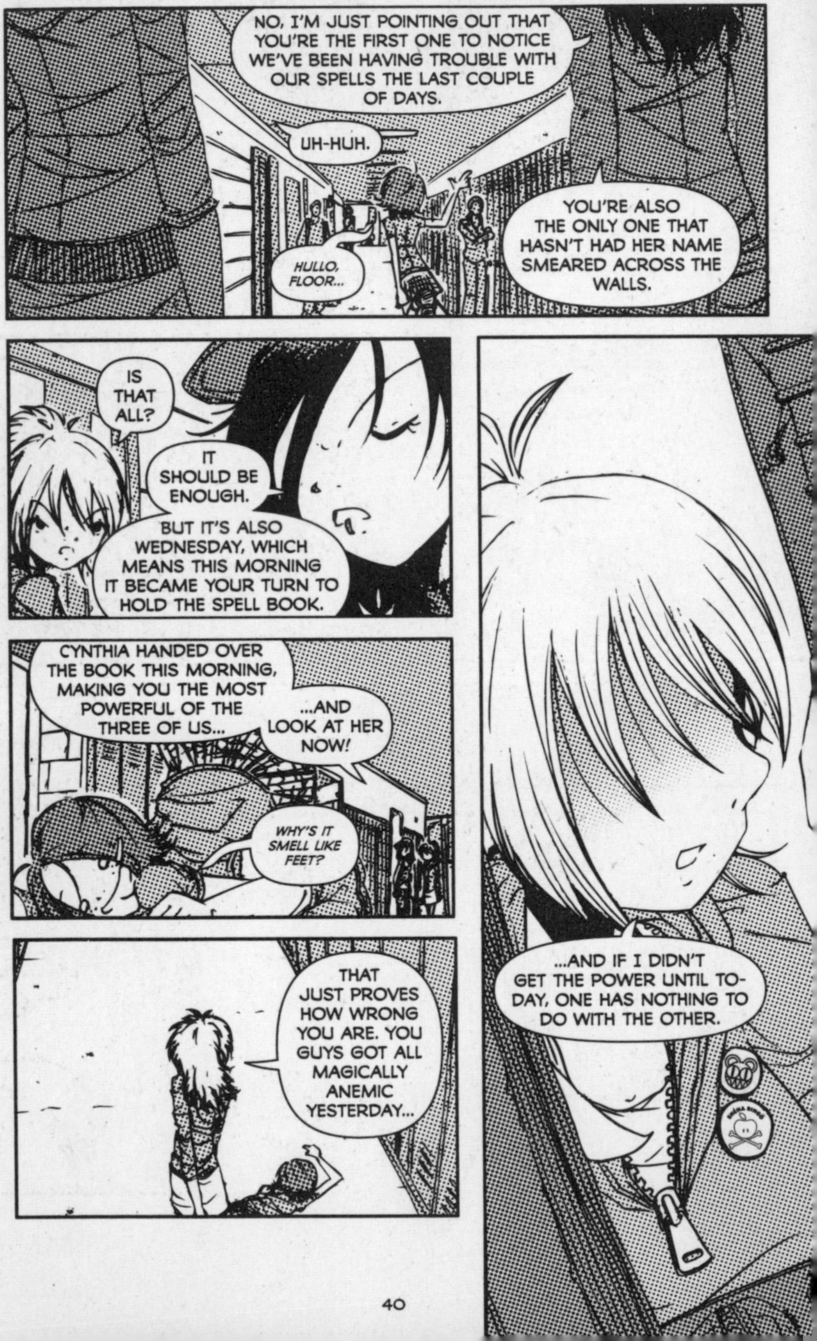
NO, I'M JUST POINTING OUT THAT YOU'RE THE FIRST ONE TO NOTICE WE'VE BEEN HAVING TROUBLE WITH OUR SPELLS THE LAST COUPLE OF DAYS.
UH-HUH.
HULLO, FLOOR...
YOU'RE ALSO THE ONLY ONE THAT HASN'T HAD HER NAME SMEARED ACROSS THE WALLS.
IS THAT ALL?
IT SHOULD BE ENOUGH.
BUT IT'S ALSO WEDNESDAY, WHICH MEANS THIS MORNING IT BECAME YOUR TURN TO HOLD THE SPELL BOOK.
CYNTHIA HANDED OVER THE BOOK THIS MORNING, MAKING YOU THE MOST POWERFUL OF THE THREE OF US...
...AND LOOK AT HER NOW!
WHY'S IT SMELL LIKE FEET?
THAT JUST PROVES HOW WRONG YOU ARE. YOU GUYS GOT ALL MAGICALLY ANEMIC YESTERDAY...
...AND IF I DIDN'T GET THE POWER UNTIL TO-DAY, ONE HAS NOTHING TO DO WITH THE OTHER.

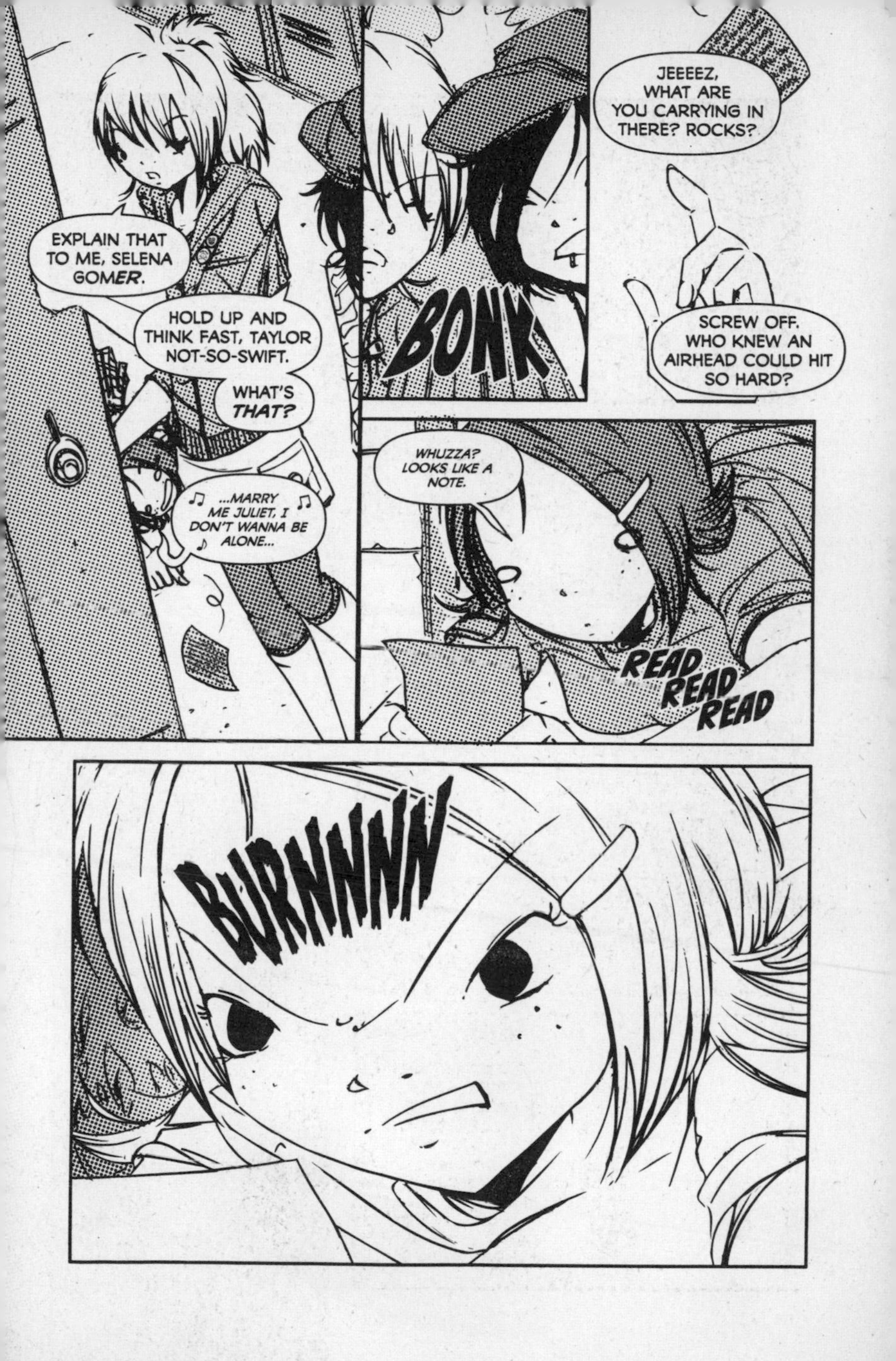
EXPLAIN THAT TO ME, SELENA GOMER.
HOLD UP AND THINK FAST, TAYLOR NOT-SO-SWIFT.
WHAT'S THAT?
♫ ...MARRY ME JULIET, I DON'T WANNA BE ALONE... ♫
BONK
JEEEEZ, WHAT ARE YOU CARRYING IN THERE? ROCKS?
SCREW OFF. WHO KNEW AN AIRHEAD COULD HIT SO HARD?
WHUZZA? LOOKS LIKE A NOTE.
READ READ READ
BURNNNN

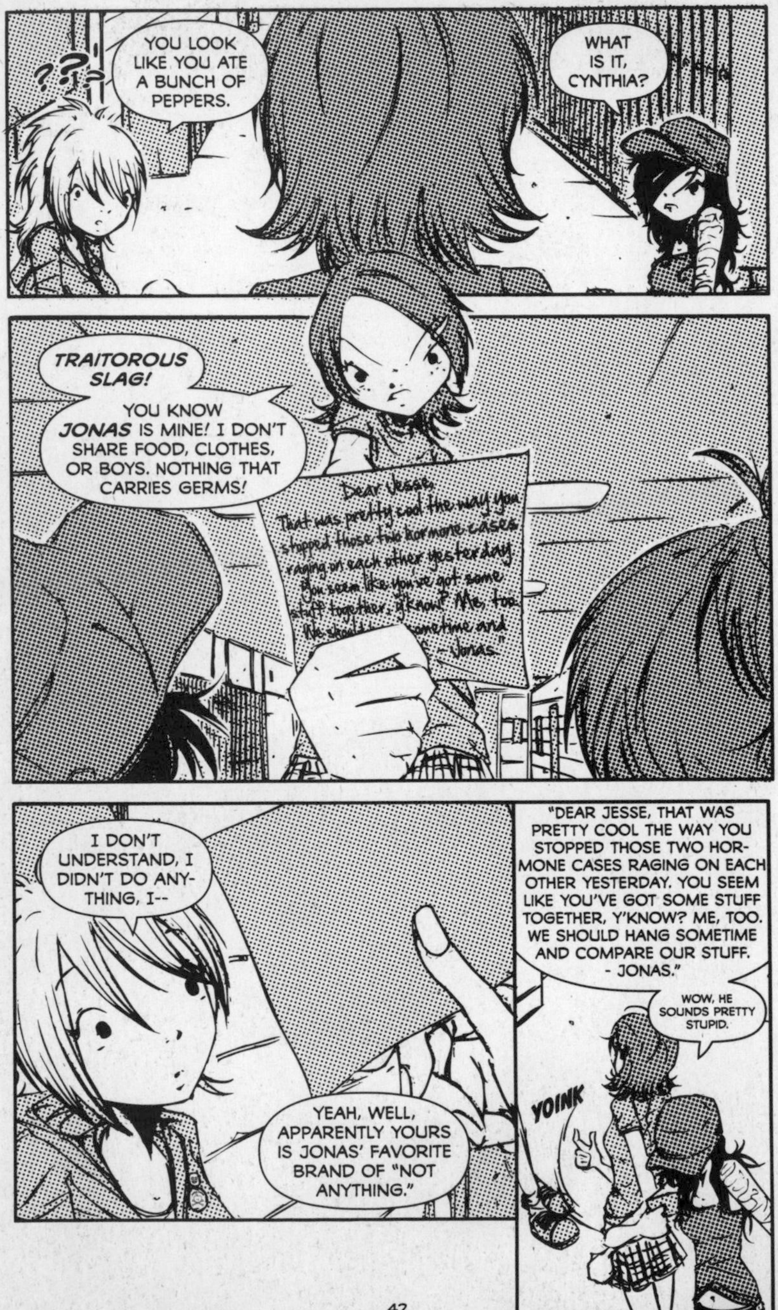

YOU LOOK LIKE YOU ATE A BUNCH OF PEPPERS.
WHAT IS IT, CYNTHIA?
TRAITOROUS SLAG!
YOU KNOW JONAS IS MINE! I DON'T SHARE FOOD, CLOTHES, OR BOYS. NOTHING THAT CARRIES GERMS!
Dear Jesse,
That was pretty cool the way you
stopped those two hormone cases
raging on each other yesterday.
You seem like you've got some
stuff together, y'know? Me, too.
sometime and
- Jonas
I DON'T UNDERSTAND, I DIDN'T DO ANY-THING, I--
YEAH, WELL, APPARENTLY YOURS IS JONAS' FAVORITE BRAND OF "NOT ANYTHING."
"DEAR JESSE, THAT WAS PRETTY COOL THE WAY YOU STOPPED THOSE TWO HOR-MONE CASES RAGING ON EACH OTHER YESTERDAY. YOU SEEM LIKE YOU'VE GOT SOME STUFF TOGETHER, Y'KNOW? ME, TOO. WE SHOULD HANG SOMETIME AND COMPARE OUR STUFF. - JONAS."
WOW, HE SOUNDS PRETTY STUPID.
YOINK

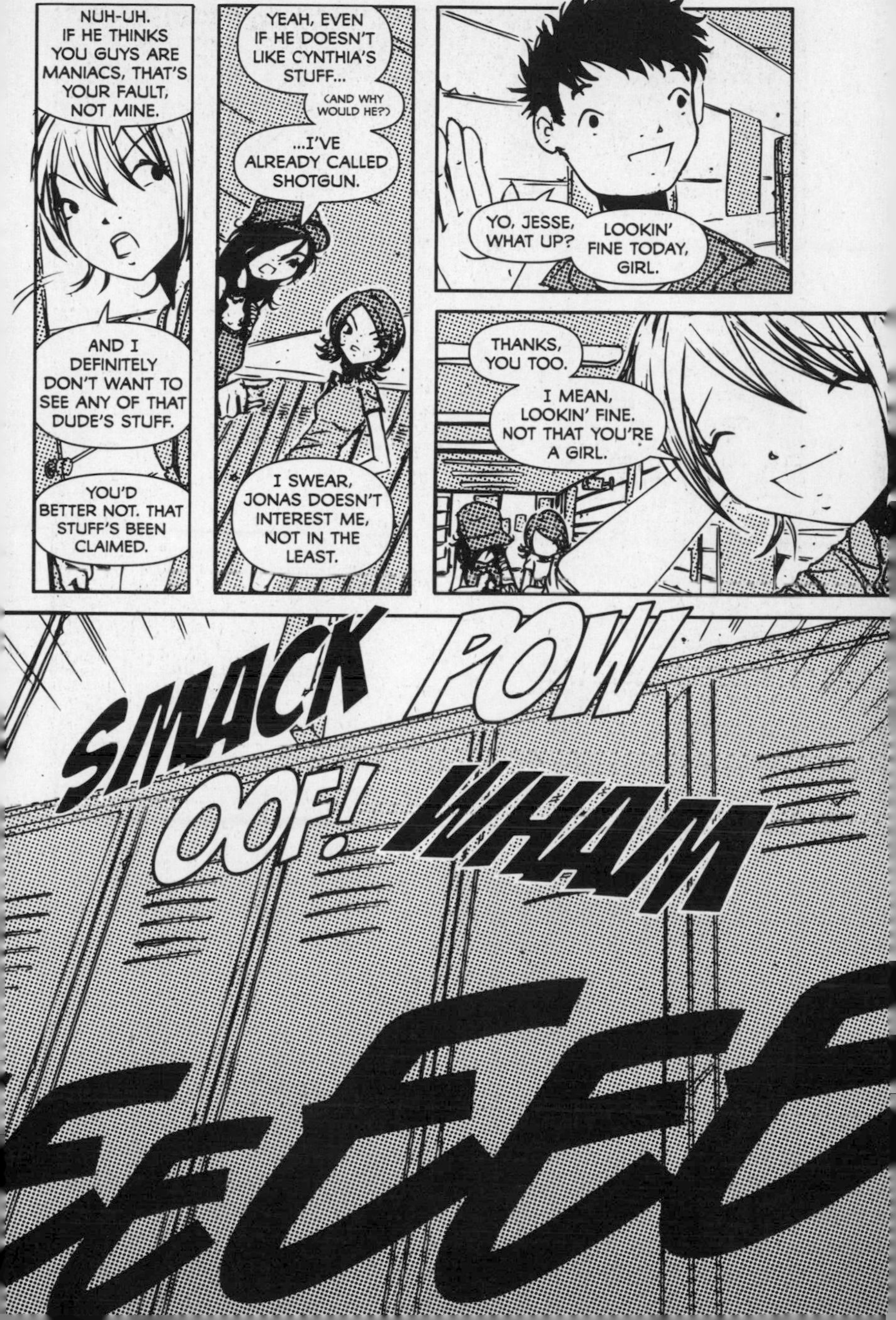
NUH-UH. IF HE THINKS YOU GUYS ARE MANIACS, THAT'S YOUR FAULT, NOT MINE.
AND I DEFINITELY DON'T WANT TO SEE ANY OF THAT DUDE'S STUFF.
YOU'D BETTER NOT. THAT STUFF'S BEEN CLAIMED.
YEAH, EVEN IF HE DOESN'T LIKE CYNTHIA'S STUFF...
(AND WHY WOULD HE?)
...I'VE ALREADY CALLED SHOTGUN.
I SWEAR, JONAS DOESN'T INTEREST ME, NOT IN THE LEAST.
YO, JESSE, WHAT UP?
LOOKIN' FINE TODAY, GIRL.
THANKS, YOU TOO.
I MEAN, LOOKIN' FINE. NOT THAT YOU'RE A GIRL.
SMACK
POW
OOF!
WHAM
EEEE

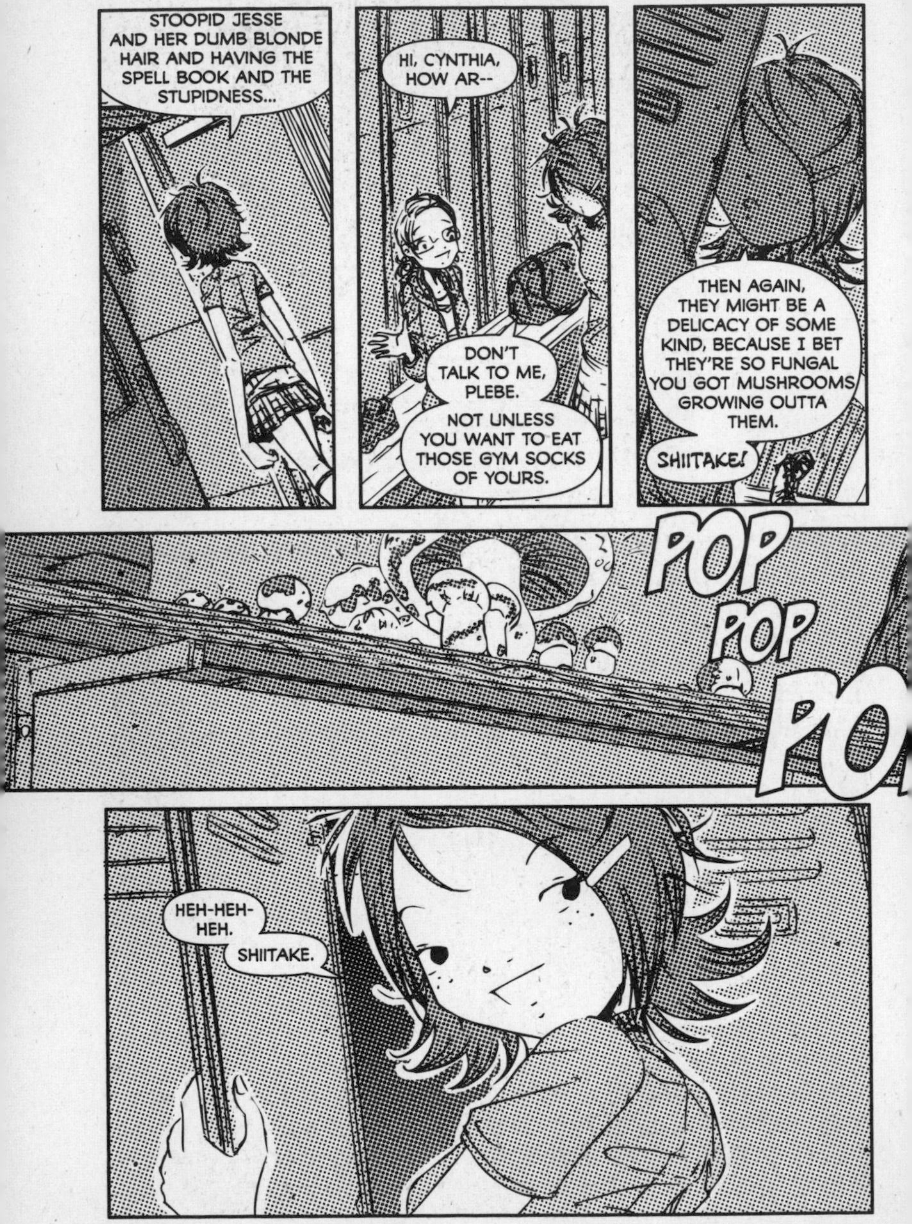
STOOPID JESSE AND HER DUMB BLONDE HAIR AND HAVING THE SPELL BOOK AND THE STUPIDNESS...
HI, CYNTHIA, HOW AR--
DON'T TALK TO ME, PLEBE.
NOT UNLESS YOU WANT TO EAT THOSE GYM SOCKS OF YOURS.
THEN AGAIN, THEY MIGHT BE A DELICACY OF SOME KIND, BECAUSE I BET THEY'RE SO FUNGAL YOU GOT MUSHROOMS GROWING OUTTA THEM.
SHIITAKE!
POP
POP
HEH-HEH-HEH.
SHIITAKE.

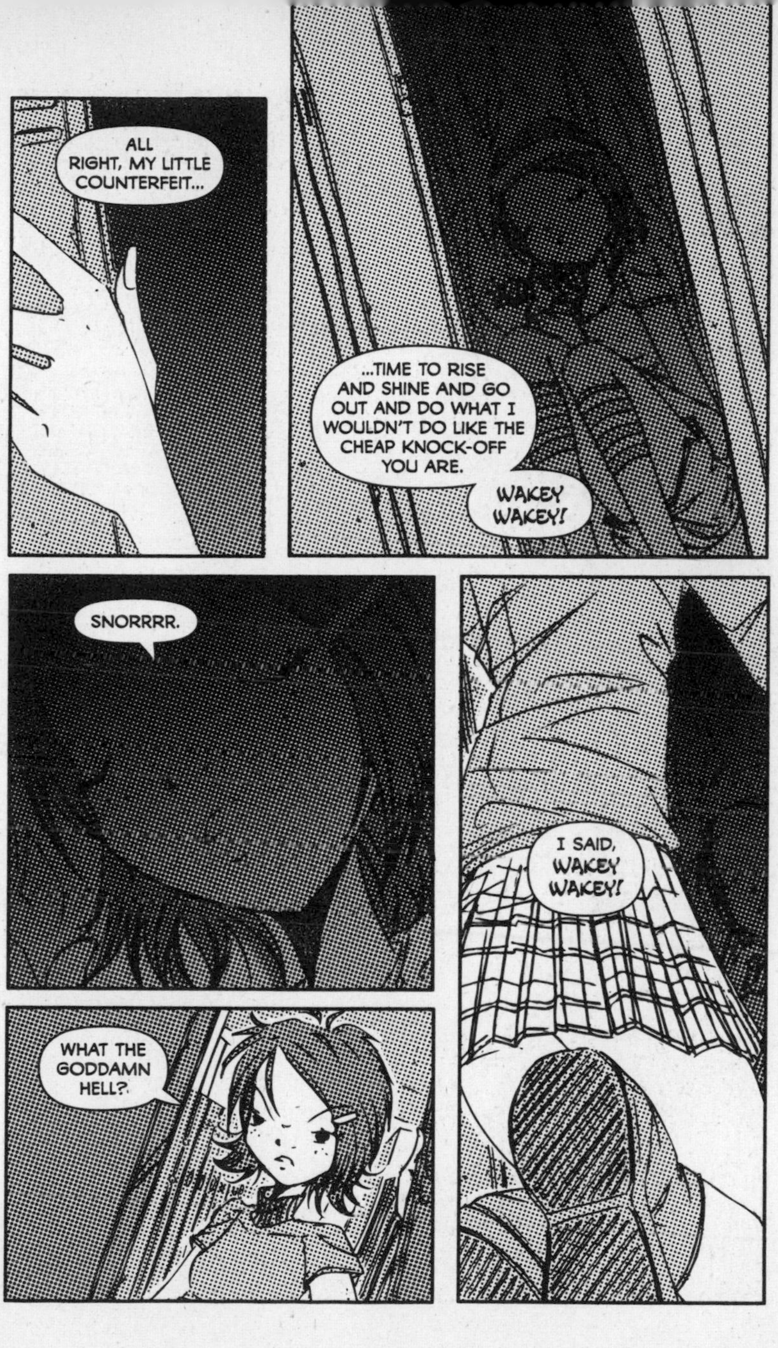
ALL RIGHT, MY LITTLE COUNTERFEIT...
...TIME TO RISE AND SHINE AND GO OUT AND DO WHAT I WOULDN'T DO LIKE THE CHEAP KNOCK-OFF YOU ARE.
WAKEY WAKEY!
SNORRRR.
I SAID, WAKEY WAKEY!
WHAT THE GODDAMN HELL?

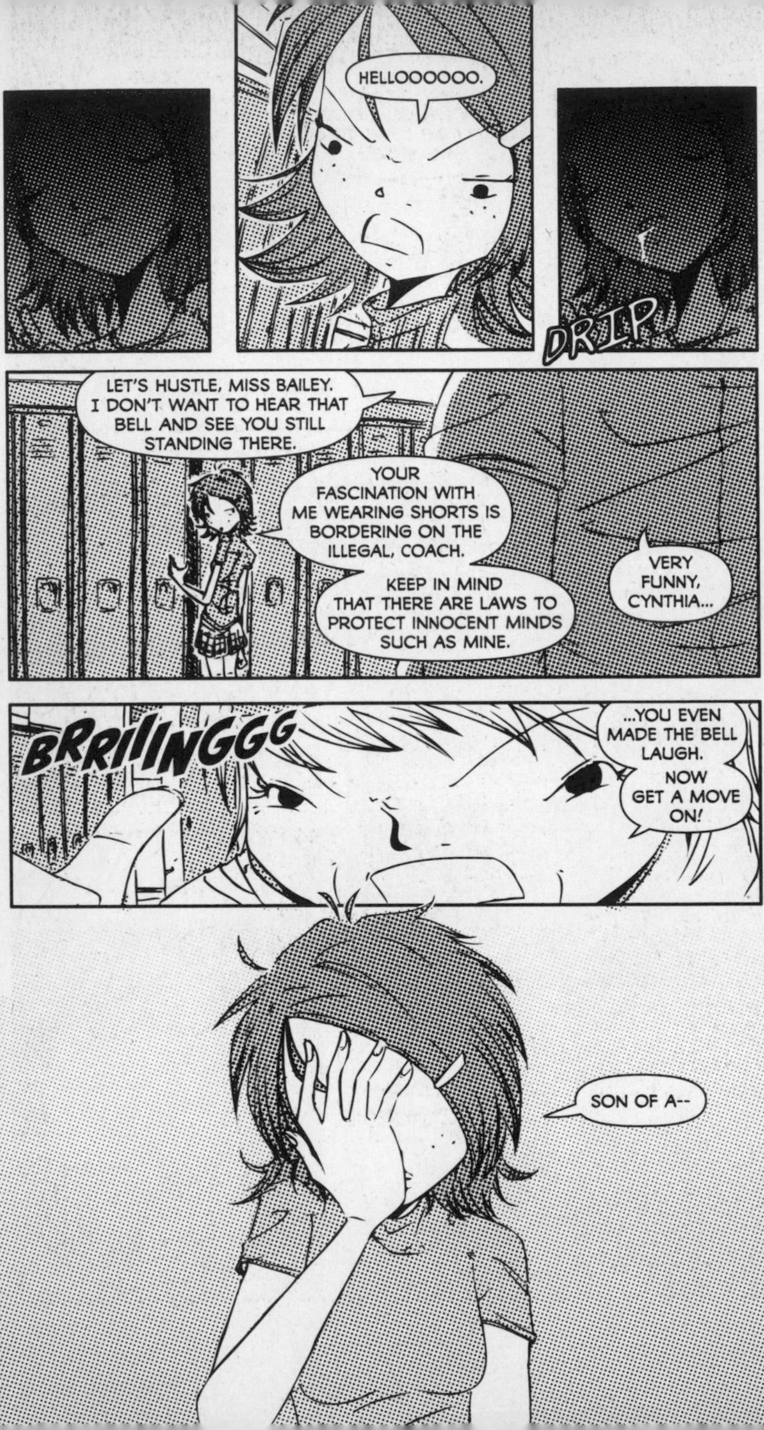
HELLOOOOOO.
DRIP
LET'S HUSTLE, MISS BAILEY. I DON'T WANT TO HEAR THAT BELL AND SEE YOU STILL STANDING THERE.
YOUR FASCINATION WITH ME WEARING SHORTS IS BORDERING ON THE ILLEGAL, COACH.
KEEP IN MIND THAT THERE ARE LAWS TO PROTECT INNOCENT MINDS SUCH AS MINE.
VERY FUNNY, CYNTHIA...
BRRIIINGGG
...YOU EVEN MADE THE BELL LAUGH.
NOW GET A MOVE ON!
SON OF A--

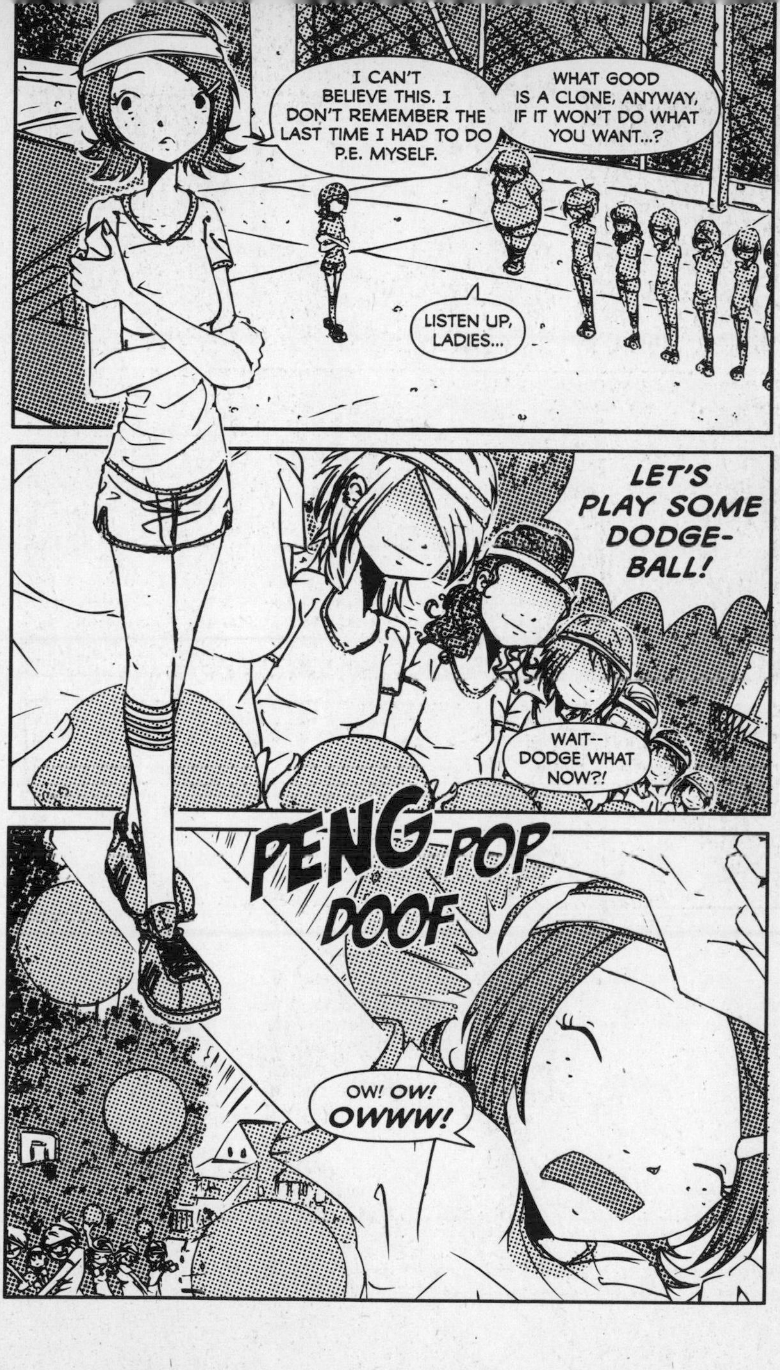
I CAN'T BELIEVE THIS. I DON'T REMEMBER THE LAST TIME I HAD TO DO P.E. MYSELF.
WHAT GOOD IS A CLONE, ANYWAY, IF IT WON'T DO WHAT YOU WANT...?
LISTEN UP, LADIES...
LET'S PLAY SOME DODGE-BALL!
WAIT-- DODGE WHAT NOW?!
PENG
POP
DOOF
OW! OW! OWWW!

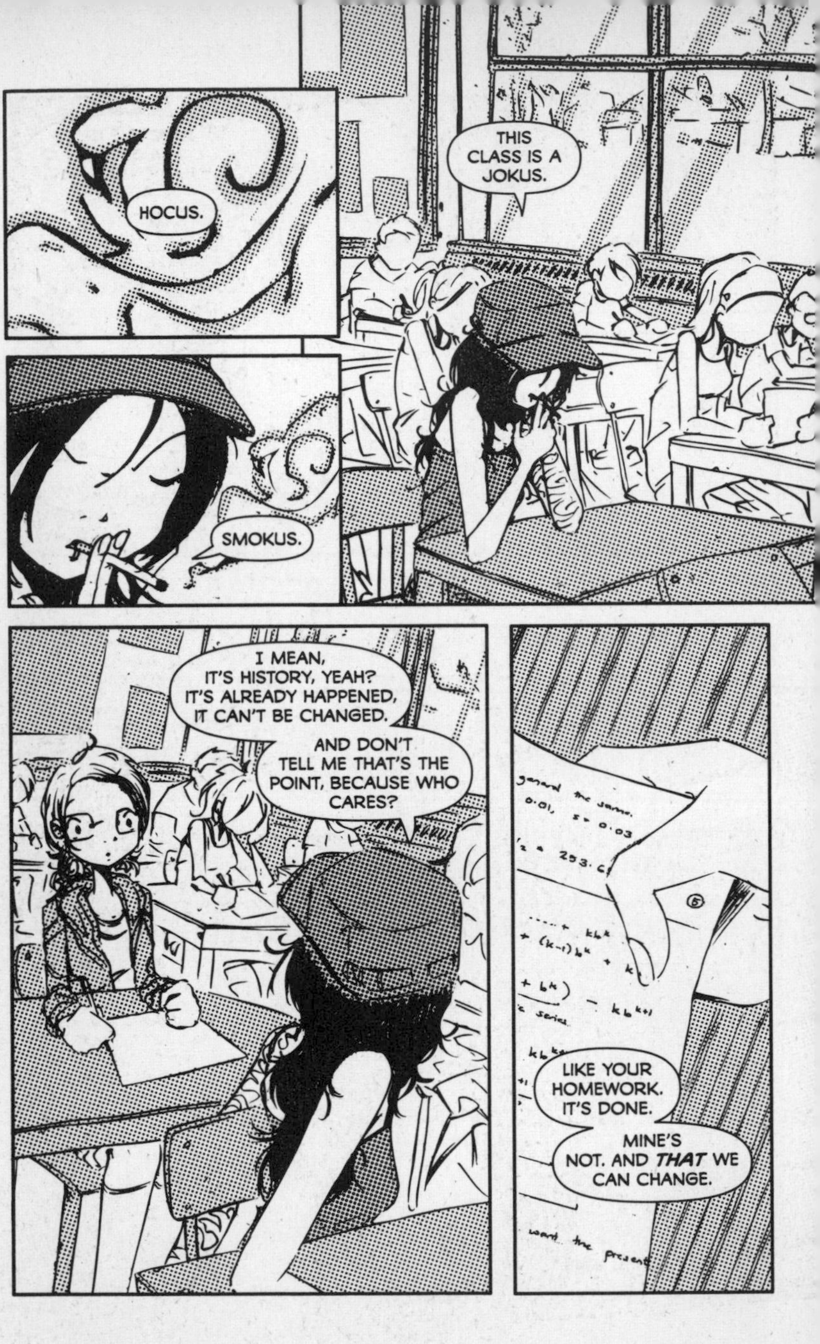
HOCUS.
SMOKUS.
THIS CLASS IS A JOKUS.
I MEAN, IT'S HISTORY, YEAH? IT'S ALREADY HAPPENED, IT CAN'T BE CHANGED.
AND DON'T TELL ME THAT'S THE POINT, BECAUSE WHO CARES?
LIKE YOUR HOMEWORK. IT'S DONE.
MINE'S NOT. AND *THAT* WE CAN CHANGE.

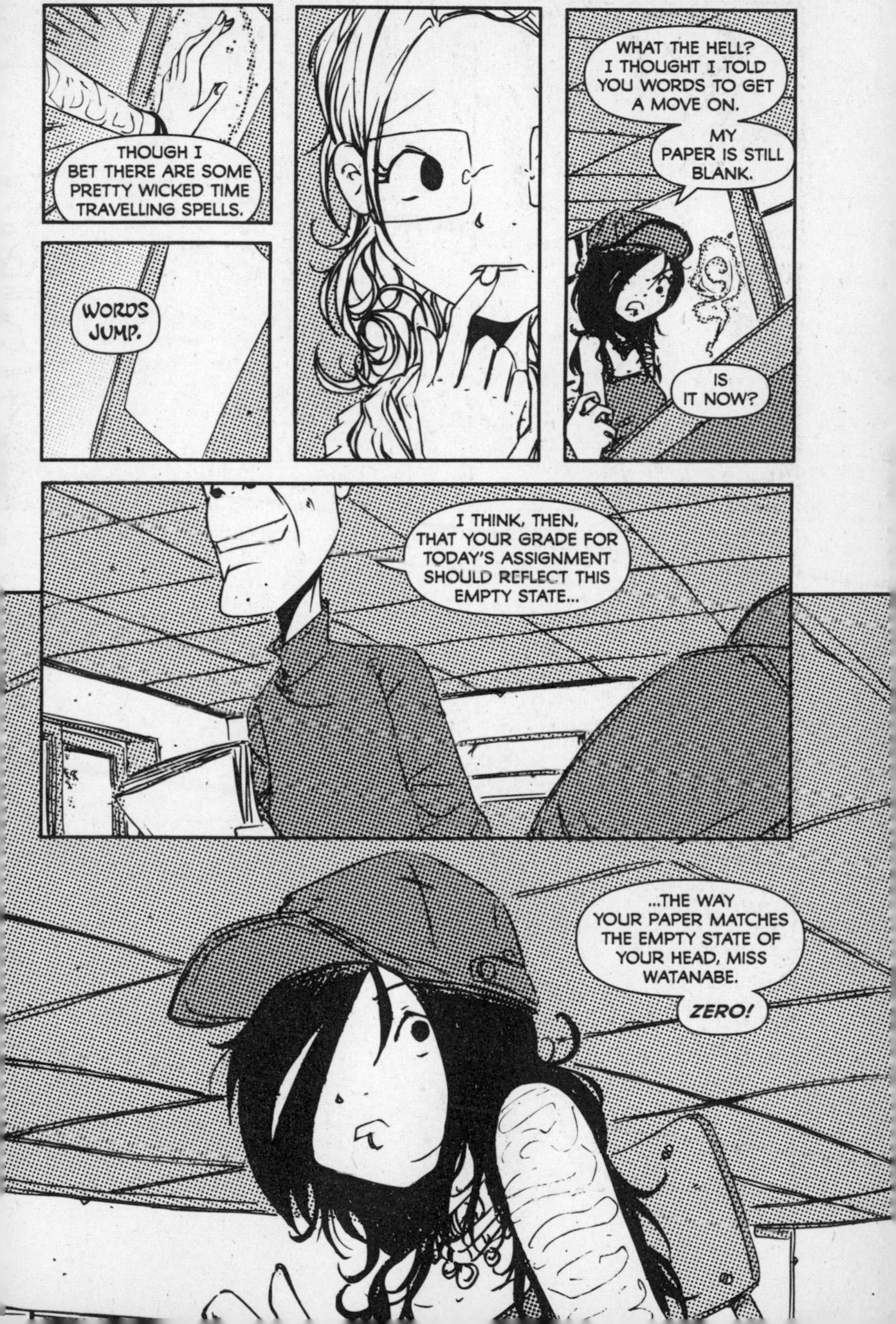
THOUGH I BET THERE ARE SOME PRETTY WICKED TIME TRAVELLING SPELLS.
WORDS JUMP.
WHAT THE HELL? I THOUGHT I TOLD YOU WORDS TO GET A MOVE ON.
MY PAPER IS STILL BLANK.
IS IT NOW?
I THINK, THEN, THAT YOUR GRADE FOR TODAY'S ASSIGNMENT SHOULD REFLECT THIS EMPTY STATE...
...THE WAY YOUR PAPER MATCHES THE EMPTY STATE OF YOUR HEAD, MISS WATANABE.
ZERO!

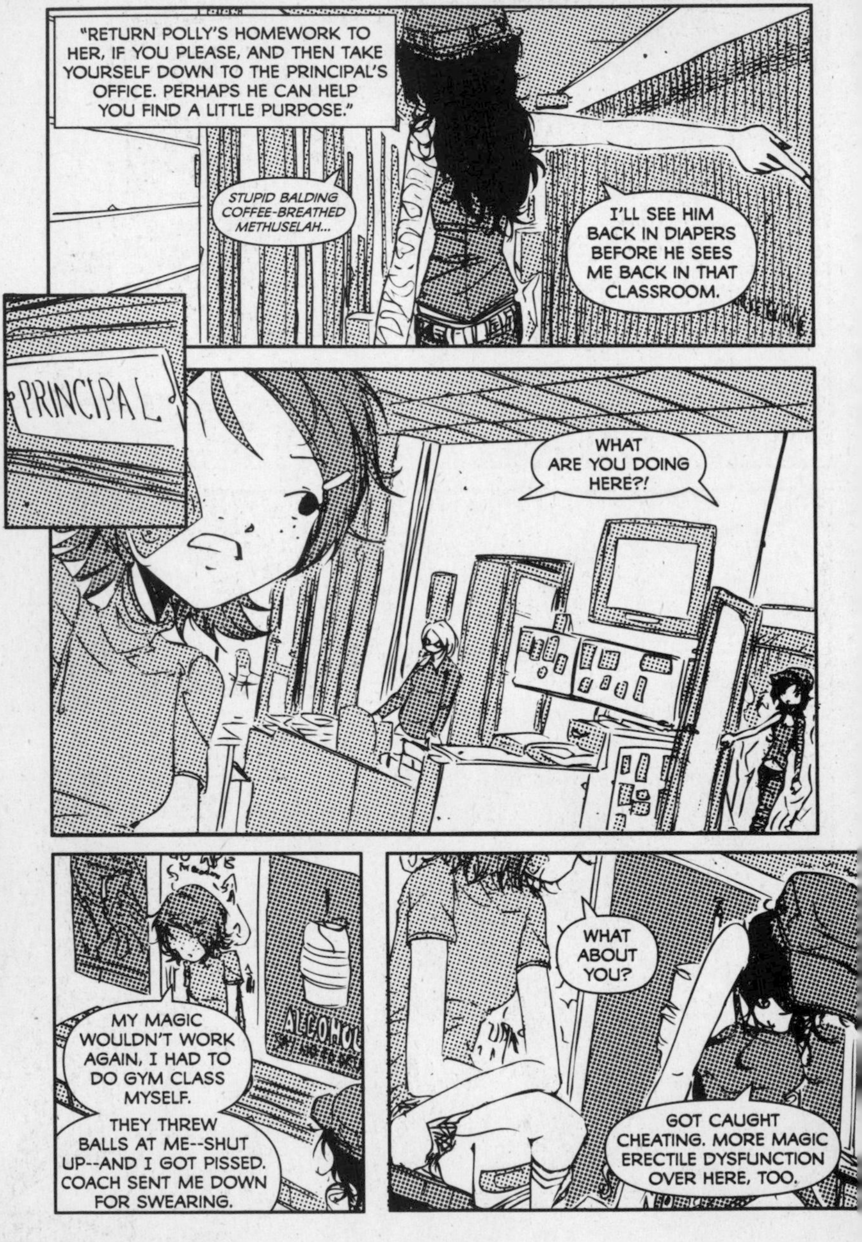
"RETURN POLLY'S HOMEWORK TO HER, IF YOU PLEASE, AND THEN TAKE YOURSELF DOWN TO THE PRINCIPAL'S OFFICE. PERHAPS HE CAN HELP YOU FIND A LITTLE PURPOSE."
STUPID BALDING COFFEE-BREATHED METHUSELAH...
I'LL SEE HIM BACK IN DIAPERS BEFORE HE SEES ME BACK IN THAT CLASSROOM.
PRINCIPAL
WHAT ARE YOU DOING HERE?!
MY MAGIC WOULDN'T WORK AGAIN. I HAD TO DO GYM CLASS MYSELF.
THEY THREW BALLS AT ME--SHUT UP--AND I GOT PISSED. COACH SENT ME DOWN FOR SWEARING.
WHAT ABOUT YOU?
GOT CAUGHT CHEATING. MORE MAGIC ERECTILE DYSFUNCTION OVER HERE, TOO.

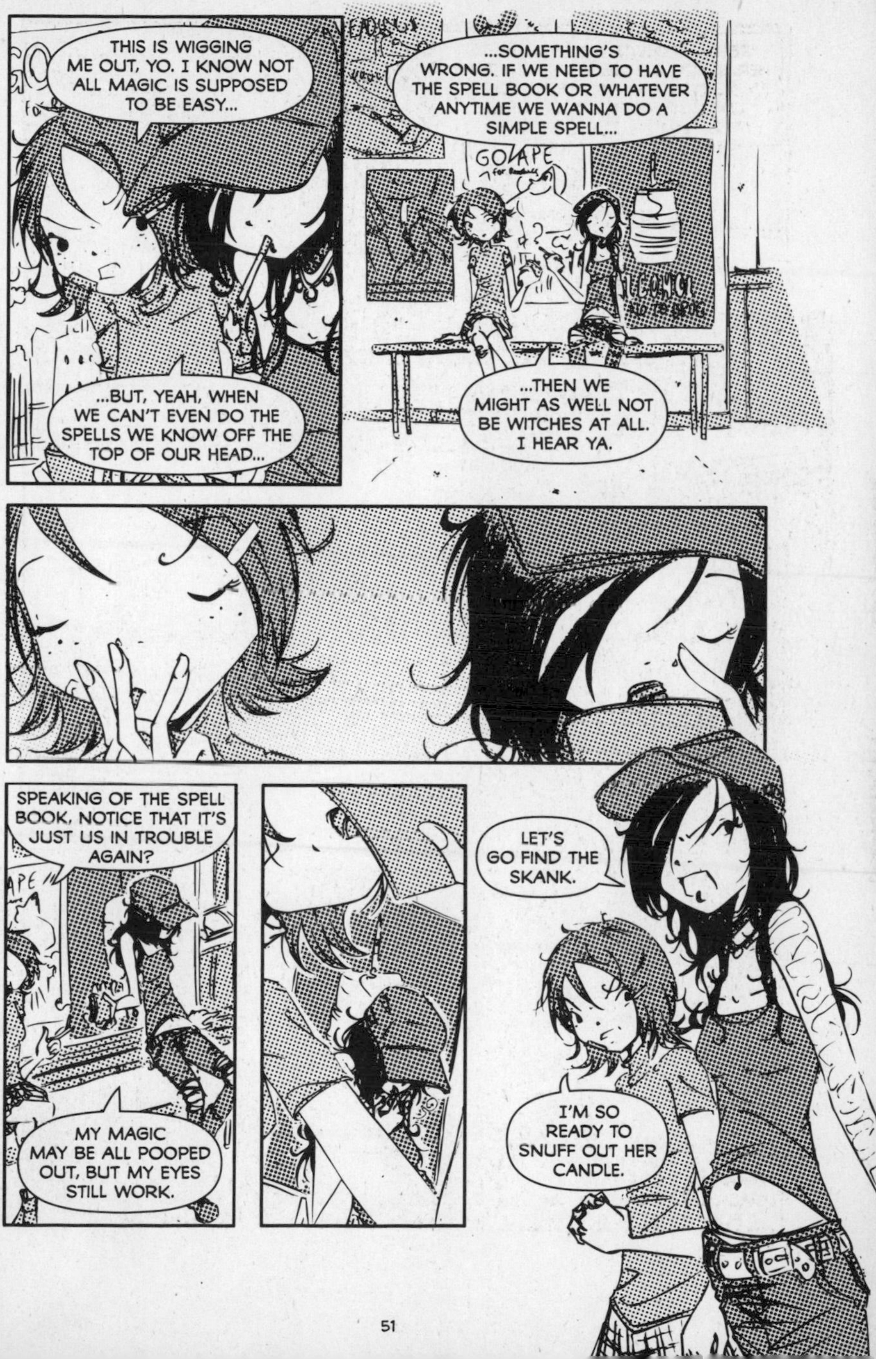
THIS IS WIGGING ME OUT, YO. I KNOW NOT ALL MAGIC IS SUPPOSED TO BE EASY...
...BUT, YEAH, WHEN WE CAN'T EVEN DO THE SPELLS WE KNOW OFF THE TOP OF OUR HEAD...
...SOMETHING'S WRONG. IF WE NEED TO HAVE THE SPELL BOOK OR WHATEVER ANYTIME WE WANNA DO A SIMPLE SPELL...
GO APE
...THEN WE MIGHT AS WELL NOT BE WITCHES AT ALL. I HEAR YA.
SPEAKING OF THE SPELL BOOK, NOTICE THAT IT'S JUST US IN TROUBLE AGAIN?
MY MAGIC MAY BE ALL POOPED OUT, BUT MY EYES STILL WORK.
LET'S GO FIND THE SKANK.
I'M SO READY TO SNUFF OUT HER CANDLE.

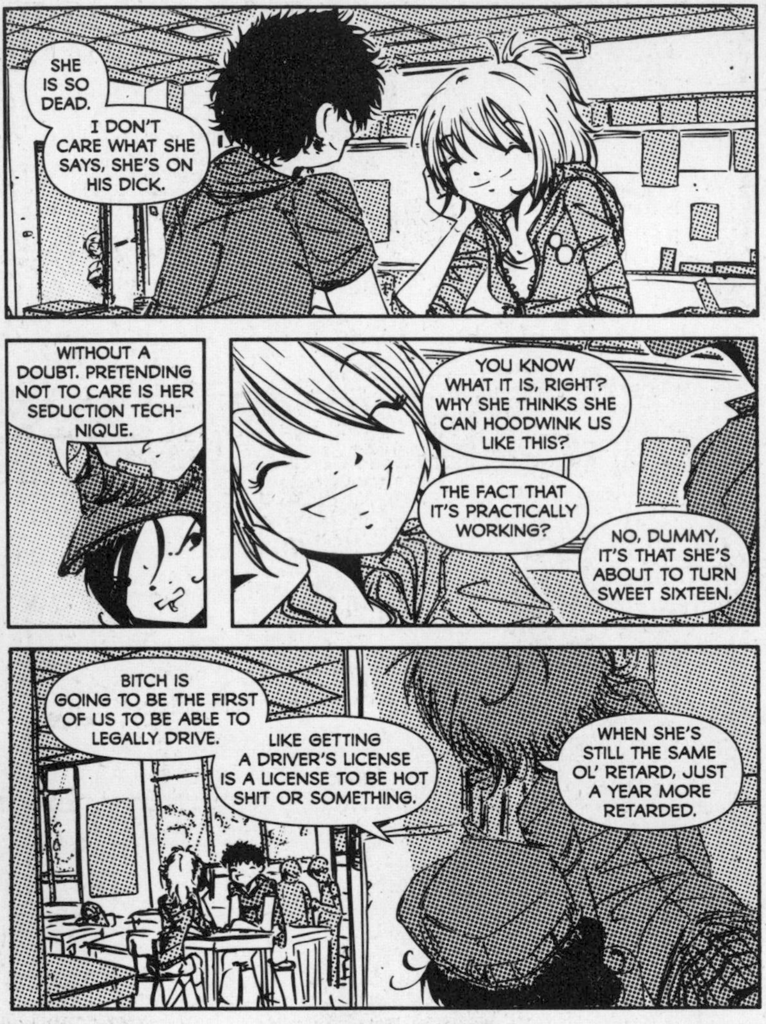
SHE IS SO DEAD.
I DON'T CARE WHAT SHE SAYS, SHE'S ON HIS DICK.
WITHOUT A DOUBT. PRETENDING NOT TO CARE IS HER SEDUCTION TECH-NIQUE.
YOU KNOW WHAT IT IS, RIGHT? WHY SHE THINKS SHE CAN HOODWINK US LIKE THIS?
THE FACT THAT IT'S PRACTICALLY WORKING?
NO, DUMMY, IT'S THAT SHE'S ABOUT TO TURN SWEET SIXTEEN.
BITCH IS GOING TO BE THE FIRST OF US TO BE ABLE TO LEGALLY DRIVE.
LIKE GETTING A DRIVER'S LICENSE IS A LICENSE TO BE HOT SHIT OR SOMETHING.
WHEN SHE'S STILL THE SAME OL' RETARD, JUST A YEAR MORE RETARDED.

"SHE'S ALWAYS ACTED LIKE SHE'S GOT NO TIME FOR ROMANCE...

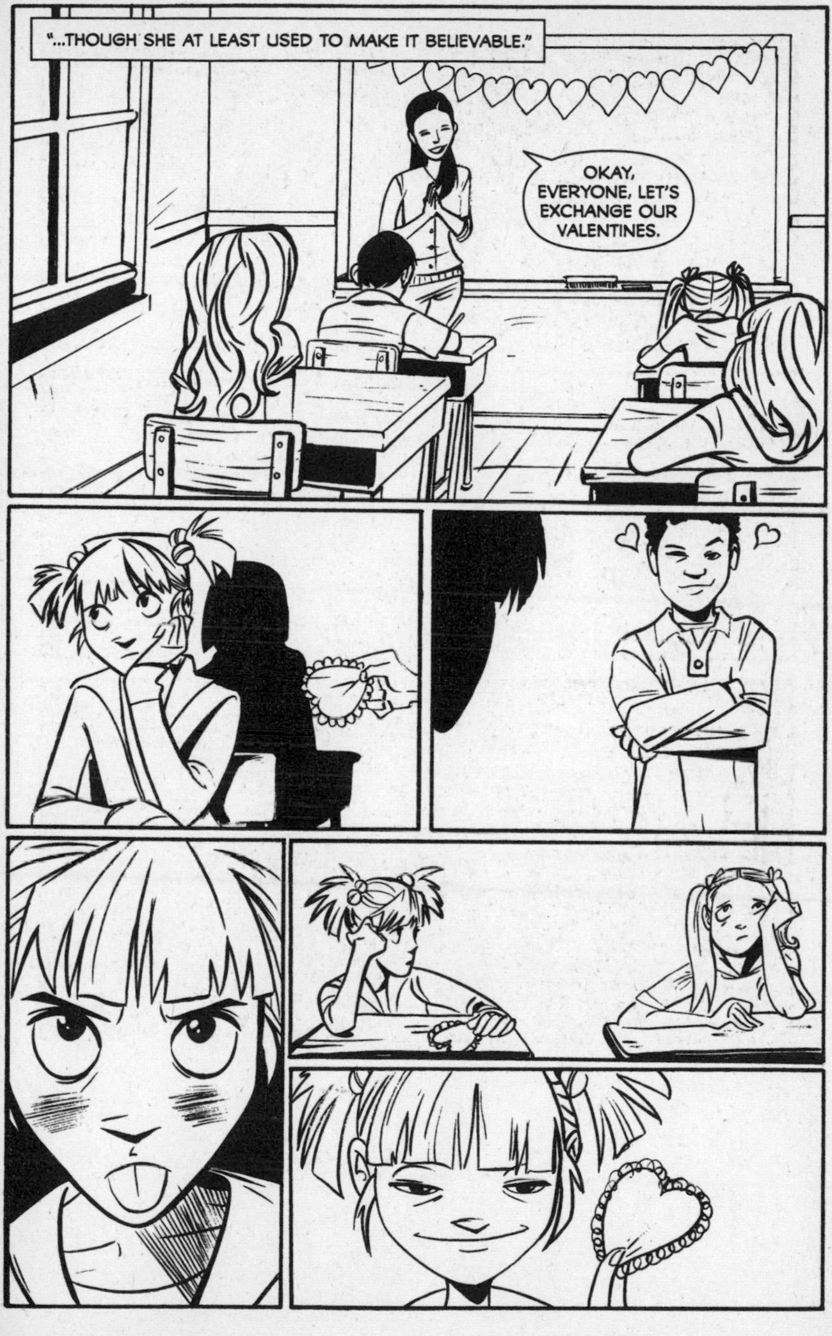
"...THOUGH SHE AT LEAST USED TO MAKE IT BELIEVABLE."
OKAY, EVERYONE, LET'S EXCHANGE OUR VALENTINES.

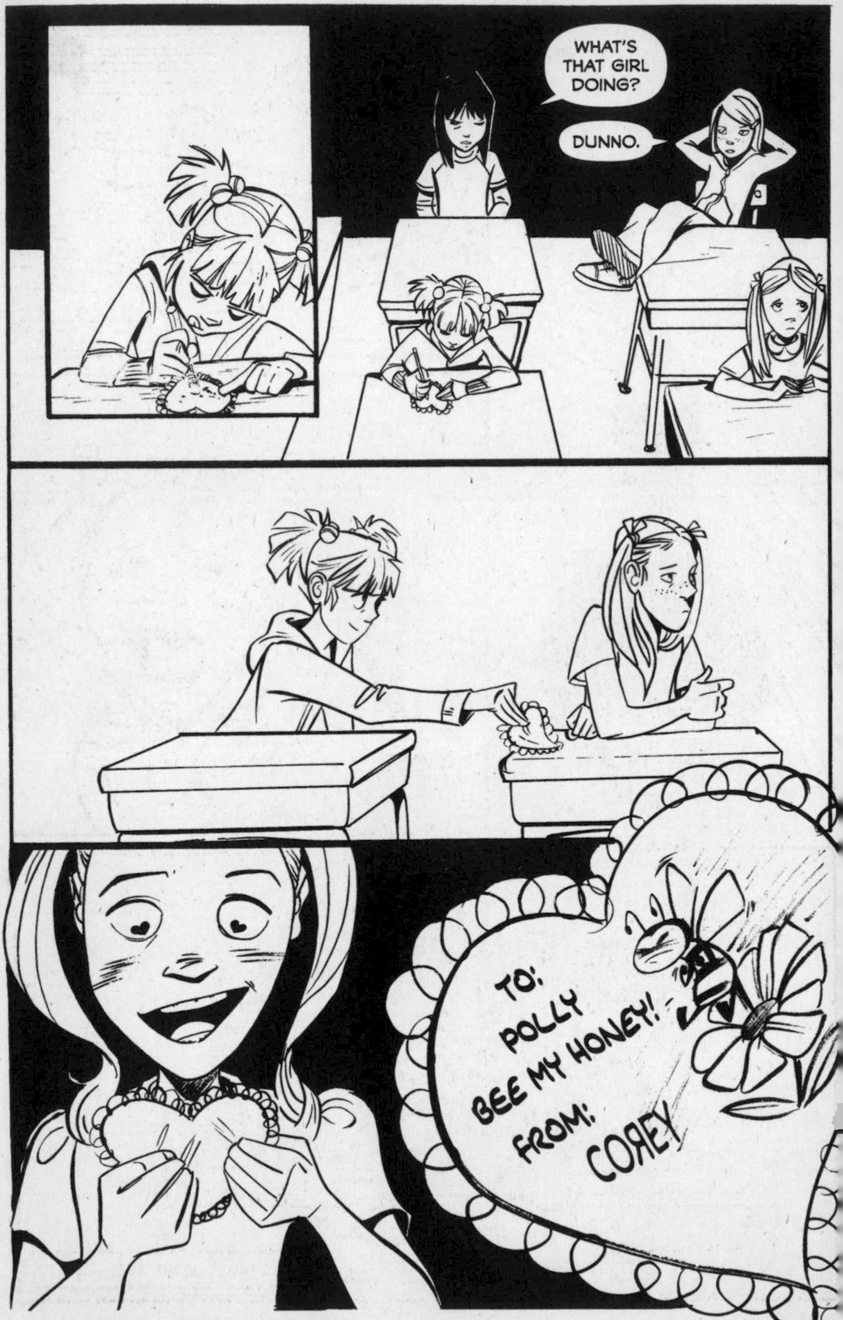
WHAT'S THAT GIRL DOING?
DUNNO.
TO: POLLY
BEE MY HONEY!
FROM: COREY

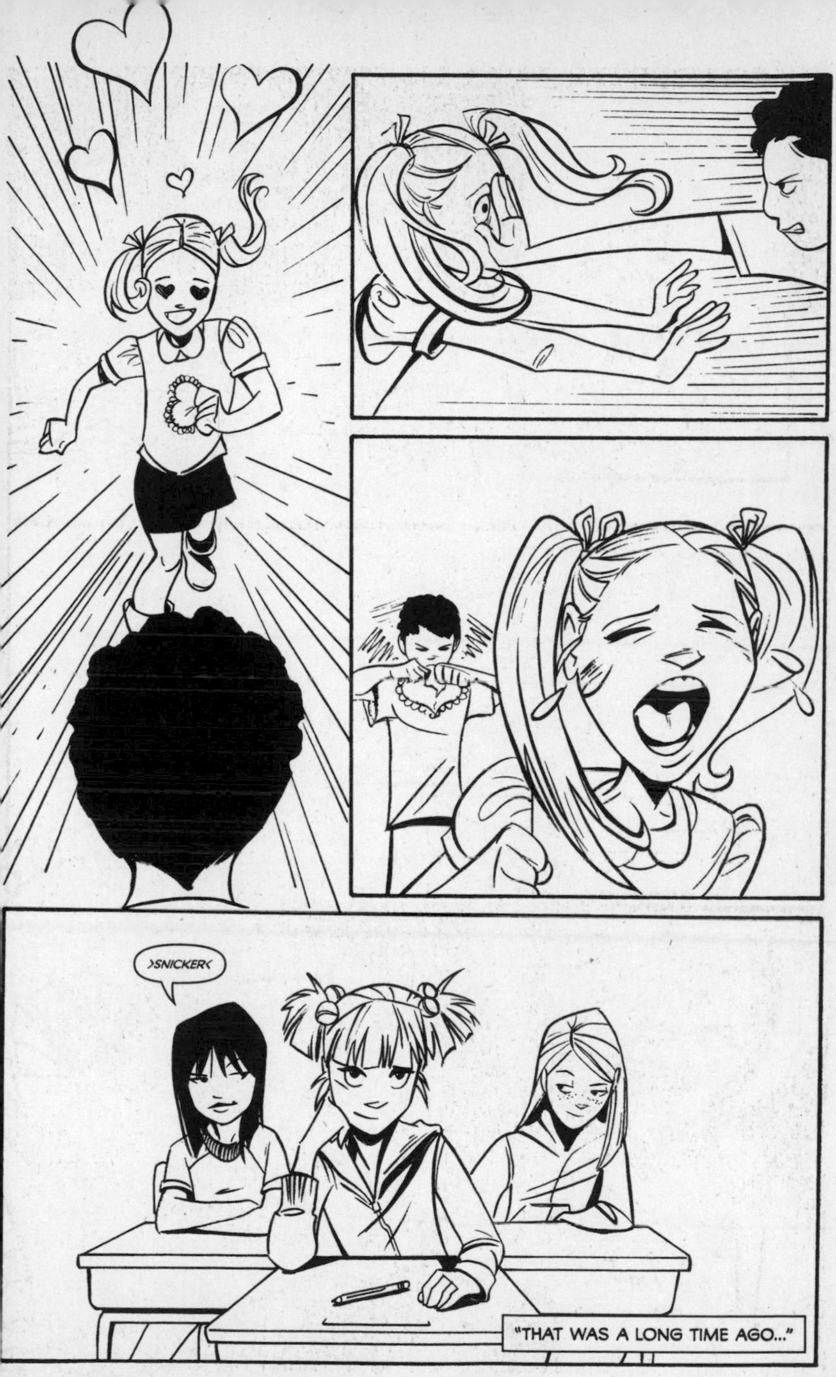
>SNICKER<
"THAT WAS A LONG TIME AGO..."

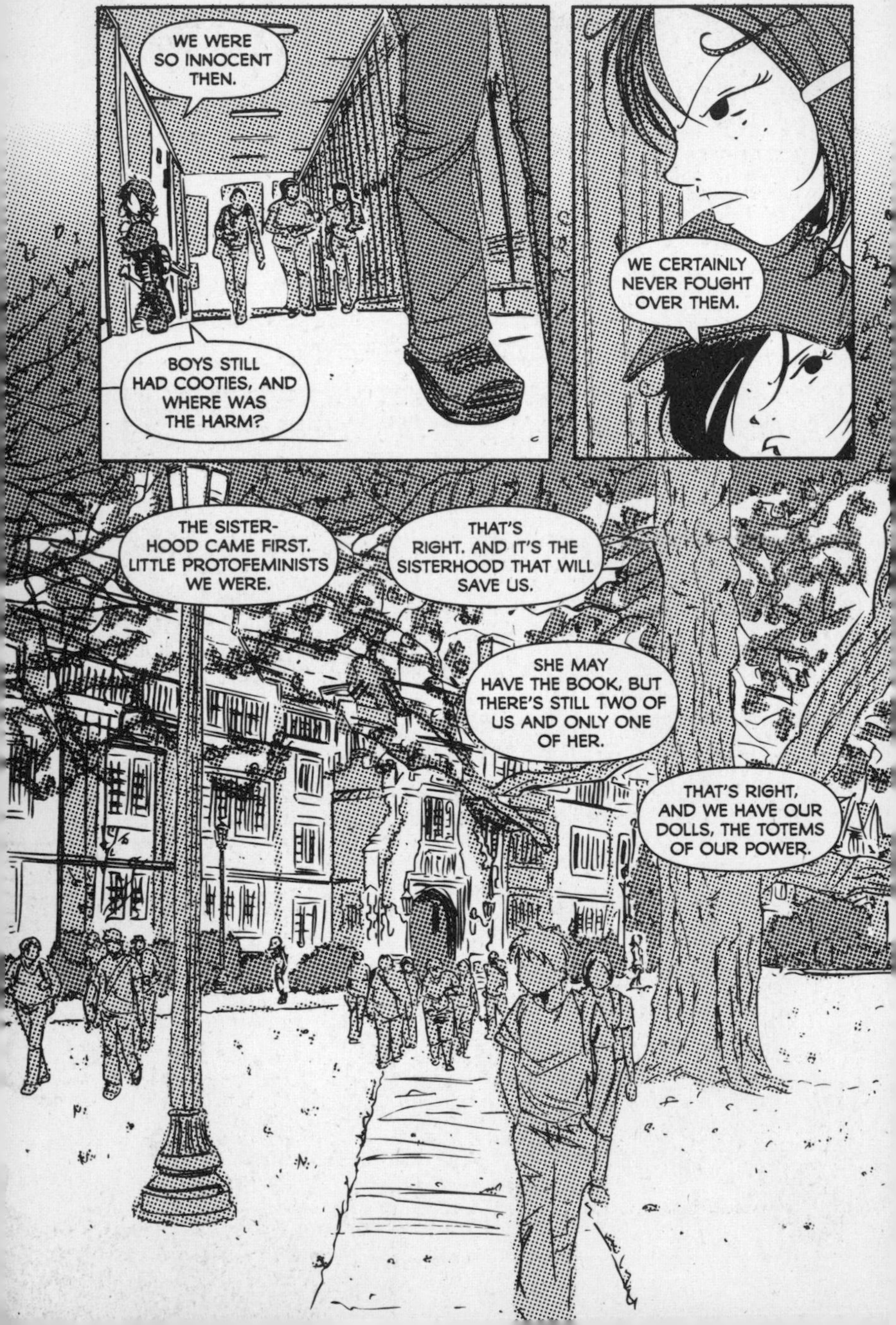
WE WERE SO INNOCENT THEN.
BOYS STILL HAD COOTIES, AND WHERE WAS THE HARM?
WE CERTAINLY NEVER FOUGHT OVER THEM.
THE SISTER-HOOD CAME FIRST. LITTLE PROTOFEMINISTS WE WERE.
THAT'S RIGHT. AND IT'S THE SISTERHOOD THAT WILL SAVE US.
SHE MAY HAVE THE BOOK, BUT THERE'S STILL TWO OF US AND ONLY ONE OF HER.
THAT'S RIGHT, AND WE HAVE OUR DOLLS, THE TOTEMS OF OUR POWER.

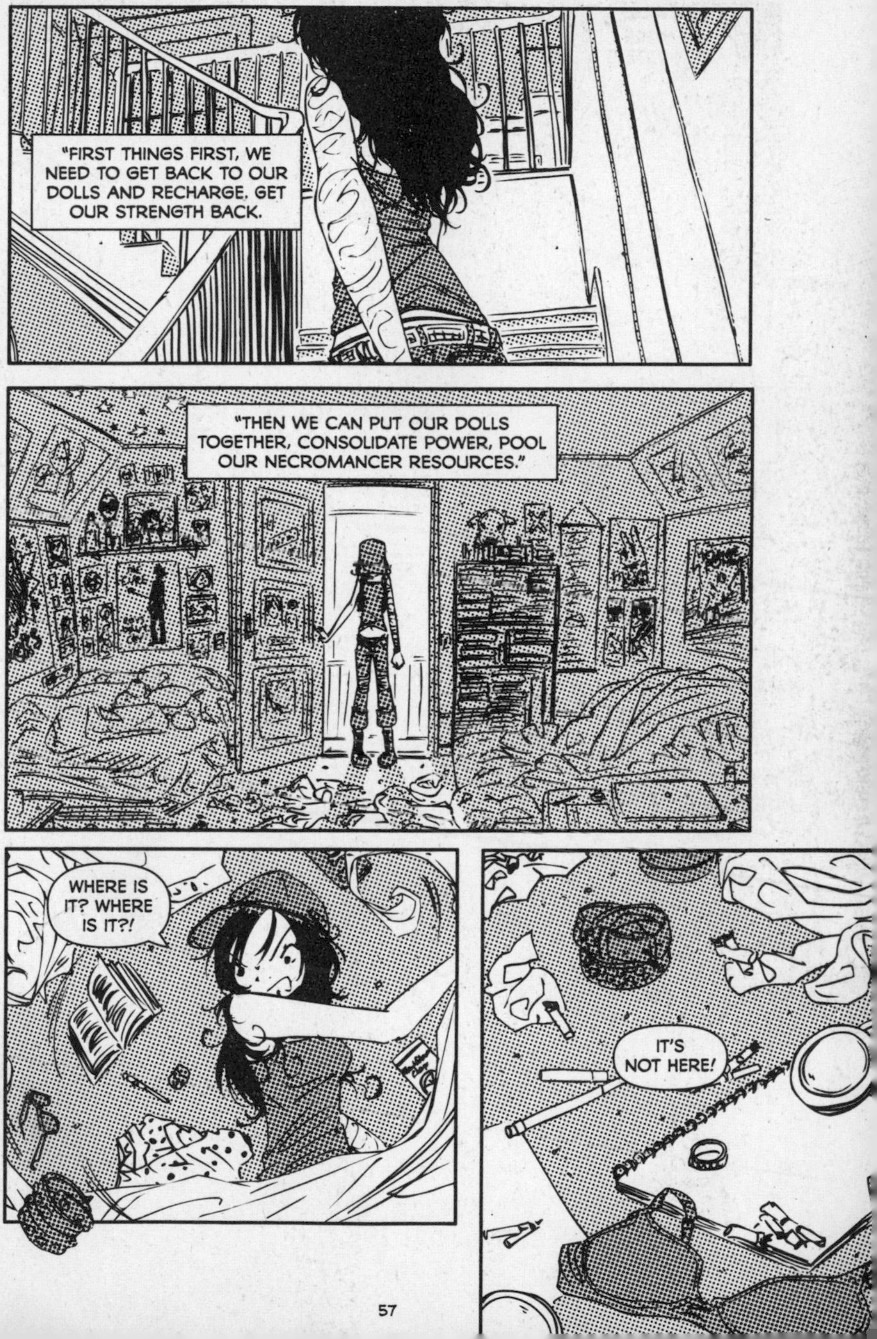
"FIRST THINGS FIRST, WE NEED TO GET BACK TO OUR DOLLS AND RECHARGE. GET OUR STRENGTH BACK.
"THEN WE CAN PUT OUR DOLLS TOGETHER, CONSOLIDATE POWER, POOL OUR NECROMANCER RESOURCES."
WHERE IS IT? WHERE IS IT?!
IT'S NOT HERE!

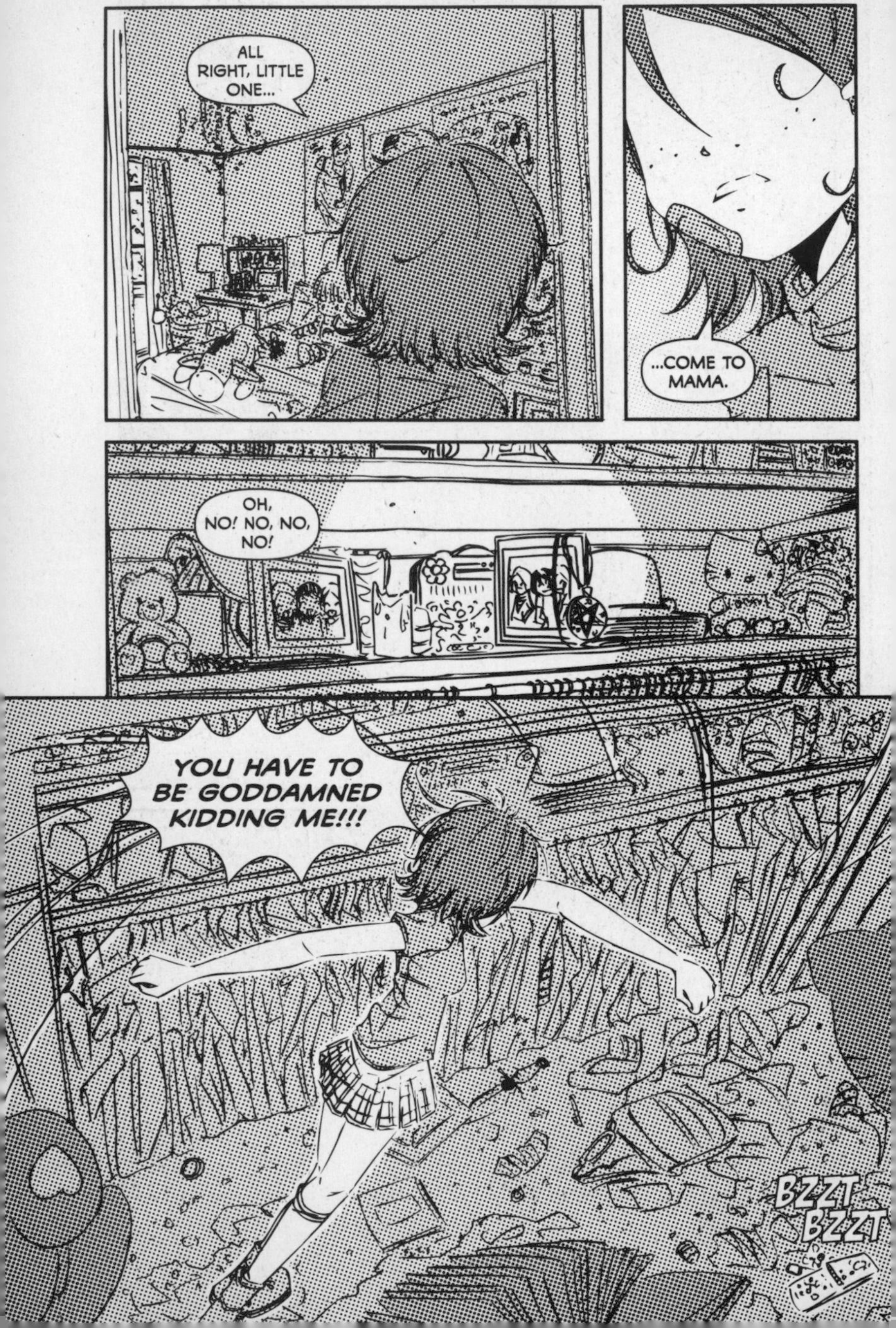
ALL RIGHT, LITTLE ONE...
...COME TO MAMA.
OH, NO! NO, NO, NO!
YOU HAVE TO BE GODDAMNED KIDDING ME!!!
BZZT BZZT

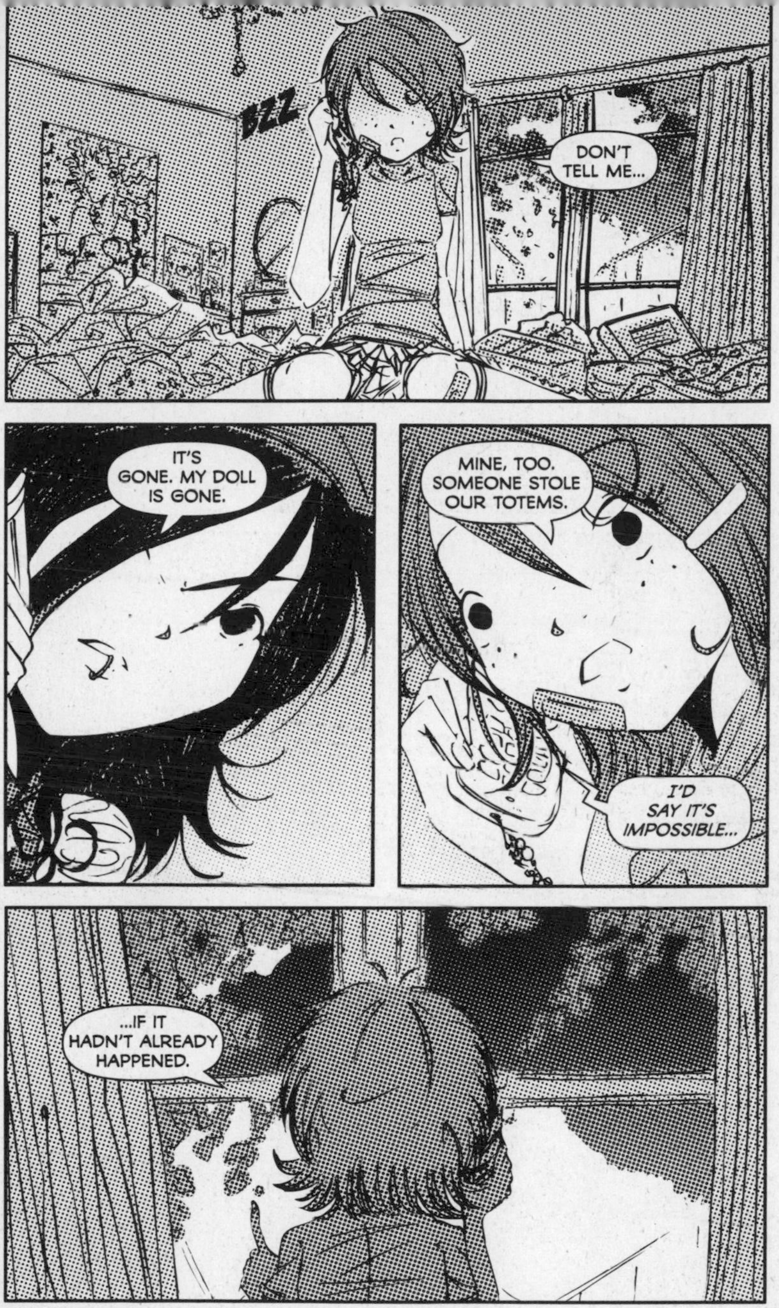
BZZ
DON'T TELL ME...
IT'S GONE. MY DOLL IS GONE.
MINE, TOO. SOMEONE STOLE OUR TOTEMS.
I'D SAY IT'S IMPOSSIBLE...
...IF IT HADN'T ALREADY HAPPENED.

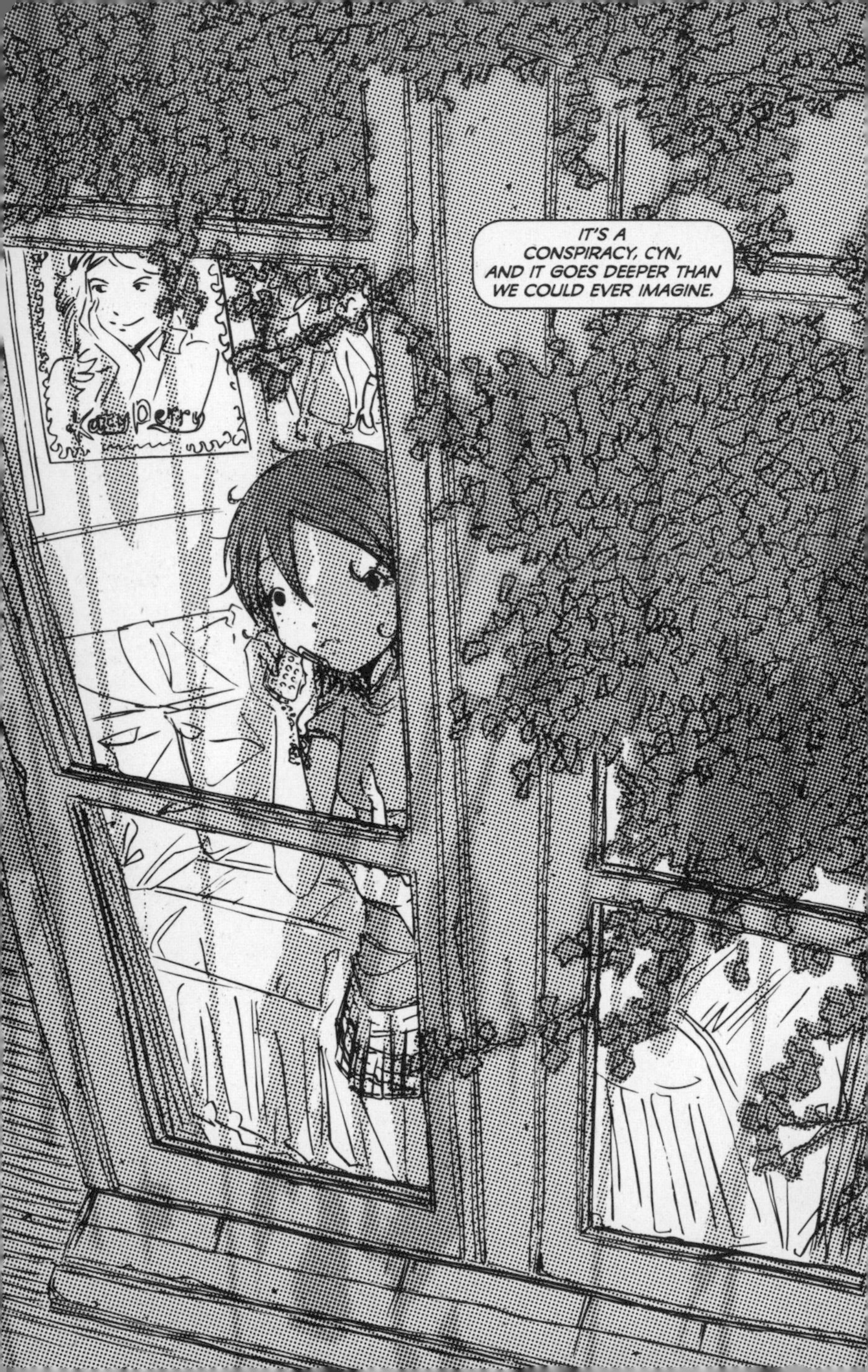
Katy Perry
IT'S A CONSPIRACY, CYN, AND IT GOES DEEPER THAN WE COULD EVER IMAGINE.

Chapter 3
"Hate Me Now"

3

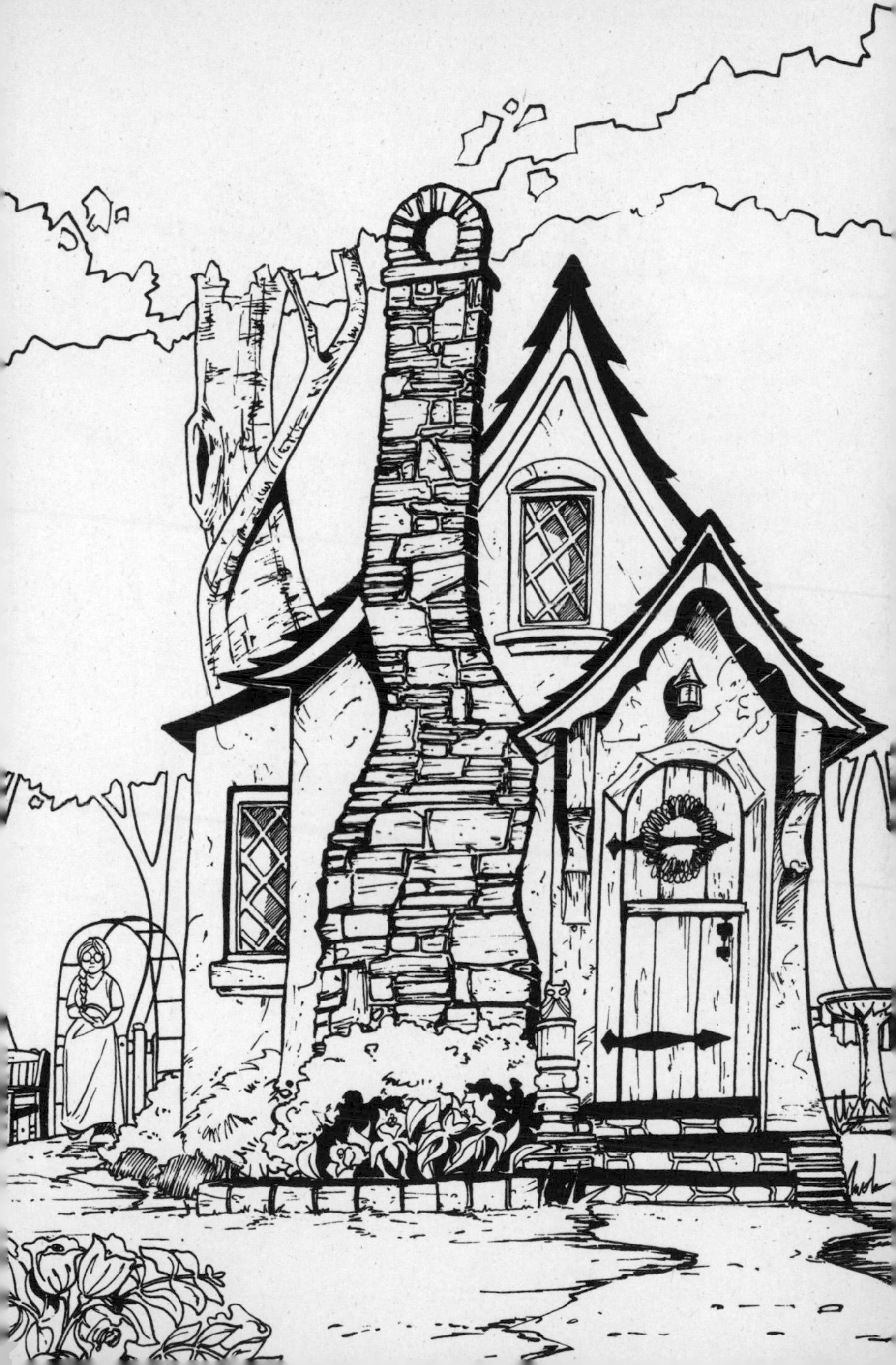

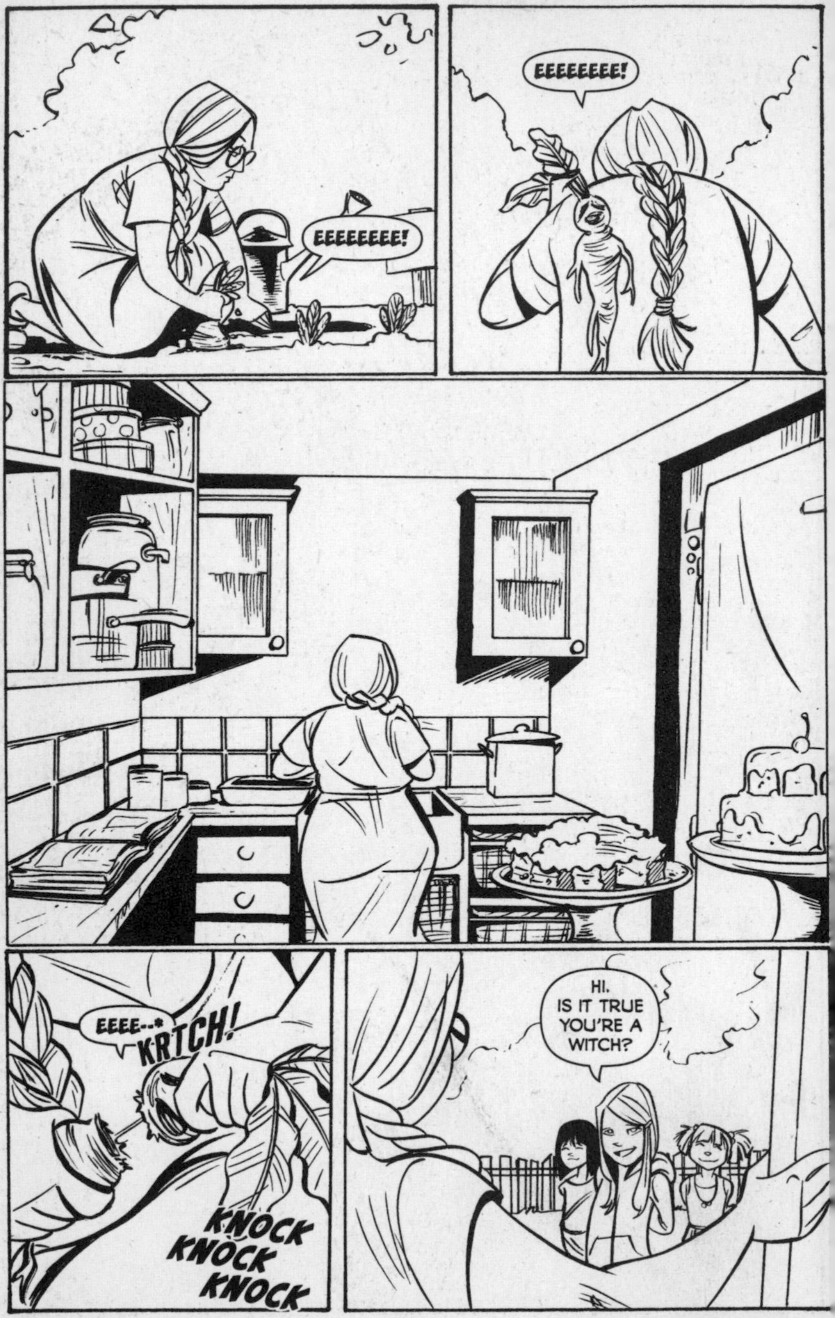
EEEEEEEE!
EEEEEEEE!
EEEE--*
KRTCH!
KNOCK
KNOCK
KNOCK
HI.
IS IT TRUE
YOU'RE A
WITCH?

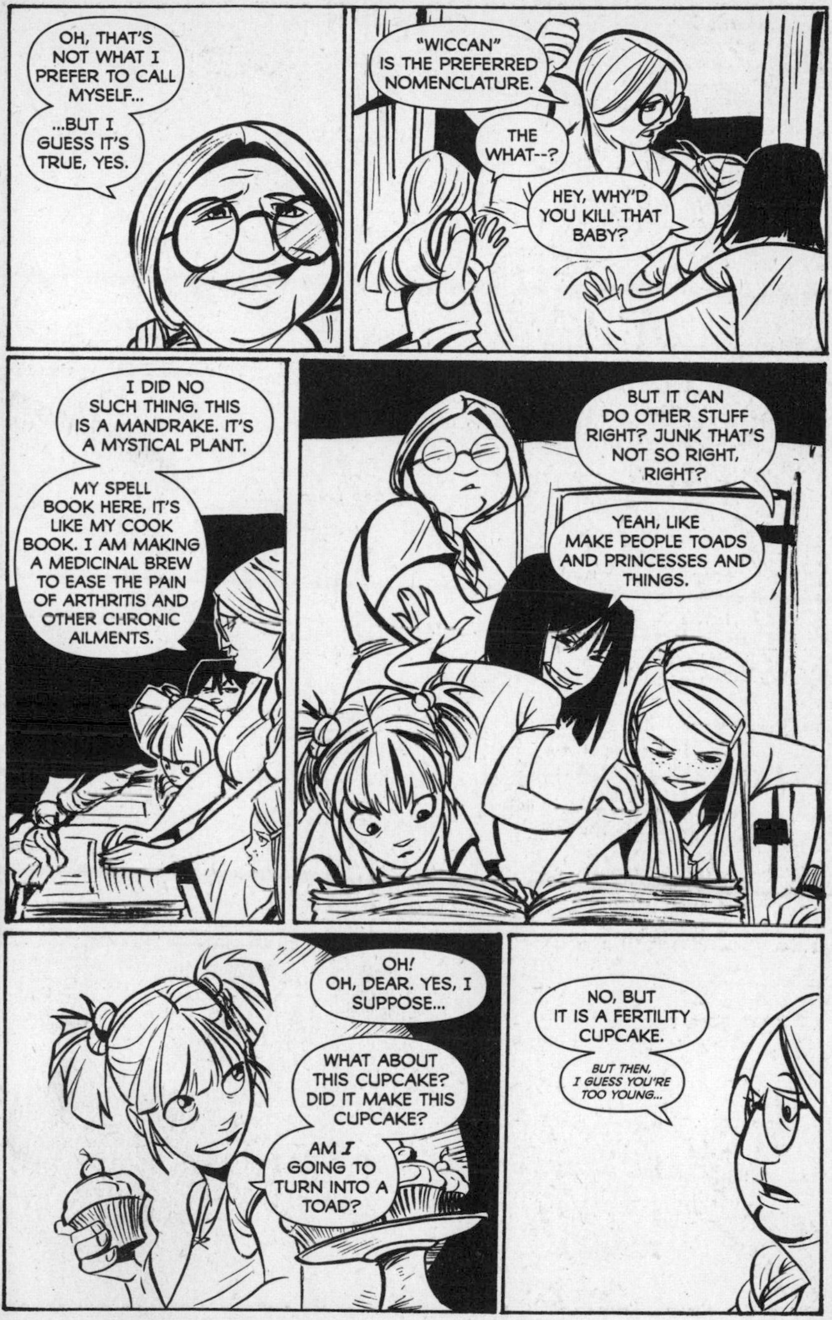
OH, THAT'S NOT WHAT I PREFER TO CALL MYSELF...
...BUT I GUESS IT'S TRUE, YES.
"WICCAN" IS THE PREFERRED NOMENCLATURE.
THE WHAT--?
HEY, WHY'D YOU KILL THAT BABY?
I DID NO SUCH THING. THIS IS A MANDRAKE. IT'S A MYSTICAL PLANT.
MY SPELL BOOK HERE, IT'S LIKE MY COOK BOOK. I AM MAKING A MEDICINAL BREW TO EASE THE PAIN OF ARTHRITIS AND OTHER CHRONIC AILMENTS.
BUT IT CAN DO OTHER STUFF RIGHT? JUNK THAT'S NOT SO RIGHT, RIGHT?
YEAH, LIKE MAKE PEOPLE TOADS AND PRINCESSES AND THINGS.
OH! OH, DEAR. YES, I SUPPOSE...
WHAT ABOUT THIS CUPCAKE? DID IT MAKE THIS CUPCAKE?
AM *I* GOING TO TURN INTO A TOAD?
NO, BUT IT IS A FERTILITY CUPCAKE.
BUT THEN, I GUESS YOU'RE TOO YOUNG...

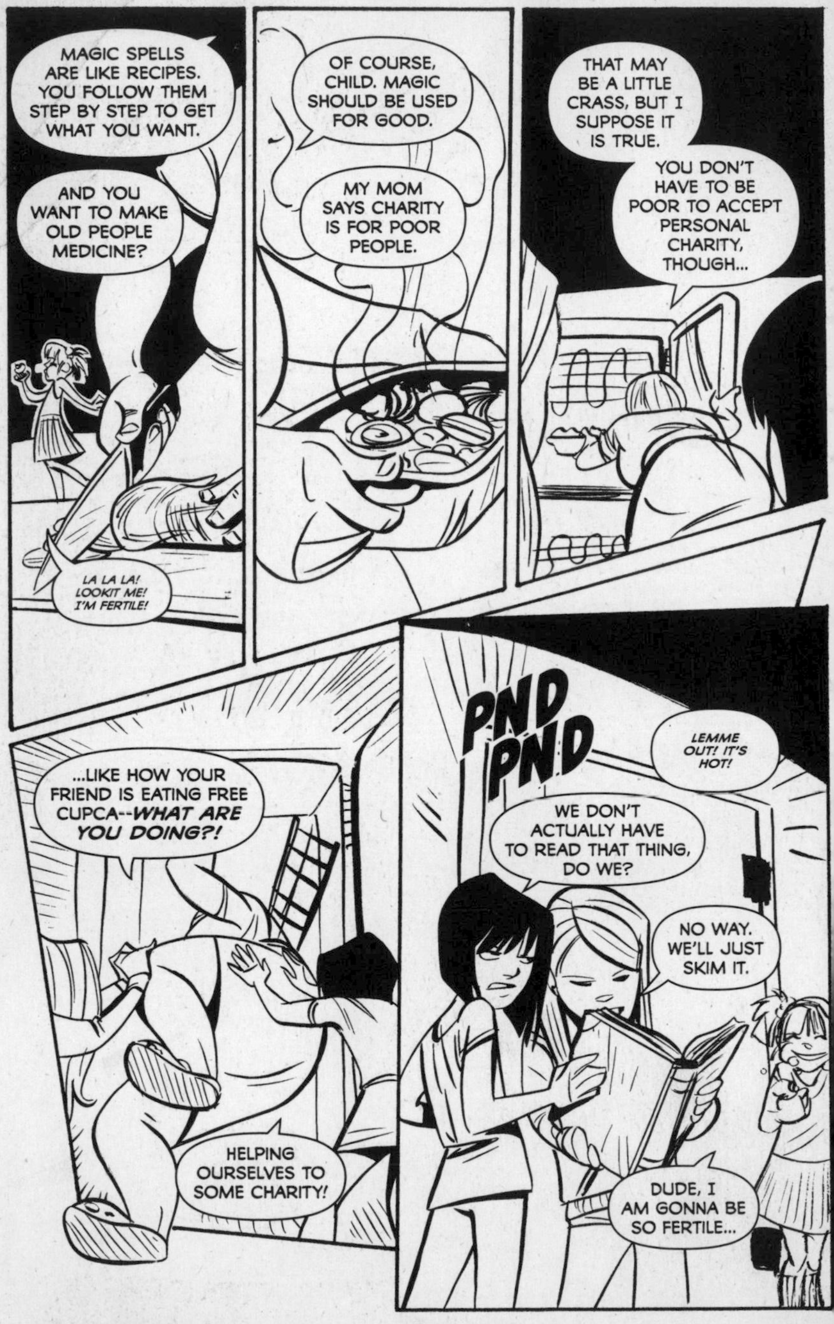
MAGIC SPELLS ARE LIKE RECIPES. YOU FOLLOW THEM STEP BY STEP TO GET WHAT YOU WANT.
AND YOU WANT TO MAKE OLD PEOPLE MEDICINE?
LA LA LA! LOOKIT ME! I'M FERTILE!
OF COURSE, CHILD. MAGIC SHOULD BE USED FOR GOOD.
MY MOM SAYS CHARITY IS FOR POOR PEOPLE.
THAT MAY BE A LITTLE CRASS, BUT I SUPPOSE IT IS TRUE.
YOU DON'T HAVE TO BE POOR TO ACCEPT PERSONAL CHARITY, THOUGH...
...LIKE HOW YOUR FRIEND IS EATING FREE CUPCA--*WHAT ARE YOU DOING?!*
HELPING OURSELVES TO SOME CHARITY!
PND PND
LEMME OUT! IT'S HOT!
WE DON'T ACTUALLY HAVE TO READ THAT THING, DO WE?
NO WAY. WE'LL JUST SKIM IT.
DUDE, I AM GONNA BE SO FERTILE...

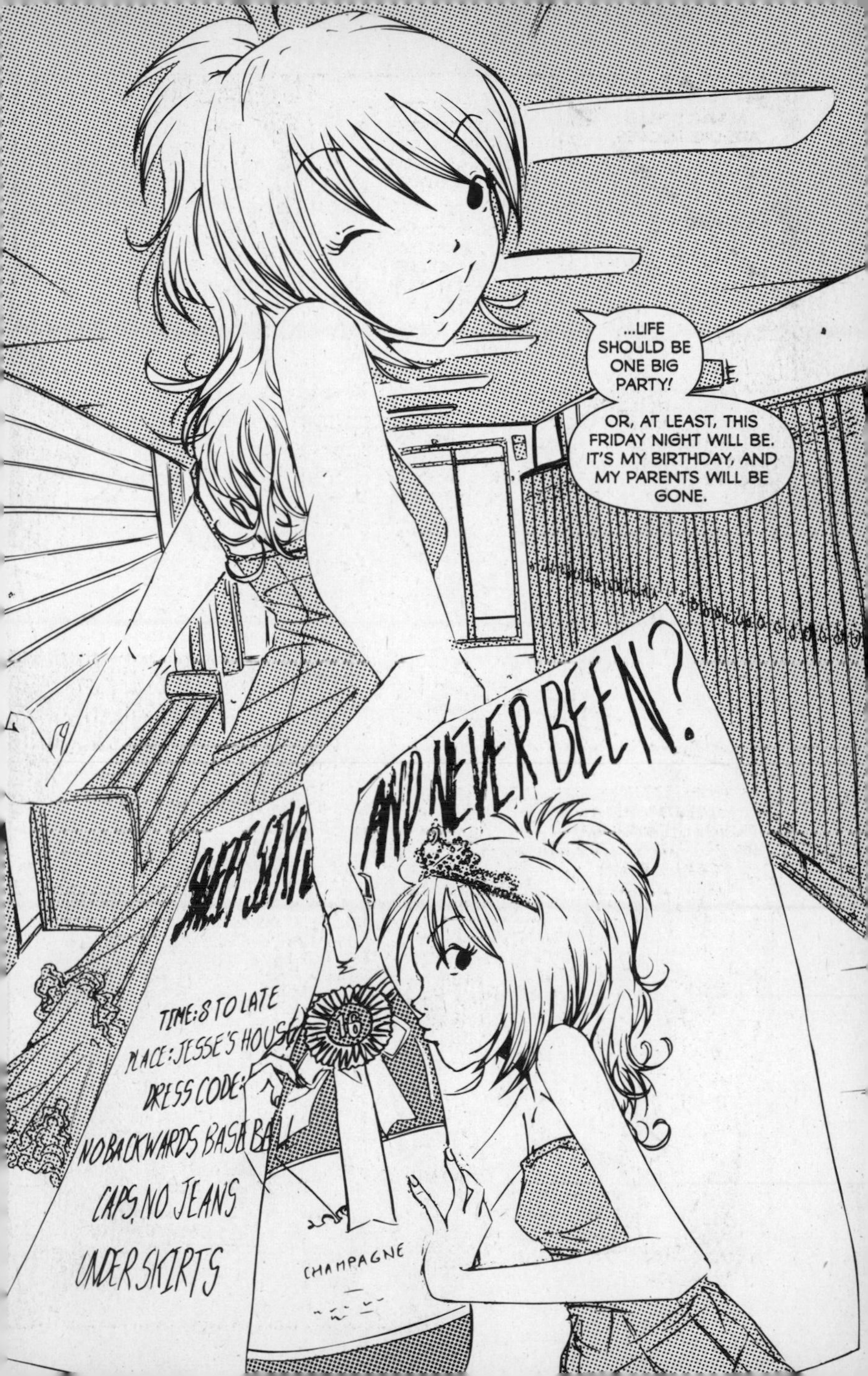
...LIFE SHOULD BE ONE BIG PARTY!
OR, AT LEAST, THIS FRIDAY NIGHT WILL BE. IT'S MY BIRTHDAY, AND MY PARENTS WILL BE GONE.
AND NEVER BEEN?
TIME: 8 TO LATE
PLACE: JESSE'S HOUS
DRESS CODE:
NO BACKWARDS BASEBA
CAPS, NO JEANS
UNDER SKIRTS
16
CHAMPAGNE

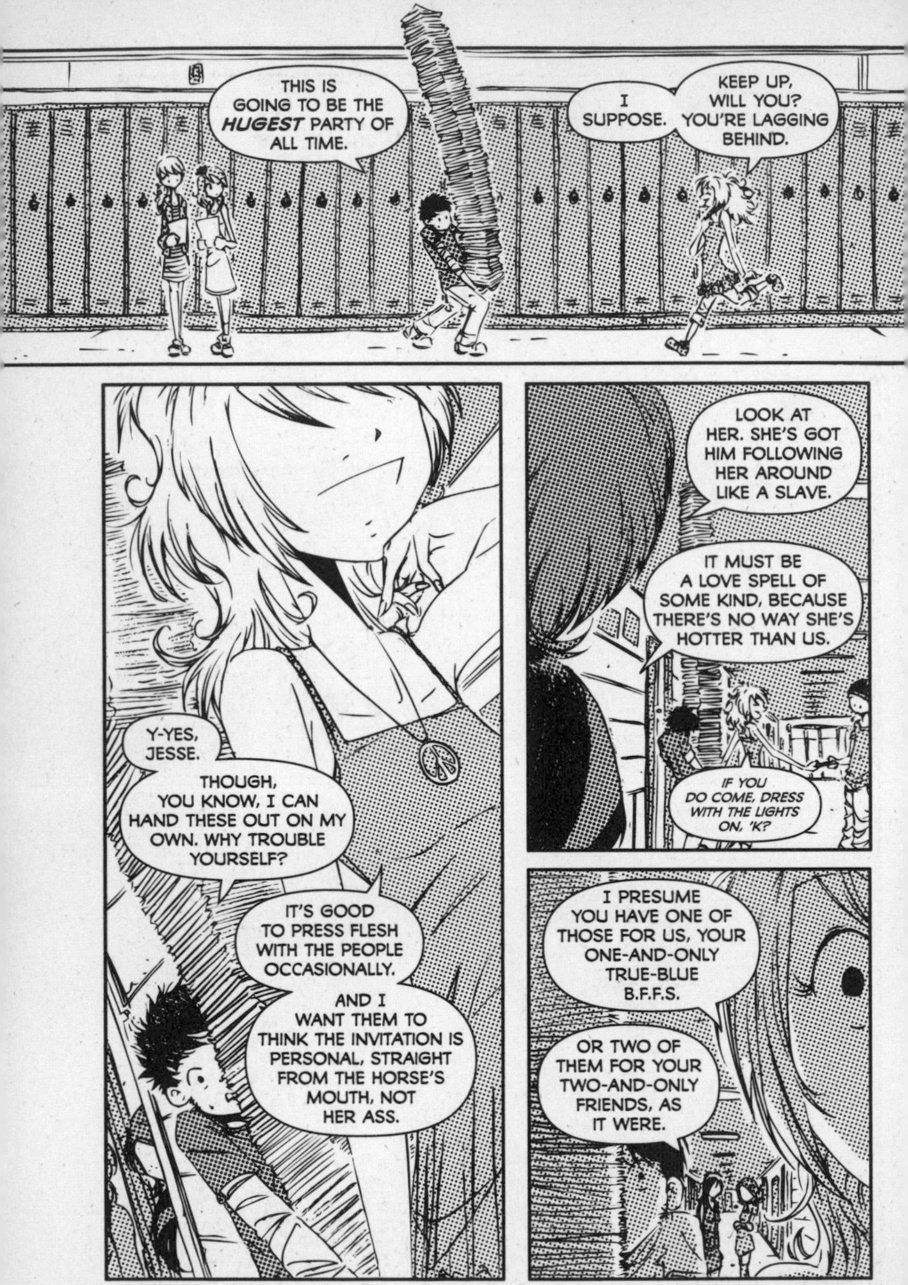
THIS IS GOING TO BE THE *HUGEST* PARTY OF ALL TIME.
I SUPPOSE.
KEEP UP, WILL YOU? YOU'RE LAGGING BEHIND.
Y-YES, JESSE.
THOUGH, YOU KNOW, I CAN HAND THESE OUT ON MY OWN. WHY TROUBLE YOURSELF?
IT'S GOOD TO PRESS FLESH WITH THE PEOPLE OCCASIONALLY.
AND I WANT THEM TO THINK THE INVITATION IS PERSONAL, STRAIGHT FROM THE HORSE'S MOUTH, NOT HER ASS.
LOOK AT HER. SHE'S GOT HIM FOLLOWING HER AROUND LIKE A SLAVE.
IT MUST BE A LOVE SPELL OF SOME KIND, BECAUSE THERE'S NO WAY SHE'S HOTTER THAN US.
IF YOU DO COME, DRESS WITH THE LIGHTS ON, 'K?
I PRESUME YOU HAVE ONE OF THOSE FOR US, YOUR ONE-AND-ONLY TRUE-BLUE B.F.F.S.
OR TWO OF THEM FOR YOUR TWO-AND-ONLY FRIENDS, AS IT WERE.

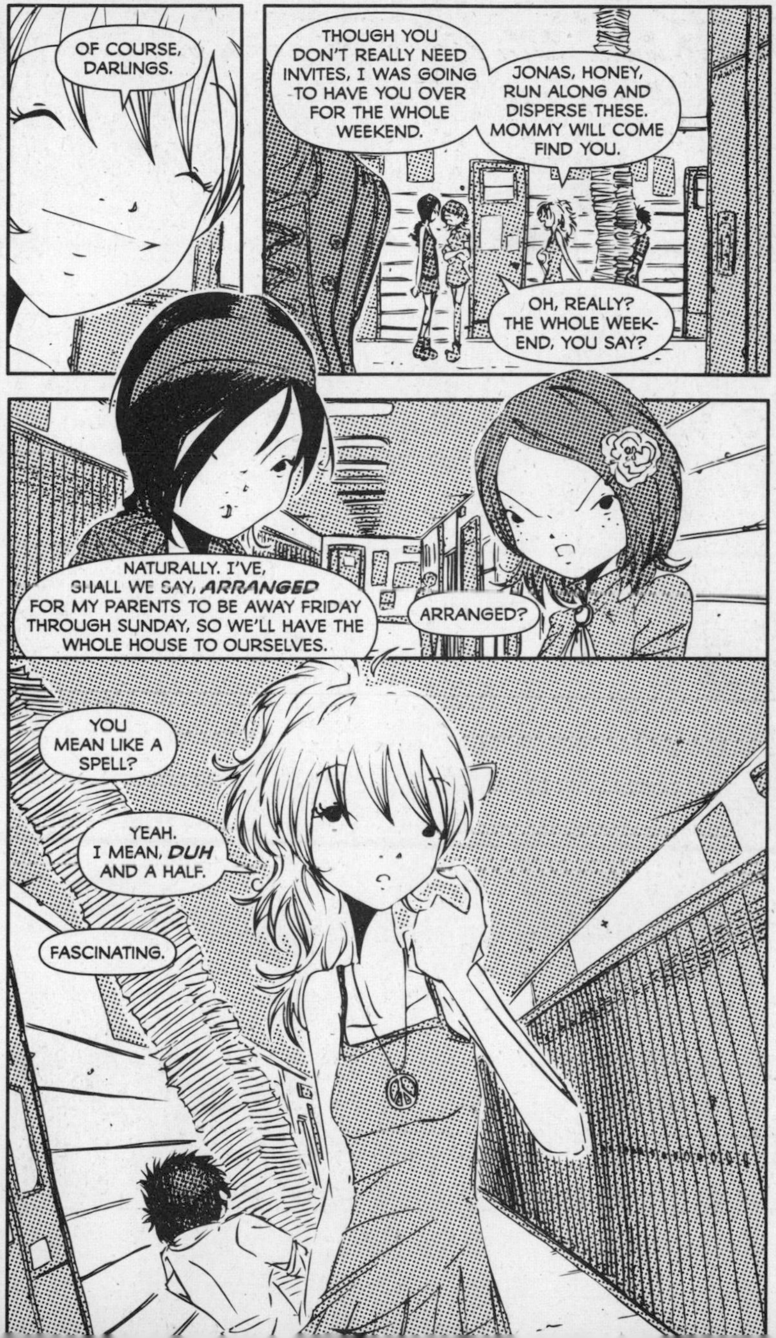
OF COURSE, DARLINGS.
THOUGH YOU DON'T REALLY NEED INVITES, I WAS GOING TO HAVE YOU OVER FOR THE WHOLE WEEKEND.
JONAS, HONEY, RUN ALONG AND DISPERSE THESE. MOMMY WILL COME FIND YOU.
OH, REALLY? THE WHOLE WEEK-END, YOU SAY?
NATURALLY. I'VE, SHALL WE SAY, *ARRANGED* FOR MY PARENTS TO BE AWAY FRIDAY THROUGH SUNDAY, SO WE'LL HAVE THE WHOLE HOUSE TO OURSELVES.
ARRANGED?
YOU MEAN LIKE A SPELL?
YEAH. I MEAN, *DUH* AND A HALF.
FASCINATING.

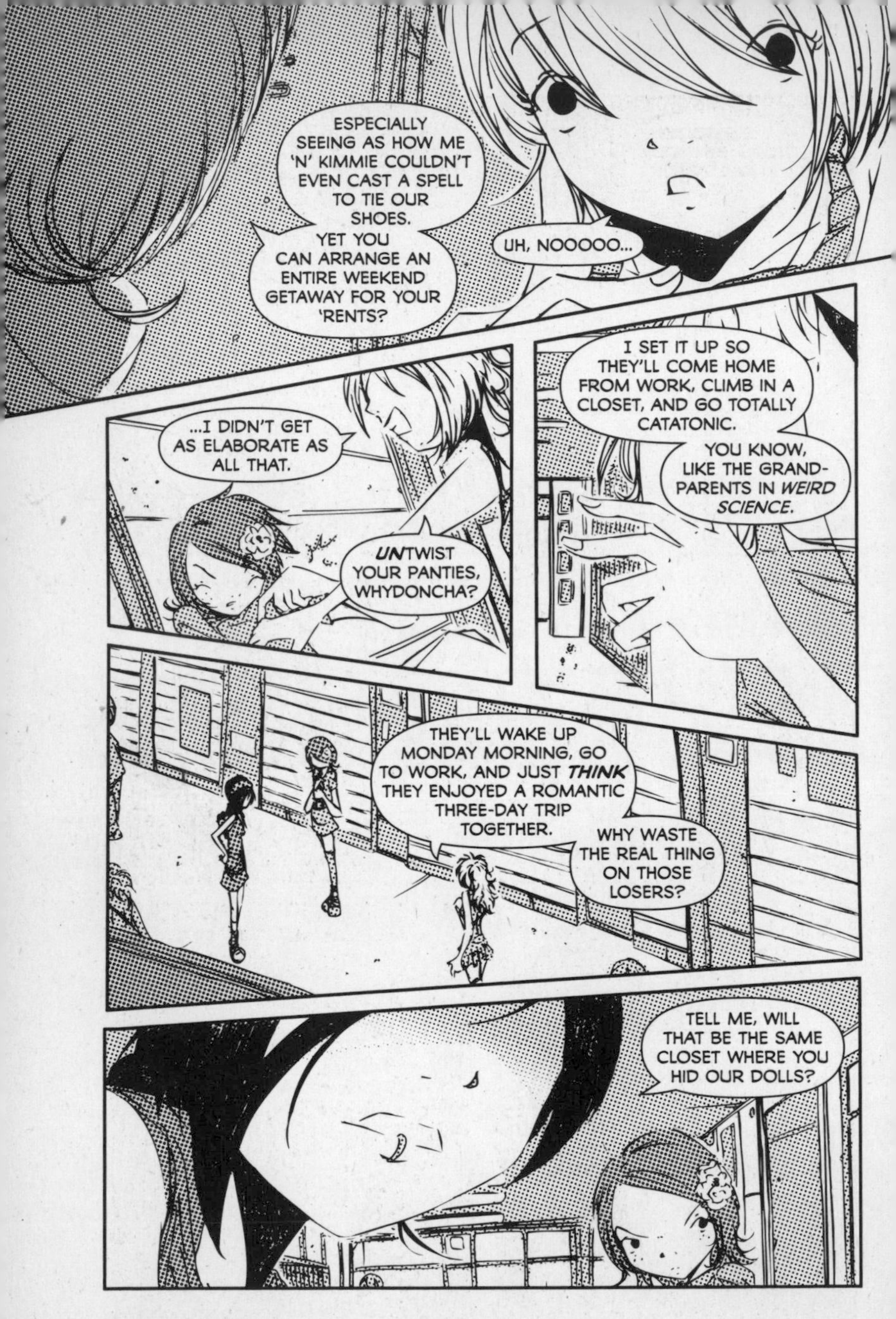
ESPECIALLY SEEING AS HOW ME 'N' KIMMIE COULDN'T EVEN CAST A SPELL TO TIE OUR SHOES.
YET YOU CAN ARRANGE AN ENTIRE WEEKEND GETAWAY FOR YOUR 'RENTS?
UH, NOOOOO...
...I DIDN'T GET AS ELABORATE AS ALL THAT.
*UN*TWIST YOUR PANTIES, WHYDONCHA?
I SET IT UP SO THEY'LL COME HOME FROM WORK, CLIMB IN A CLOSET, AND GO TOTALLY CATATONIC.
YOU KNOW, LIKE THE GRAND-PARENTS IN *WEIRD SCIENCE.*
THEY'LL WAKE UP MONDAY MORNING, GO TO WORK, AND JUST *THINK* THEY ENJOYED A ROMANTIC THREE-DAY TRIP TOGETHER.
WHY WASTE THE REAL THING ON THOSE LOSERS?
TELL ME, WILL THAT BE THE SAME CLOSET WHERE YOU HID OUR DOLLS?

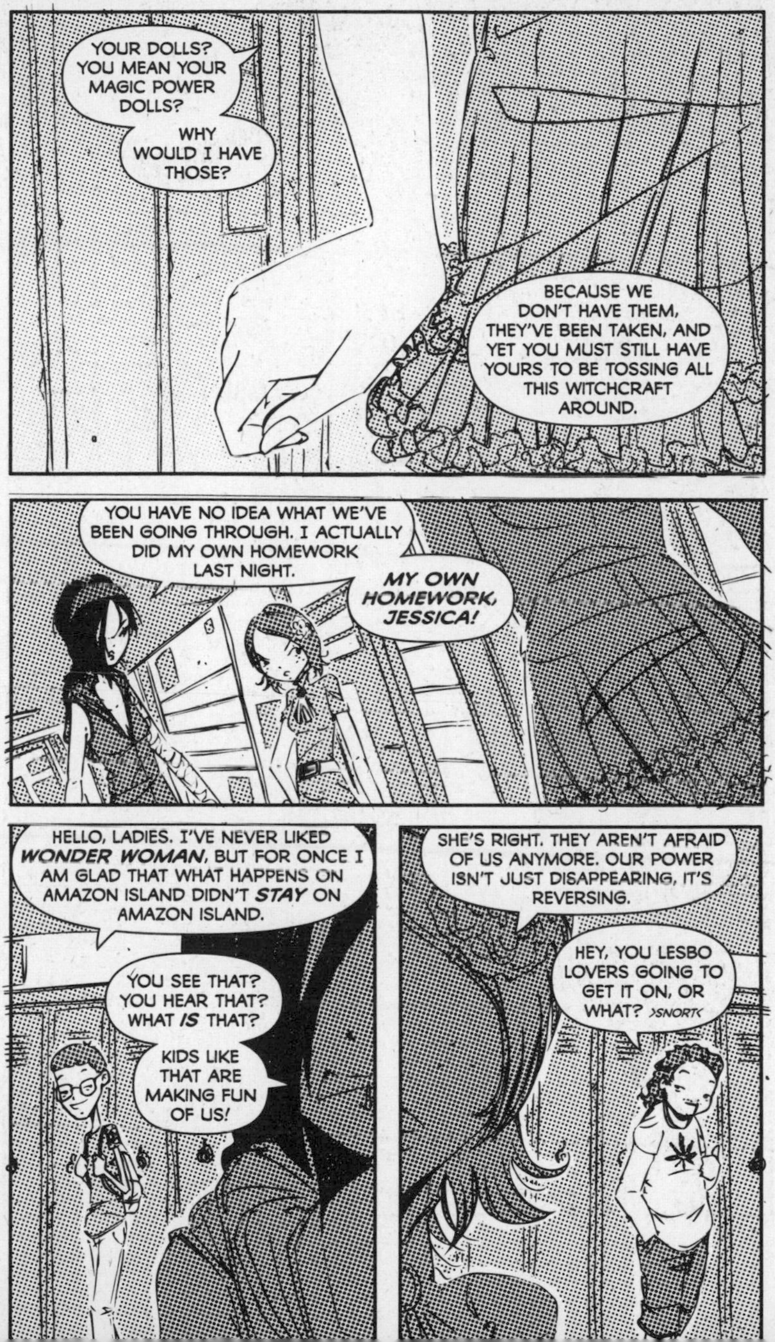

YOUR DOLLS? YOU MEAN YOUR MAGIC POWER DOLLS?
WHY WOULD I HAVE THOSE?
BECAUSE WE DON'T HAVE THEM, THEY'VE BEEN TAKEN, AND YET YOU MUST STILL HAVE YOURS TO BE TOSSING ALL THIS WITCHCRAFT AROUND.
YOU HAVE NO IDEA WHAT WE'VE BEEN GOING THROUGH. I ACTUALLY DID MY OWN HOMEWORK LAST NIGHT.
MY OWN HOMEWORK, JESSICA!
HELLO, LADIES. I'VE NEVER LIKED WONDER WOMAN, BUT FOR ONCE I AM GLAD THAT WHAT HAPPENS ON AMAZON ISLAND DIDN'T STAY ON AMAZON ISLAND.
YOU SEE THAT? YOU HEAR THAT? WHAT IS THAT?
KIDS LIKE THAT ARE MAKING FUN OF US!
SHE'S RIGHT. THEY AREN'T AFRAID OF US ANYMORE. OUR POWER ISN'T JUST DISAPPEARING, IT'S REVERSING.
HEY, YOU LESBO LOVERS GOING TO GET IT ON, OR WHAT? >SNORT<

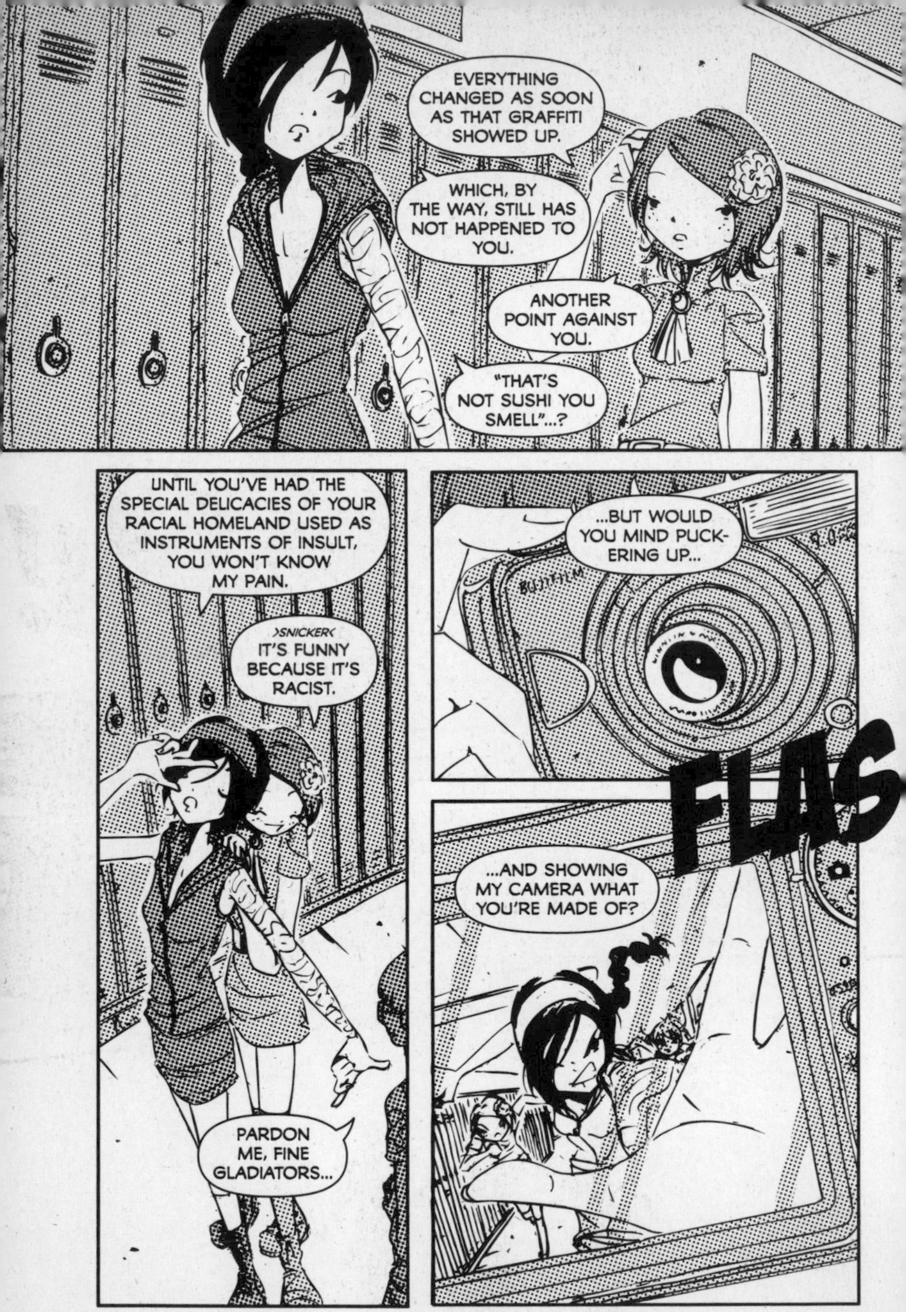
EVERYTHING CHANGED AS SOON AS THAT GRAFFITI SHOWED UP.
WHICH, BY THE WAY, STILL HAS NOT HAPPENED TO YOU.
ANOTHER POINT AGAINST YOU.
"THAT'S NOT SUSHI YOU SMELL"...?
UNTIL YOU'VE HAD THE SPECIAL DELICACIES OF YOUR RACIAL HOMELAND USED AS INSTRUMENTS OF INSULT, YOU WON'T KNOW MY PAIN.
>SNICKER< IT'S FUNNY BECAUSE IT'S RACIST.
PARDON ME, FINE GLADIATORS...
...BUT WOULD YOU MIND PUCK-ERING UP...
FLAS
...AND SHOWING MY CAMERA WHAT YOU'RE MADE OF?

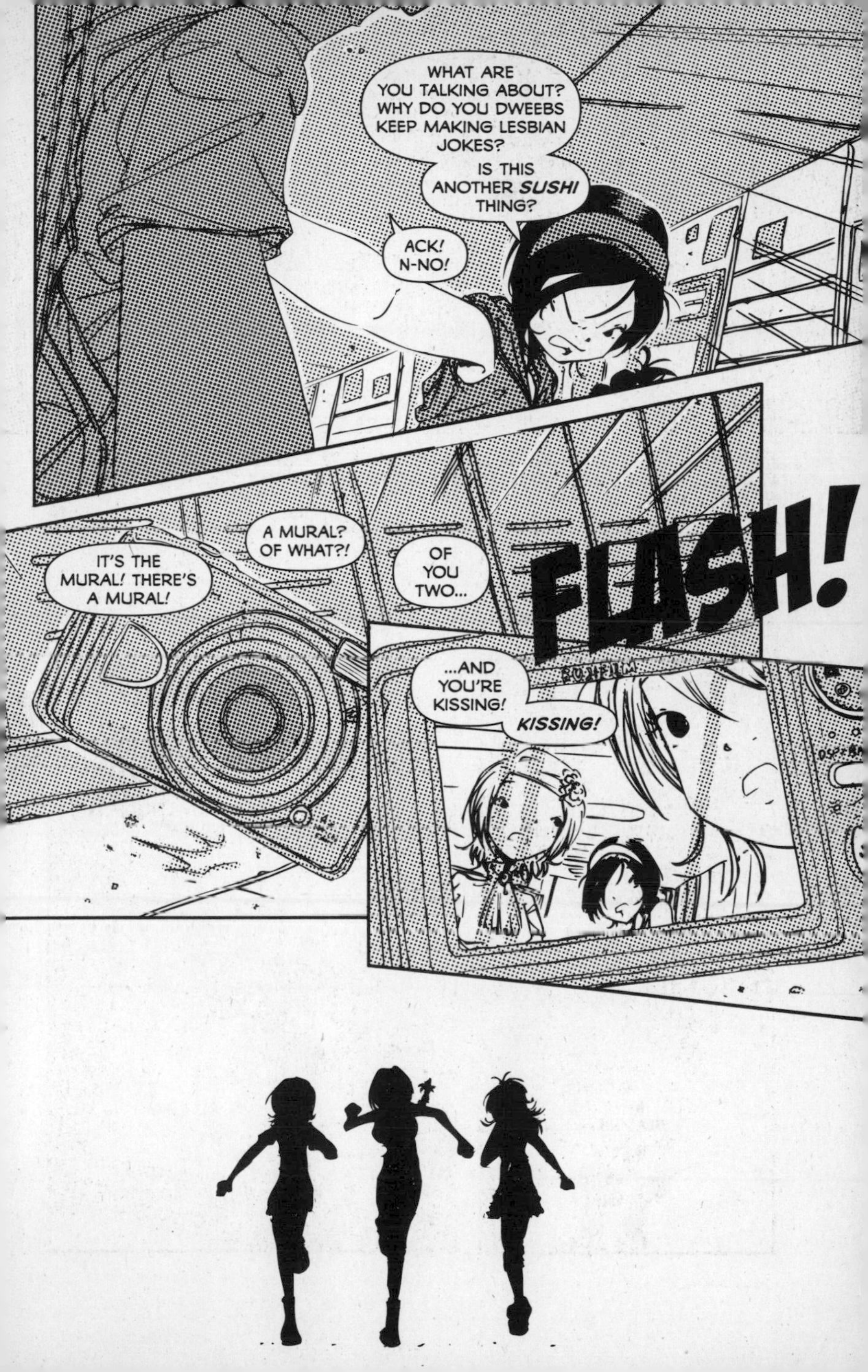
WHAT ARE YOU TALKING ABOUT? WHY DO YOU DWEEBS KEEP MAKING LESBIAN JOKES?
IS THIS ANOTHER *SUSHI* THING?
ACK! N-NO!
IT'S THE MURAL! THERE'S A MURAL!
A MURAL? OF WHAT?!
OF YOU TWO...
FLASH!
...AND YOU'RE KISSING!
KISSING!

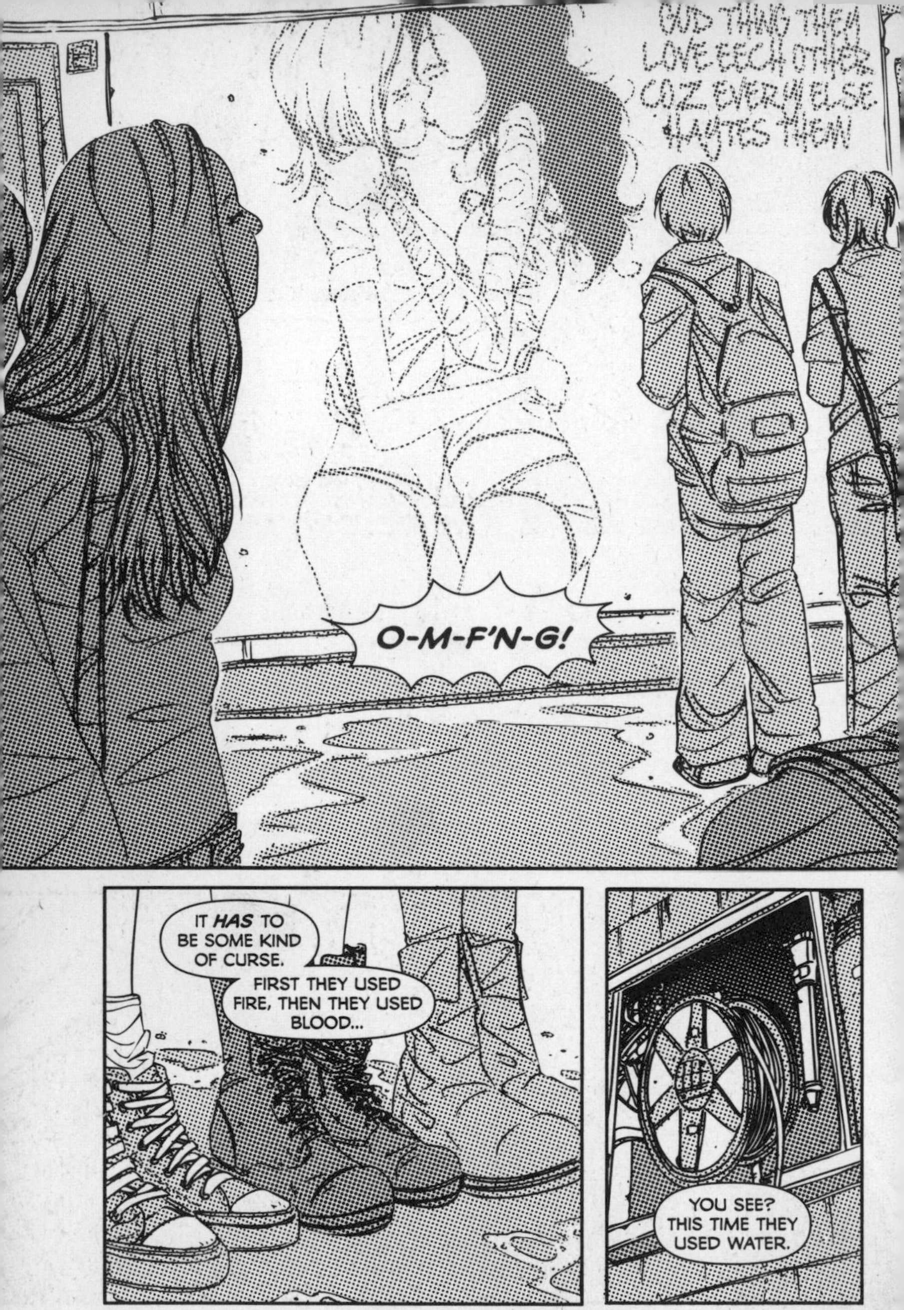
GUD THING THEY LOVE EECH OTHER COZ EVERY ELSE HAYTES THEM
O-M-F'N-G!
IT *HAS* TO BE SOME KIND OF CURSE.
FIRST THEY USED FIRE, THEN THEY USED BLOOD...
YOU SEE? THIS TIME THEY USED WATER.

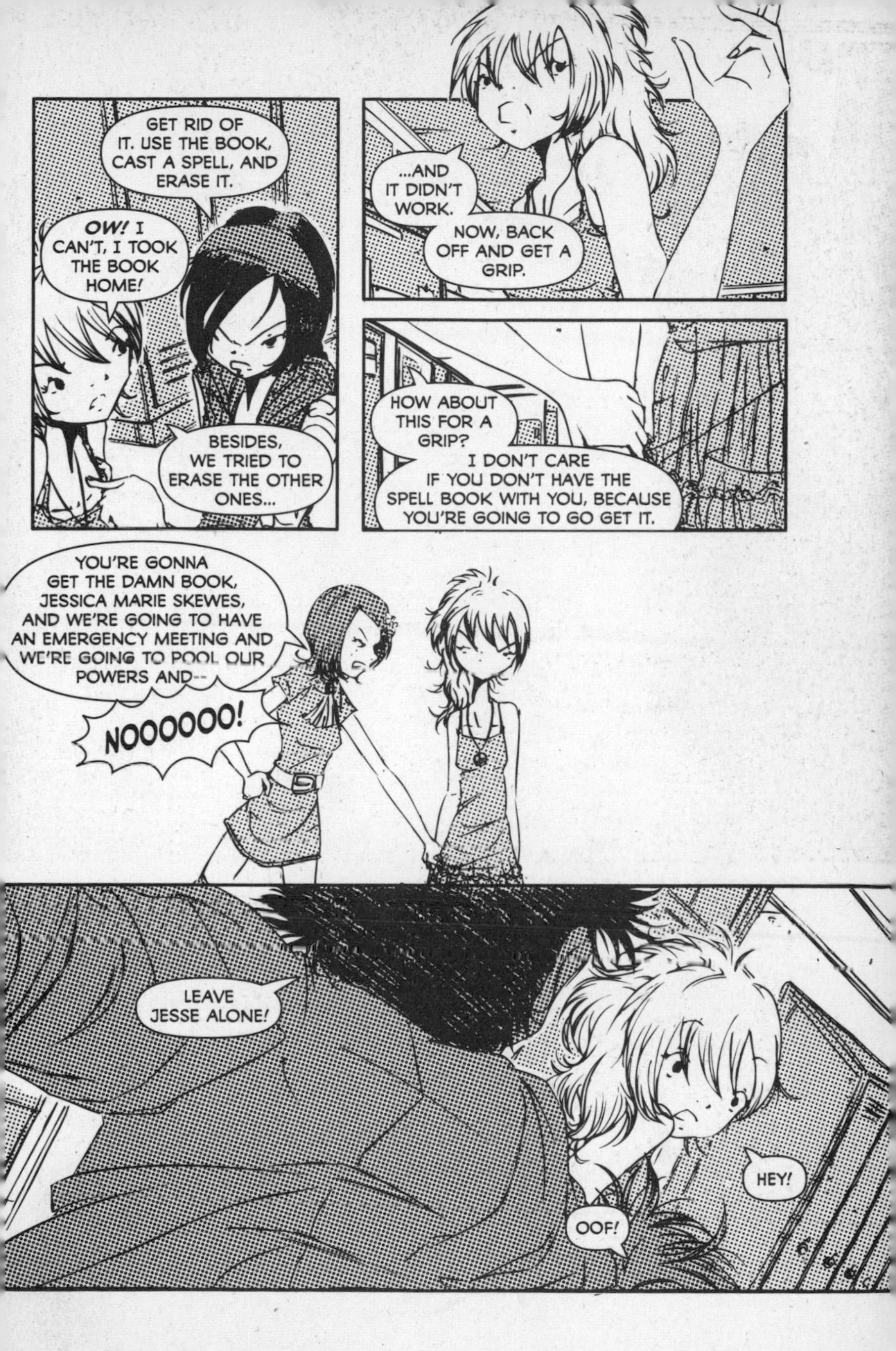
GET RID OF IT. USE THE BOOK, CAST A SPELL, AND ERASE IT.
OW! I CAN'T, I TOOK THE BOOK HOME!
BESIDES, WE TRIED TO ERASE THE OTHER ONES...
...AND IT DIDN'T WORK.
NOW, BACK OFF AND GET A GRIP.
HOW ABOUT THIS FOR A GRIP?
I DON'T CARE IF YOU DON'T HAVE THE SPELL BOOK WITH YOU, BECAUSE YOU'RE GOING TO GO GET IT.
YOU'RE GONNA GET THE DAMN BOOK, JESSICA MARIE SKEWES, AND WE'RE GOING TO HAVE AN EMERGENCY MEETING AND WE'RE GOING TO POOL OUR POWERS AND--
NOOOOOO!
LEAVE JESSE ALONE!
HEY!
OOF!

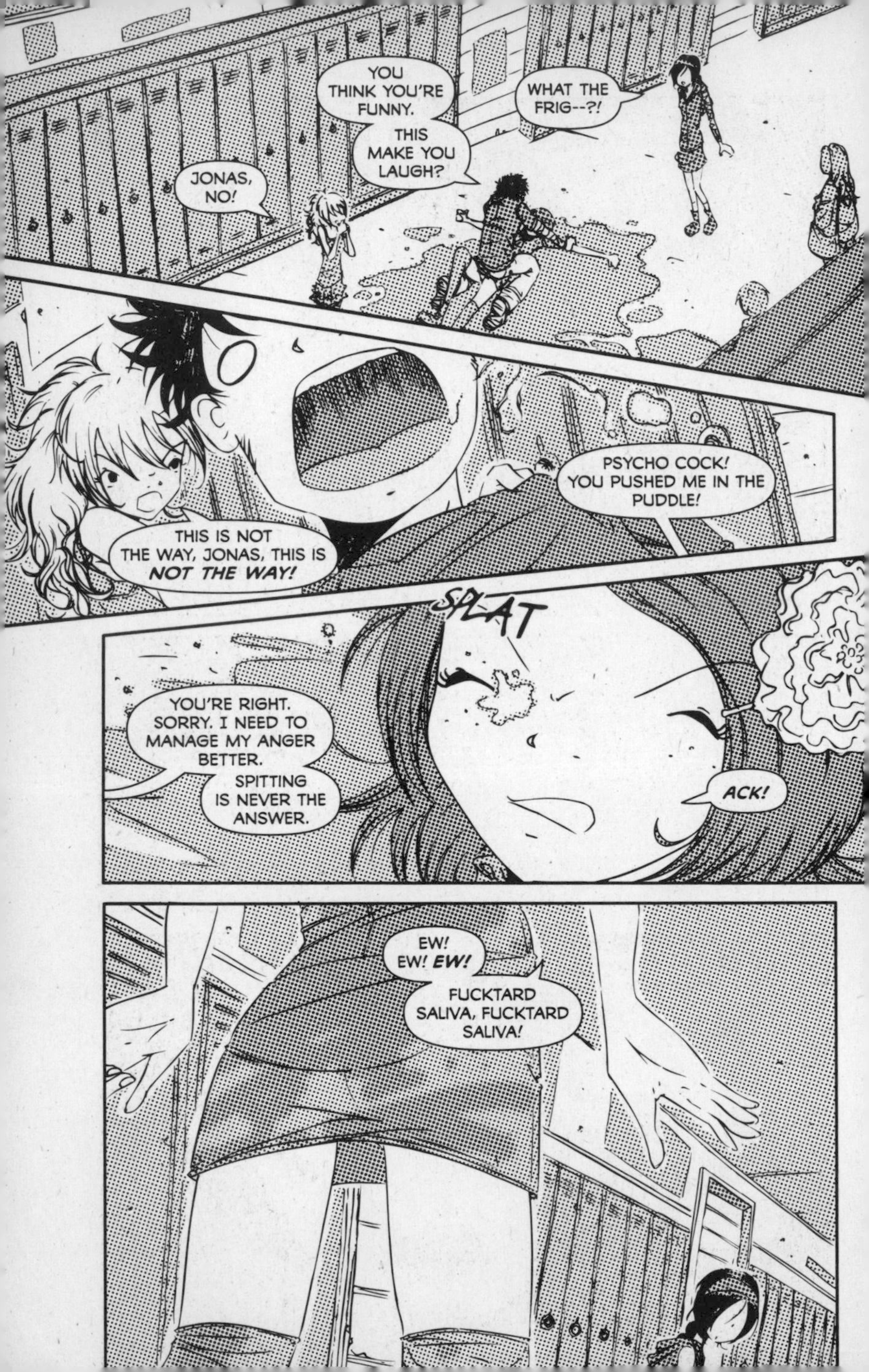
WHAT THE FRIG--?!
YOU THINK YOU'RE FUNNY.
THIS MAKE YOU LAUGH?
JONAS, NO!
PSYCHO COCK! YOU PUSHED ME IN THE PUDDLE!
THIS IS NOT THE WAY, JONAS, THIS IS *NOT THE WAY!*
SPLAT
ACK!
YOU'RE RIGHT. SORRY. I NEED TO MANAGE MY ANGER BETTER.
SPITTING IS NEVER THE ANSWER.
EW! EW! *EW!*
FUCKTARD SALIVA, FUCKTARD SALIVA!

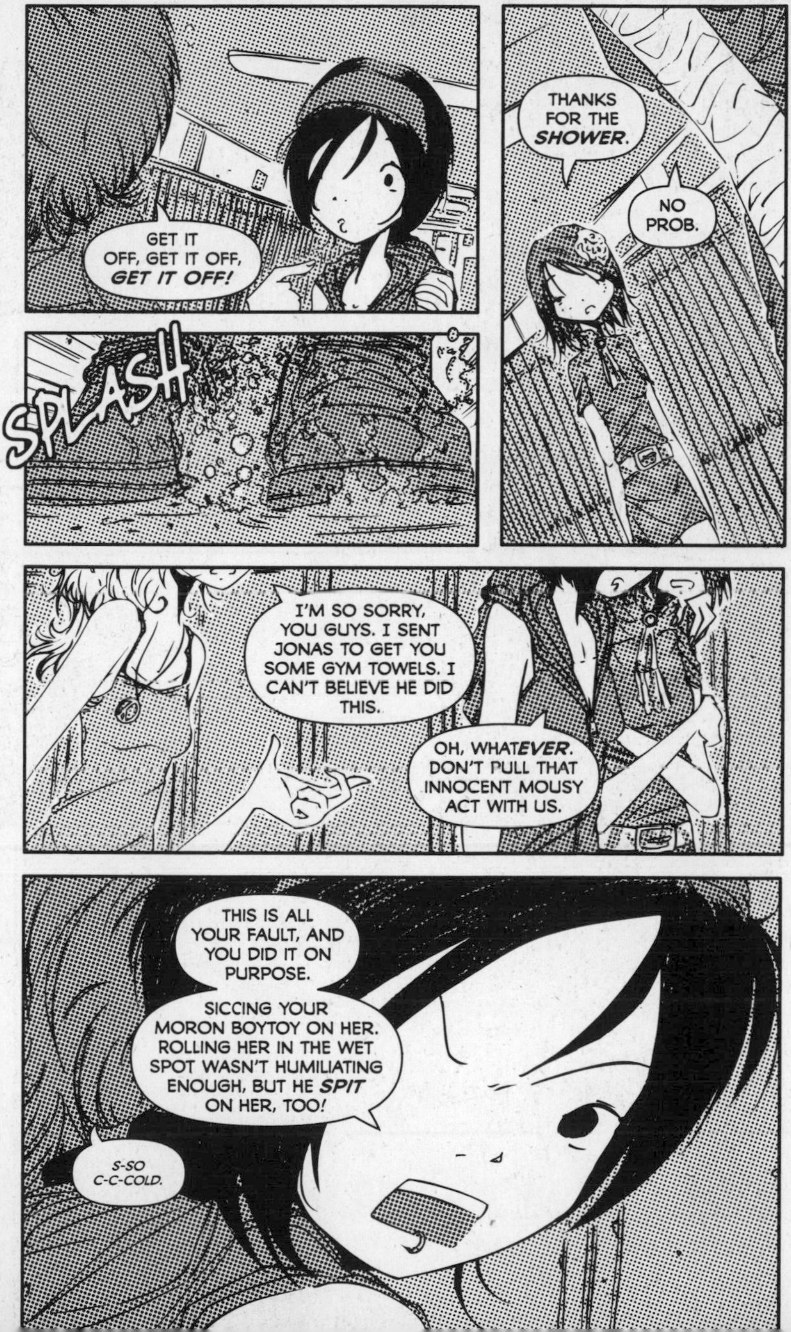

GET IT OFF, GET IT OFF, GET IT OFF!
SPLASH
THANKS FOR THE SHOWER.
NO PROB.
I'M SO SORRY, YOU GUYS. I SENT JONAS TO GET YOU SOME GYM TOWELS. I CAN'T BELIEVE HE DID THIS.
OH, WHATEVER. DON'T PULL THAT INNOCENT MOUSY ACT WITH US.
THIS IS ALL YOUR FAULT, AND YOU DID IT ON PURPOSE.
SICCING YOUR MORON BOYTOY ON HER. ROLLING HER IN THE WET SPOT WASN'T HUMILIATING ENOUGH, BUT HE SPIT ON HER, TOO!
S-SO C-C-COLD.

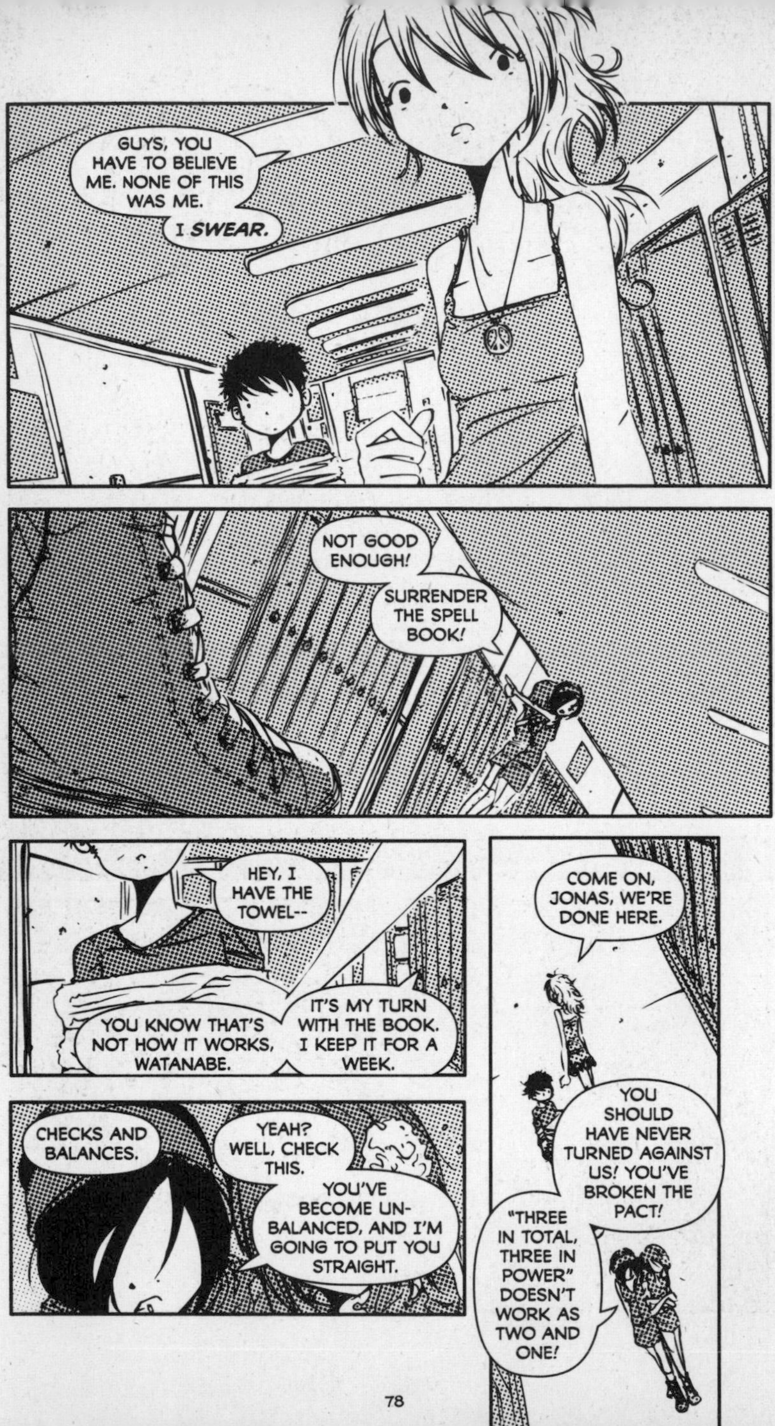

GUYS, YOU HAVE TO BELIEVE ME. NONE OF THIS WAS ME.
I SWEAR.
NOT GOOD ENOUGH!
SURRENDER THE SPELL BOOK!
HEY, I HAVE THE TOWEL--
IT'S MY TURN WITH THE BOOK. I KEEP IT FOR A WEEK.
YOU KNOW THAT'S NOT HOW IT WORKS, WATANABE.
CHECKS AND BALANCES.
YEAH? WELL, CHECK THIS.
YOU'VE BECOME UN-BALANCED, AND I'M GOING TO PUT YOU STRAIGHT.
COME ON, JONAS, WE'RE DONE HERE.
YOU SHOULD HAVE NEVER TURNED AGAINST US! YOU'VE BROKEN THE PACT!
"THREE IN TOTAL, THREE IN POWER" DOESN'T WORK AS TWO AND ONE!

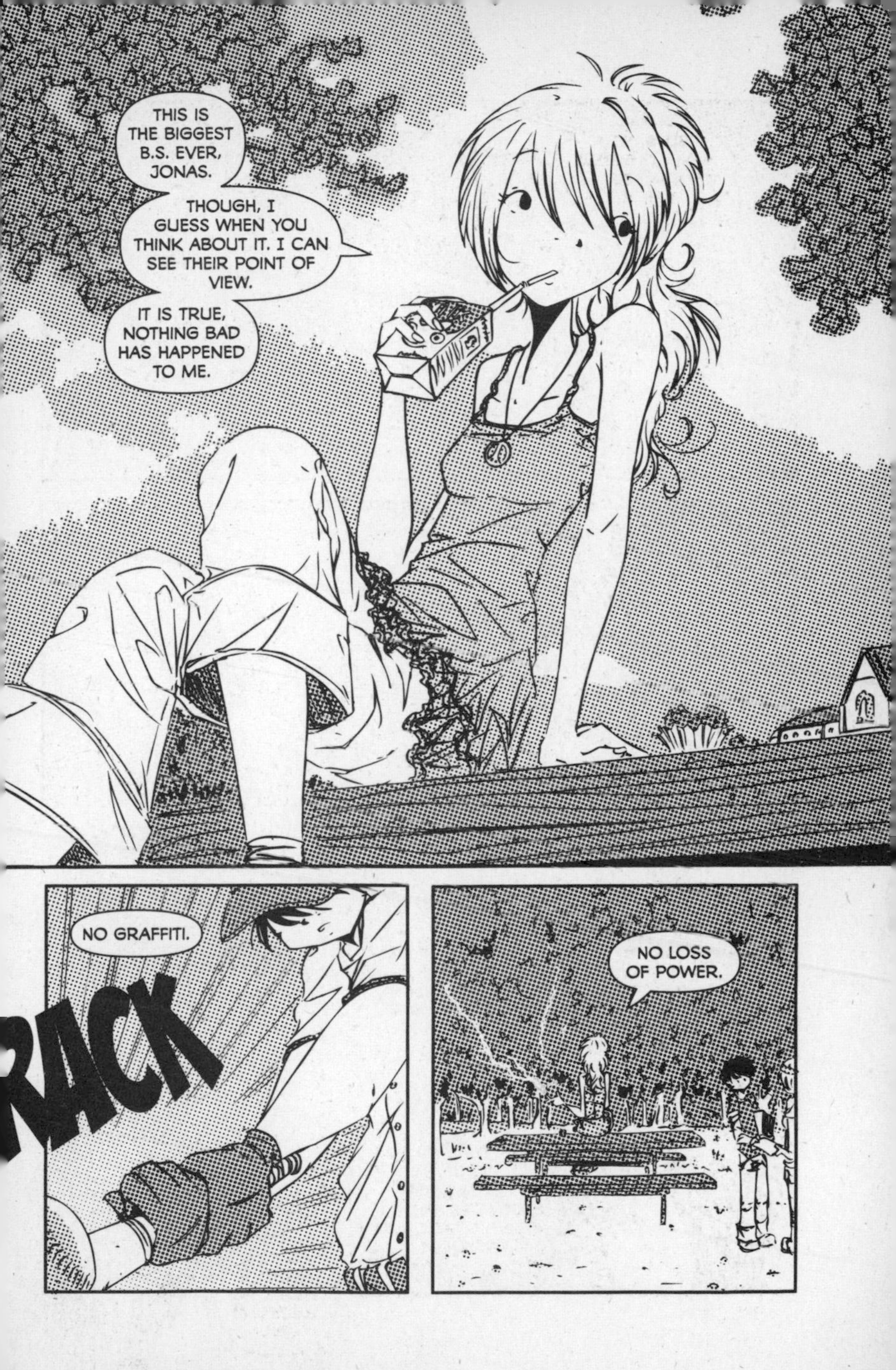
THIS IS THE BIGGEST B.S. EVER, JONAS.
THOUGH, I GUESS WHEN YOU THINK ABOUT IT. I CAN SEE THEIR POINT OF VIEW.
IT IS TRUE, NOTHING BAD HAS HAPPENED TO ME.
NO GRAFFITI.
RACK
NO LOSS OF POWER.

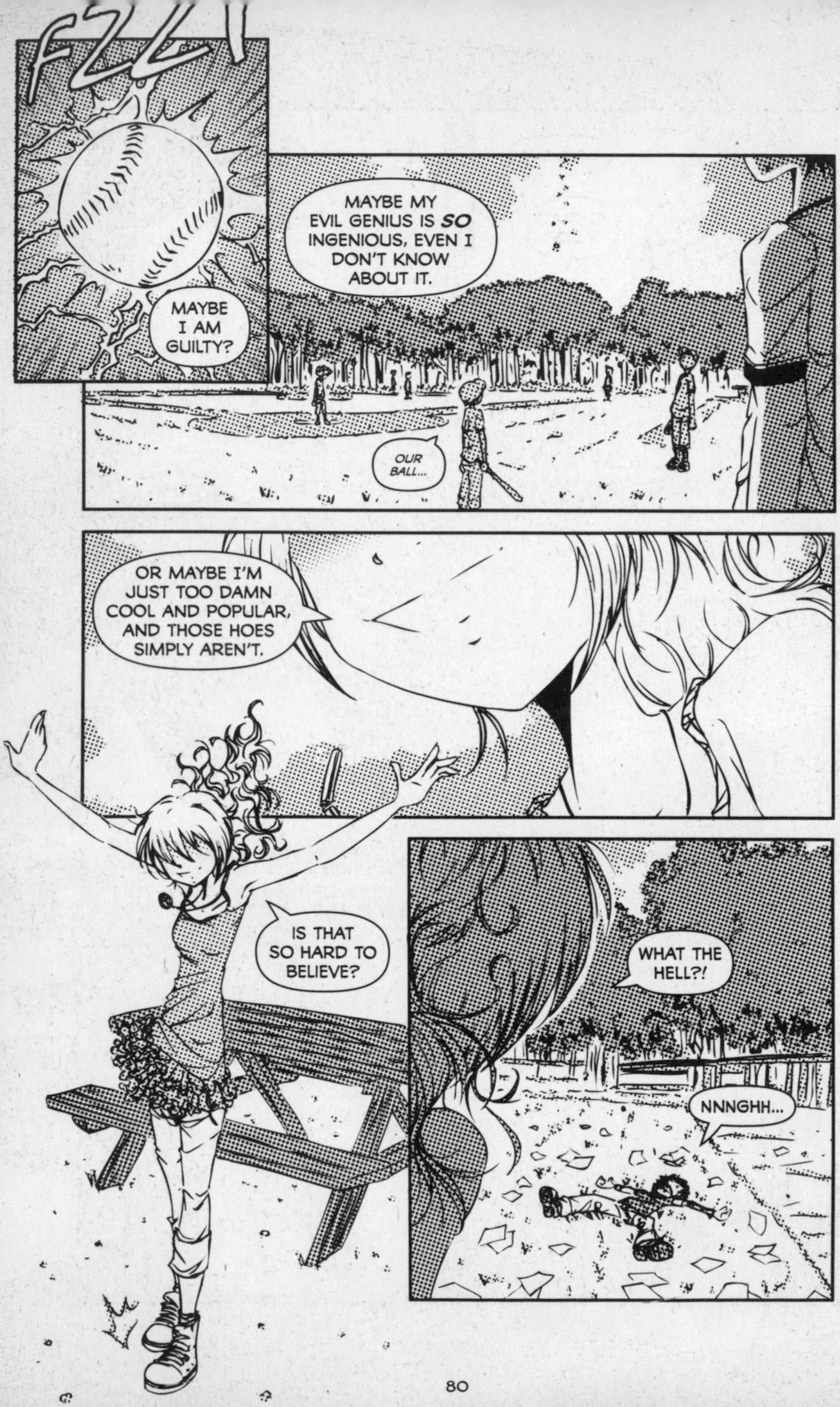
FZZT
MAYBE I AM GUILTY?
MAYBE MY EVIL GENIUS IS SO INGENIOUS, EVEN I DON'T KNOW ABOUT IT.
OUR BALL...
OR MAYBE I'M JUST TOO DAMN COOL AND POPULAR, AND THOSE HOES SIMPLY AREN'T.
IS THAT SO HARD TO BELIEVE?
WHAT THE HELL?!
NNNGHH...

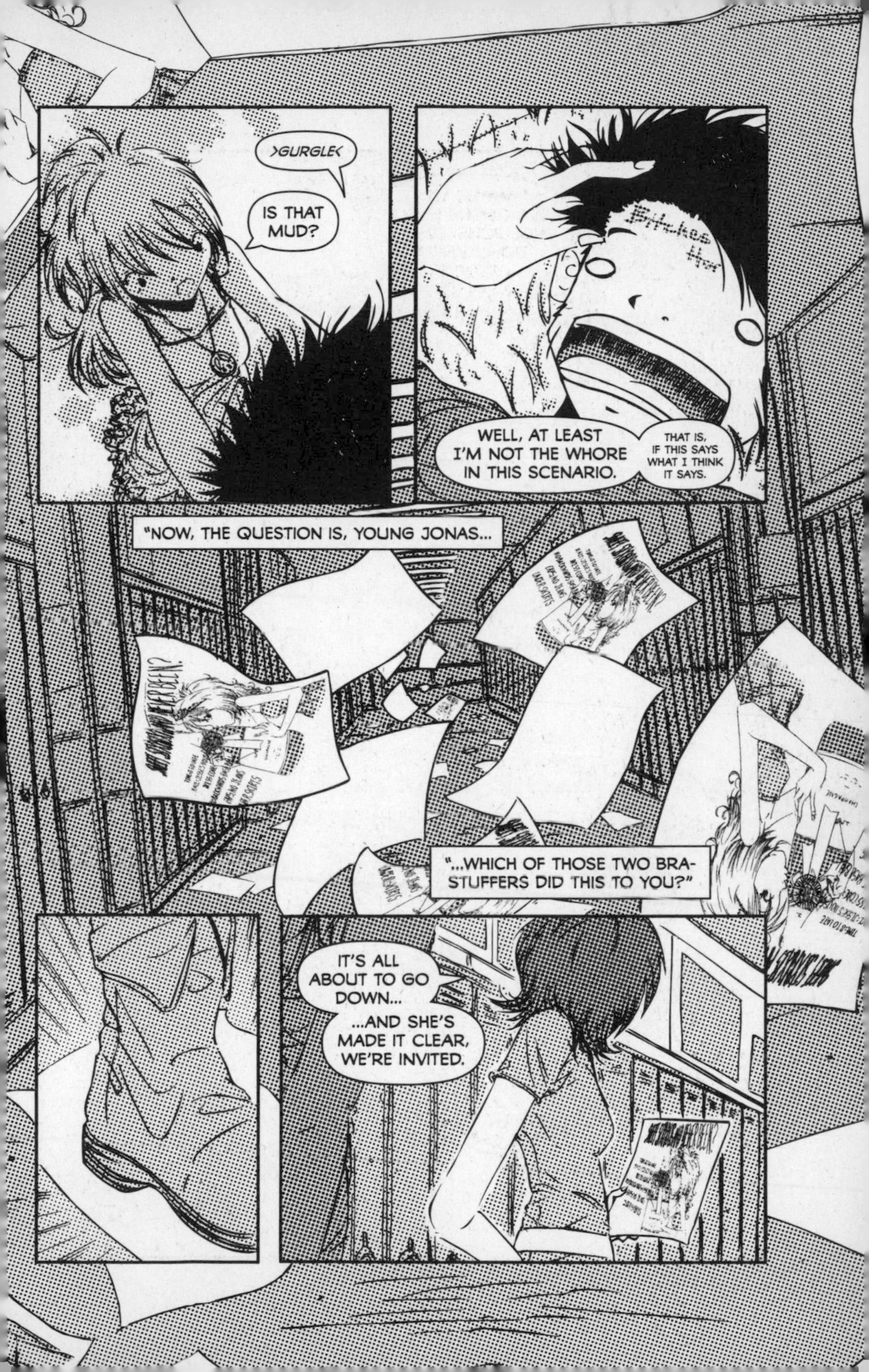

>GURGLE<
IS THAT MUD?
WELL, AT LEAST I'M NOT THE WHORE IN THIS SCENARIO.
THAT IS, IF THIS SAYS WHAT I THINK IT SAYS.
"NOW, THE QUESTION IS, YOUNG JONAS...
"...WHICH OF THOSE TWO BRA-STUFFERS DID THIS TO YOU?"
IT'S ALL ABOUT TO GO DOWN...
...AND SHE'S MADE IT CLEAR, WE'RE INVITED.

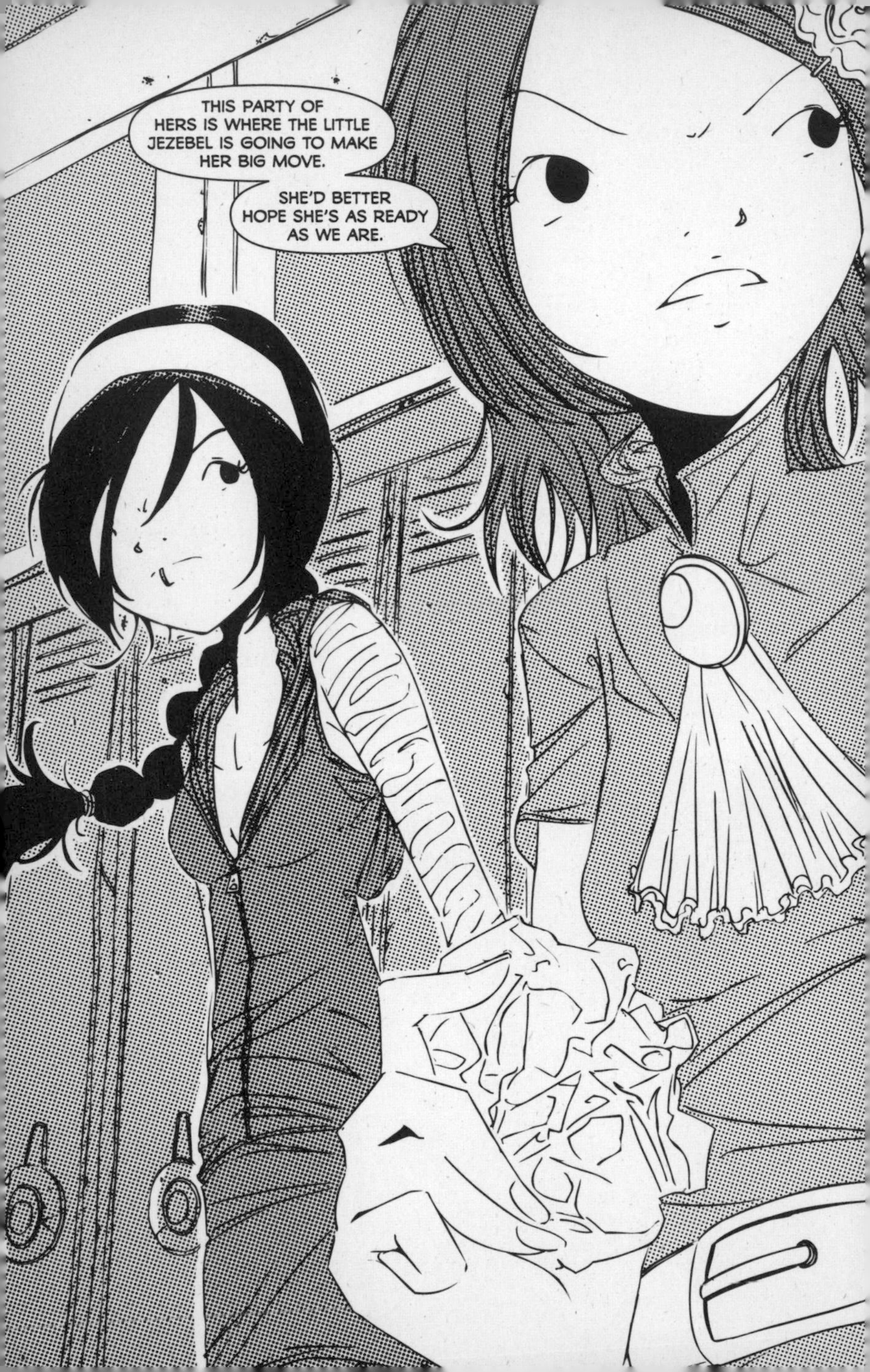
THIS PARTY OF HERS IS WHERE THE LITTLE JEZEBEL IS GOING TO MAKE HER BIG MOVE.
SHE'D BETTER HOPE SHE'S AS READY AS WE ARE.

Chapter 4
"Everyone's At It"

4

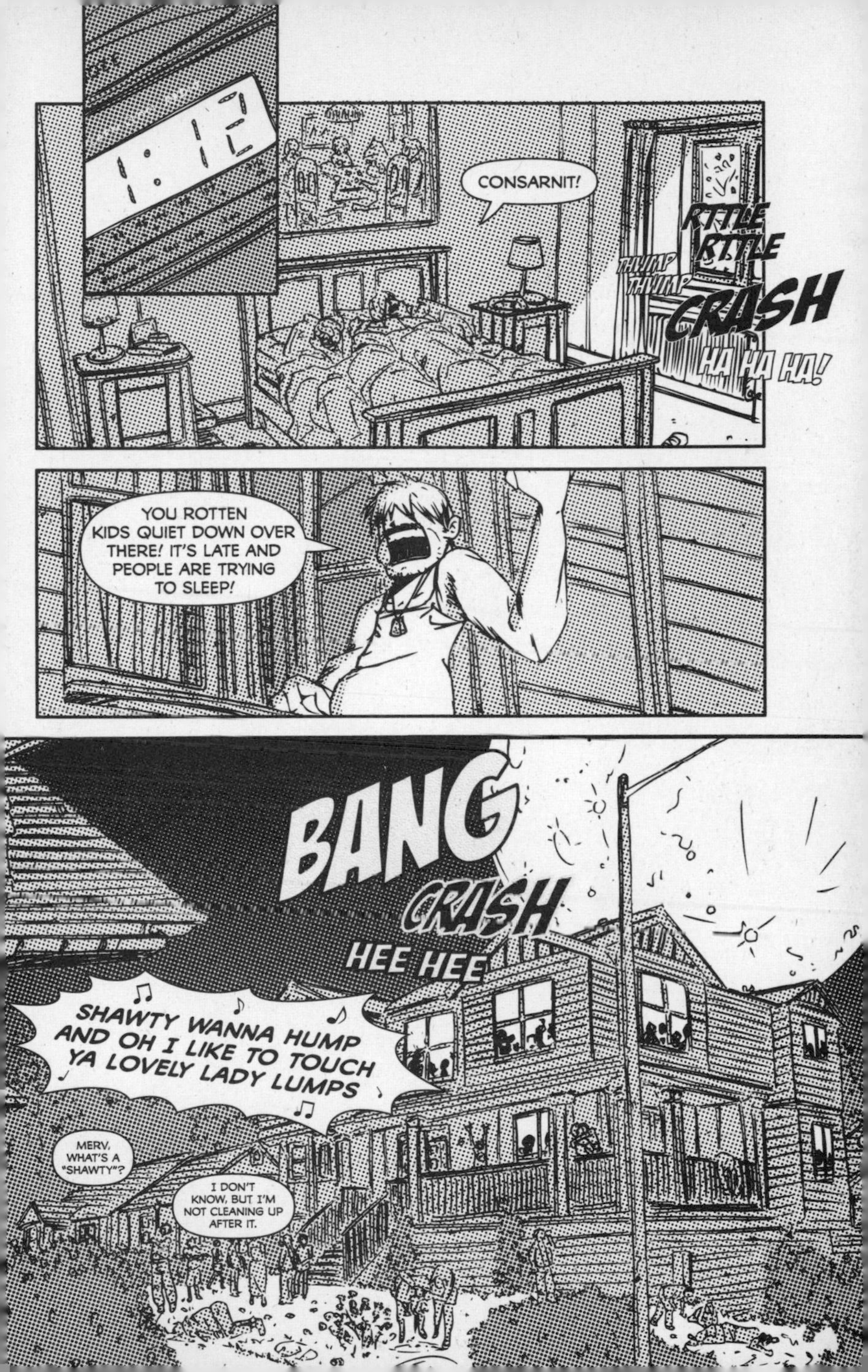
1:12
CONSARNIT!
RTTLE RTTLE
THUMP THUMP
CRASH
HA HA HA!
YOU ROTTEN KIDS QUIET DOWN OVER THERE! IT'S LATE AND PEOPLE ARE TRYING TO SLEEP!
BANG
CRASH
HEE HEE
SHAWTY WANNA HUMP AND OH I LIKE TO TOUCH YA LOVELY LADY LUMPS
MERV, WHAT'S A "SHAWTY"?
I DON'T KNOW, BUT I'M NOT CLEANING UP AFTER IT.

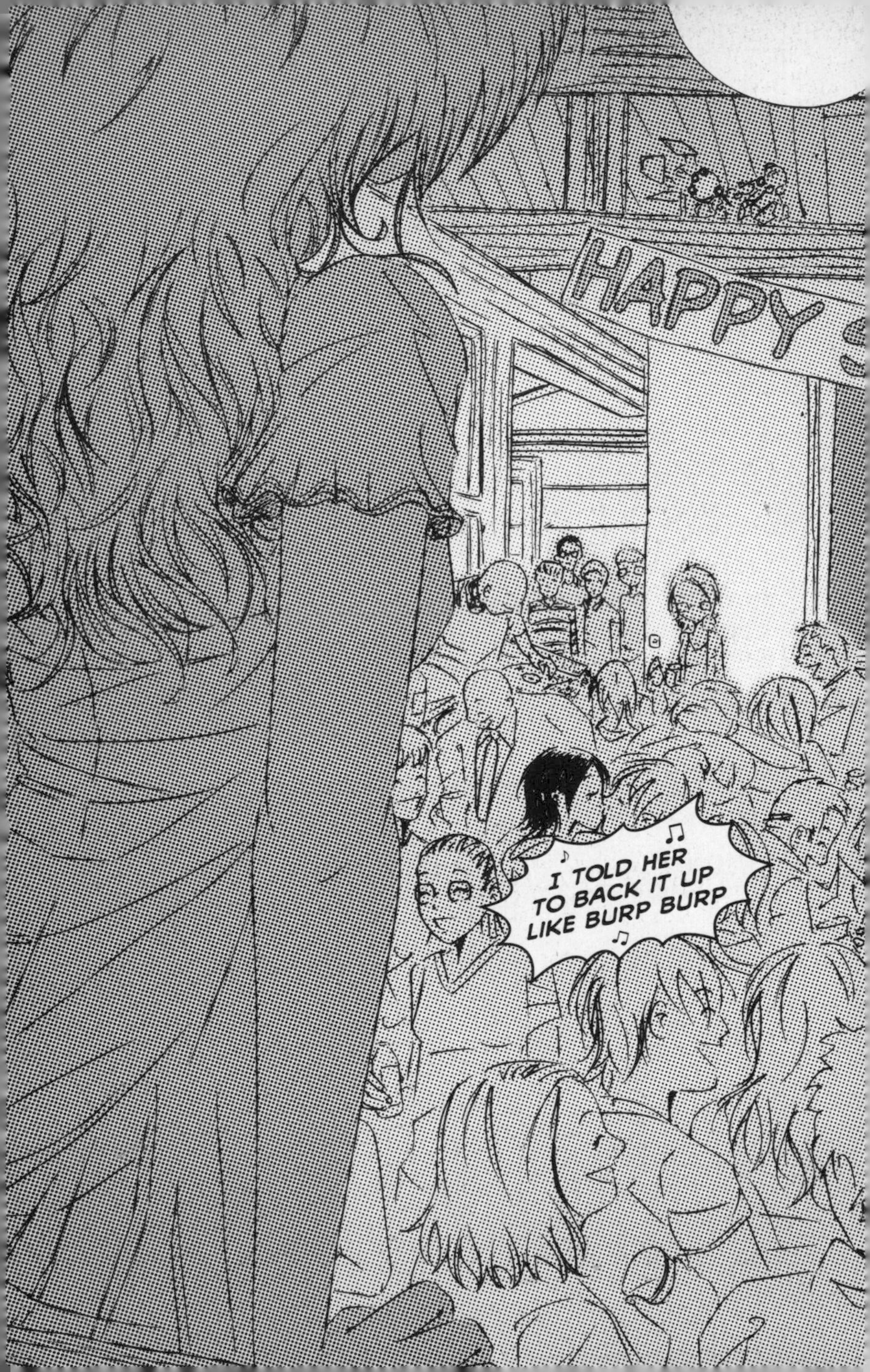
HAPPY S
I TOLD HER TO BACK IT UP LIKE BURP BURP

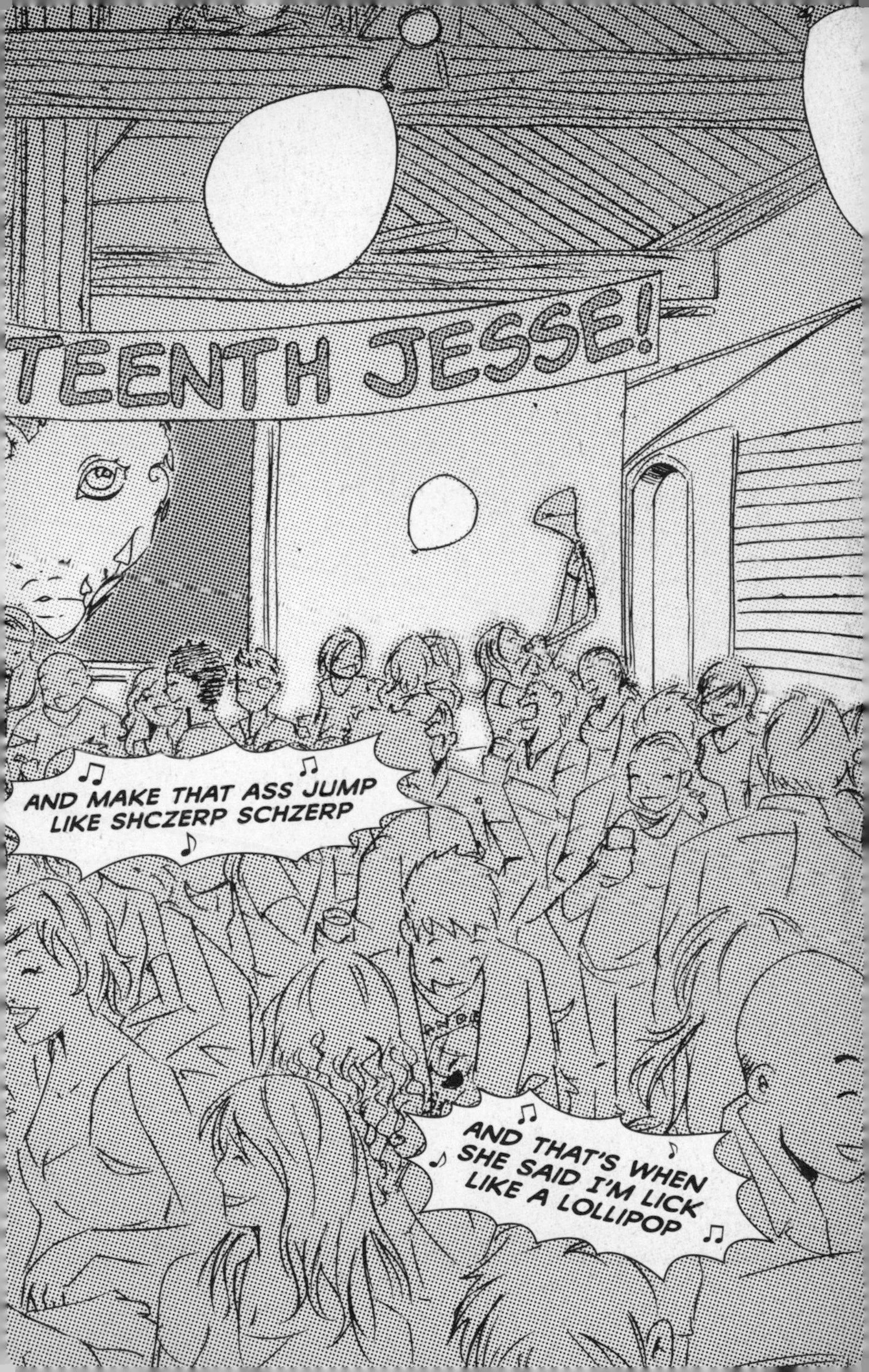
TEENTH JESSE!
AND MAKE THAT ASS JUMP LIKE SHCZERP SCHZERP
AND THAT'S WHEN SHE SAID I'M LICK LIKE A LOLLIPOP

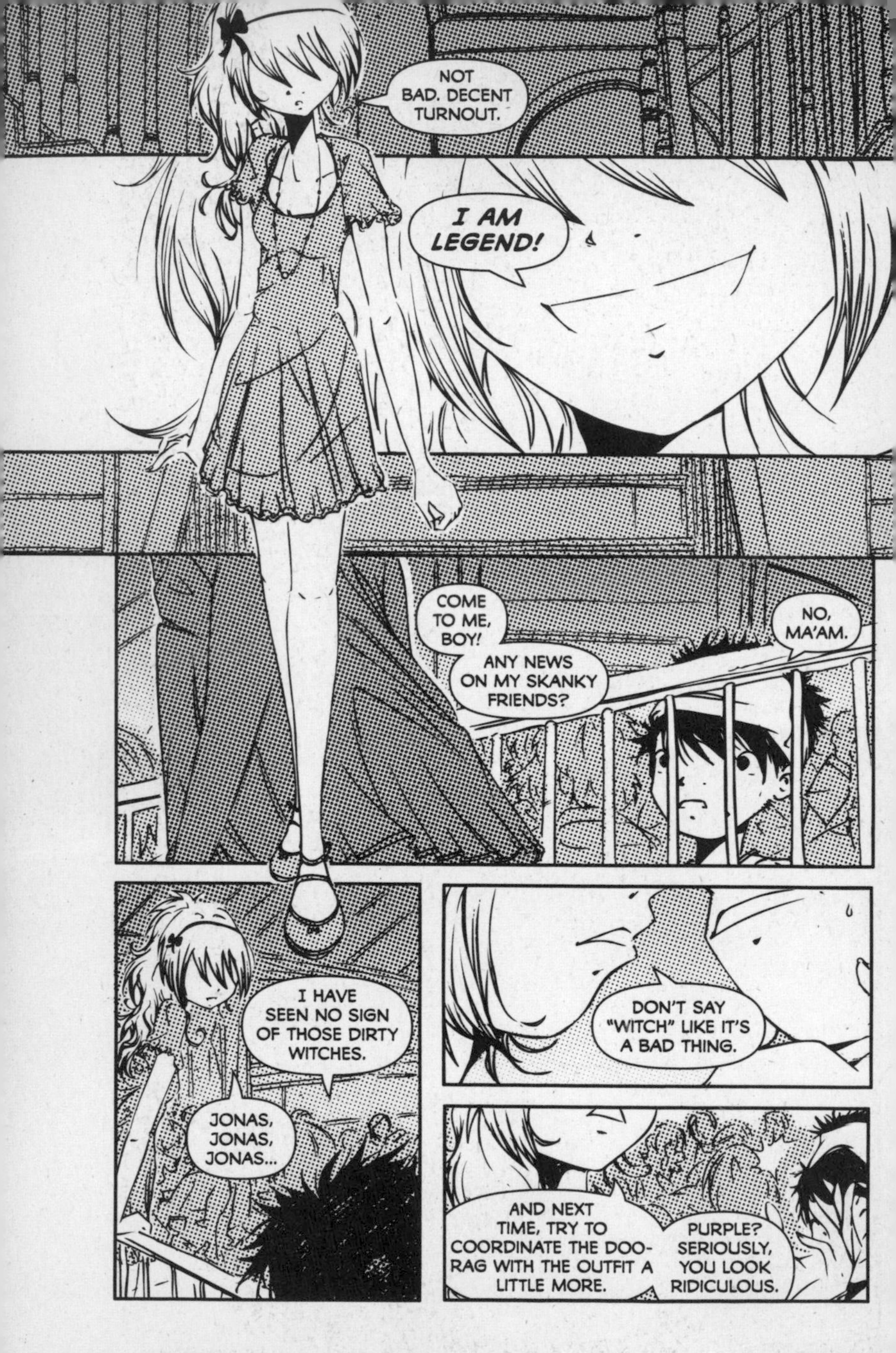
NOT BAD. DECENT TURNOUT.
I AM LEGEND!
COME TO ME, BOY!
ANY NEWS ON MY SKANKY FRIENDS?
NO, MA'AM.
I HAVE SEEN NO SIGN OF THOSE DIRTY WITCHES.
JONAS, JONAS, JONAS...
DON'T SAY "WITCH" LIKE IT'S A BAD THING.
AND NEXT TIME, TRY TO COORDINATE THE DOO-RAG WITH THE OUTFIT A LITTLE MORE.
PURPLE? SERIOUSLY, YOU LOOK RIDICULOUS.

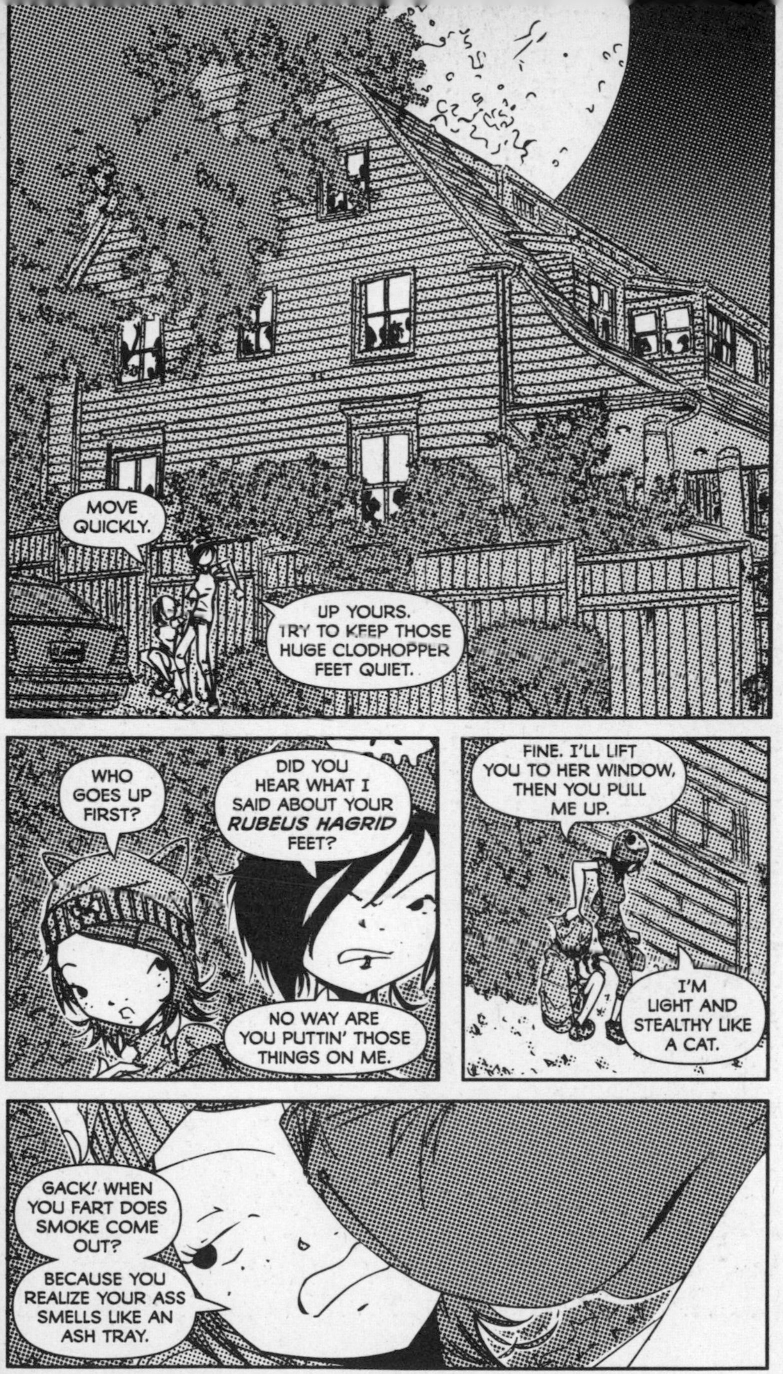
MOVE QUICKLY.
UP YOURS. TRY TO KEEP THOSE HUGE CLODHOPPER FEET QUIET.
WHO GOES UP FIRST?
DID YOU HEAR WHAT I SAID ABOUT YOUR *RUBEUS HAGRID* FEET?
NO WAY ARE YOU PUTTIN' THOSE THINGS ON ME.
FINE. I'LL LIFT YOU TO HER WINDOW, THEN YOU PULL ME UP.
I'M LIGHT AND STEALTHY LIKE A CAT.
GACK! WHEN YOU FART DOES SMOKE COME OUT?
BECAUSE YOU REALIZE YOUR ASS SMELLS LIKE AN ASH TRAY.

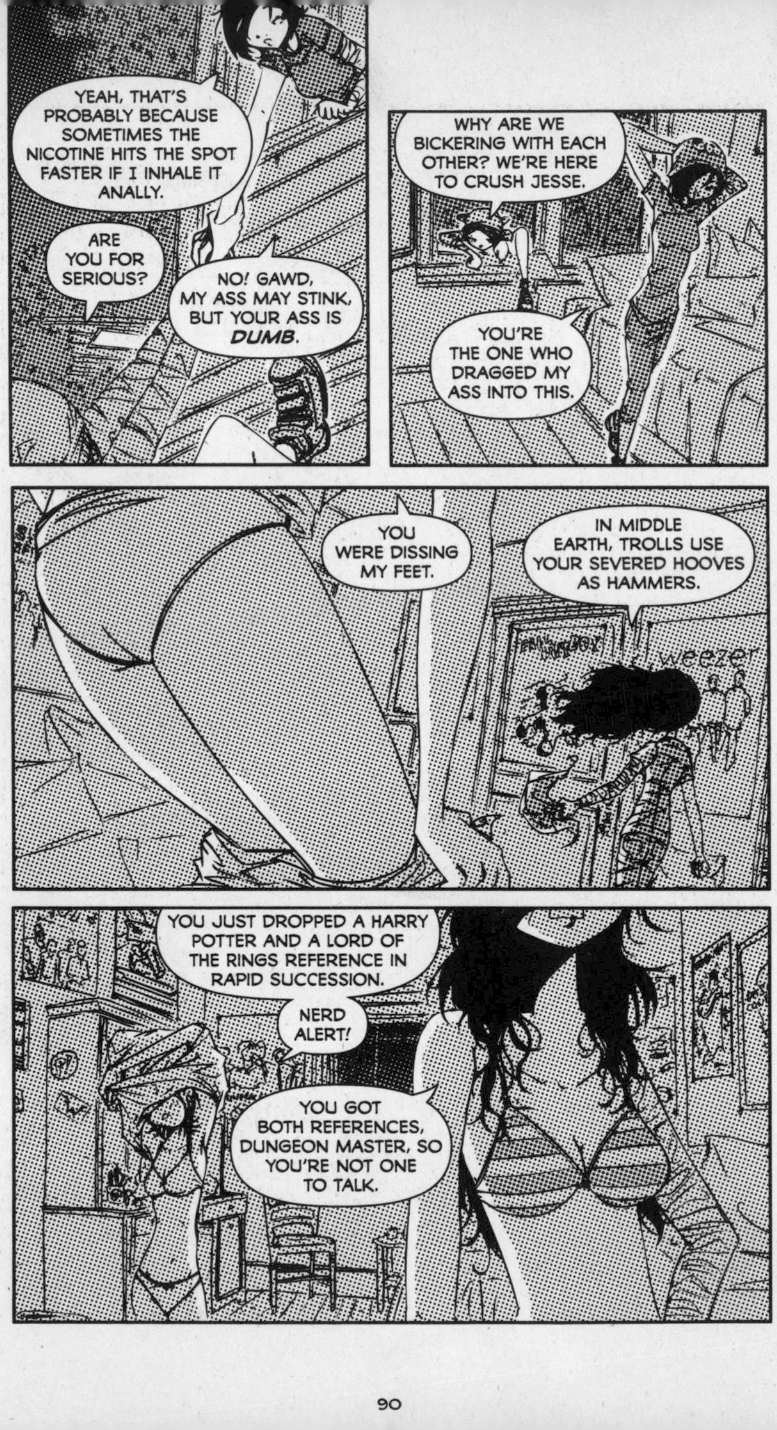
YEAH, THAT'S PROBABLY BECAUSE SOMETIMES THE NICOTINE HITS THE SPOT FASTER IF I INHALE IT ANALLY.
ARE YOU FOR SERIOUS?
NO! GAWD, MY ASS MAY STINK, BUT YOUR ASS IS *DUMB*.
WHY ARE WE BICKERING WITH EACH OTHER? WE'RE HERE TO CRUSH JESSE.
YOU'RE THE ONE WHO DRAGGED MY ASS INTO THIS.
YOU WERE DISSING MY FEET.
IN MIDDLE EARTH, TROLLS USE YOUR SEVERED HOOVES AS HAMMERS.
weezer
YOU JUST DROPPED A HARRY POTTER AND A LORD OF THE RINGS REFERENCE IN RAPID SUCCESSION.
NERD ALERT!
YOU GOT BOTH REFERENCES, DUNGEON MASTER, SO YOU'RE NOT ONE TO TALK.

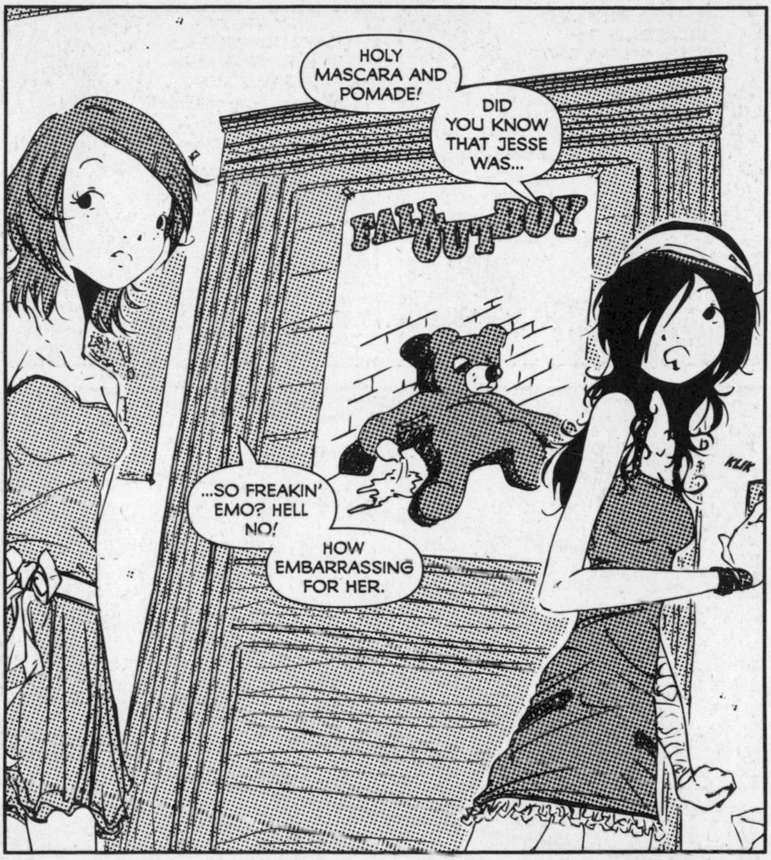
HOLY MASCARA AND POMADE!
DID YOU KNOW THAT JESSE WAS...
FALL OUT BOY
...SO FREAKIN' EMO? HELL NO!
HOW EMBARRASSING FOR HER.
KLIK

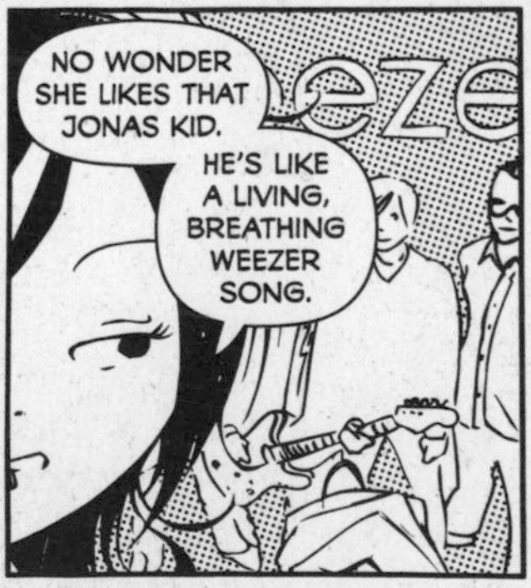
NO WONDER SHE LIKES THAT JONAS KID.
HE'S LIKE A LIVING, BREATHING WEEZER SONG.

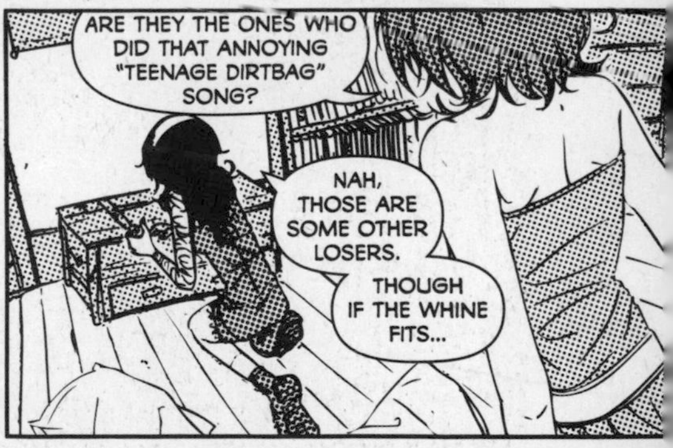
ARE THEY THE ONES WHO DID THAT ANNOYING "TEENAGE DIRTBAG" SONG?
NAH, THOSE ARE SOME OTHER LOSERS.
THOUGH IF THE WHINE FITS...

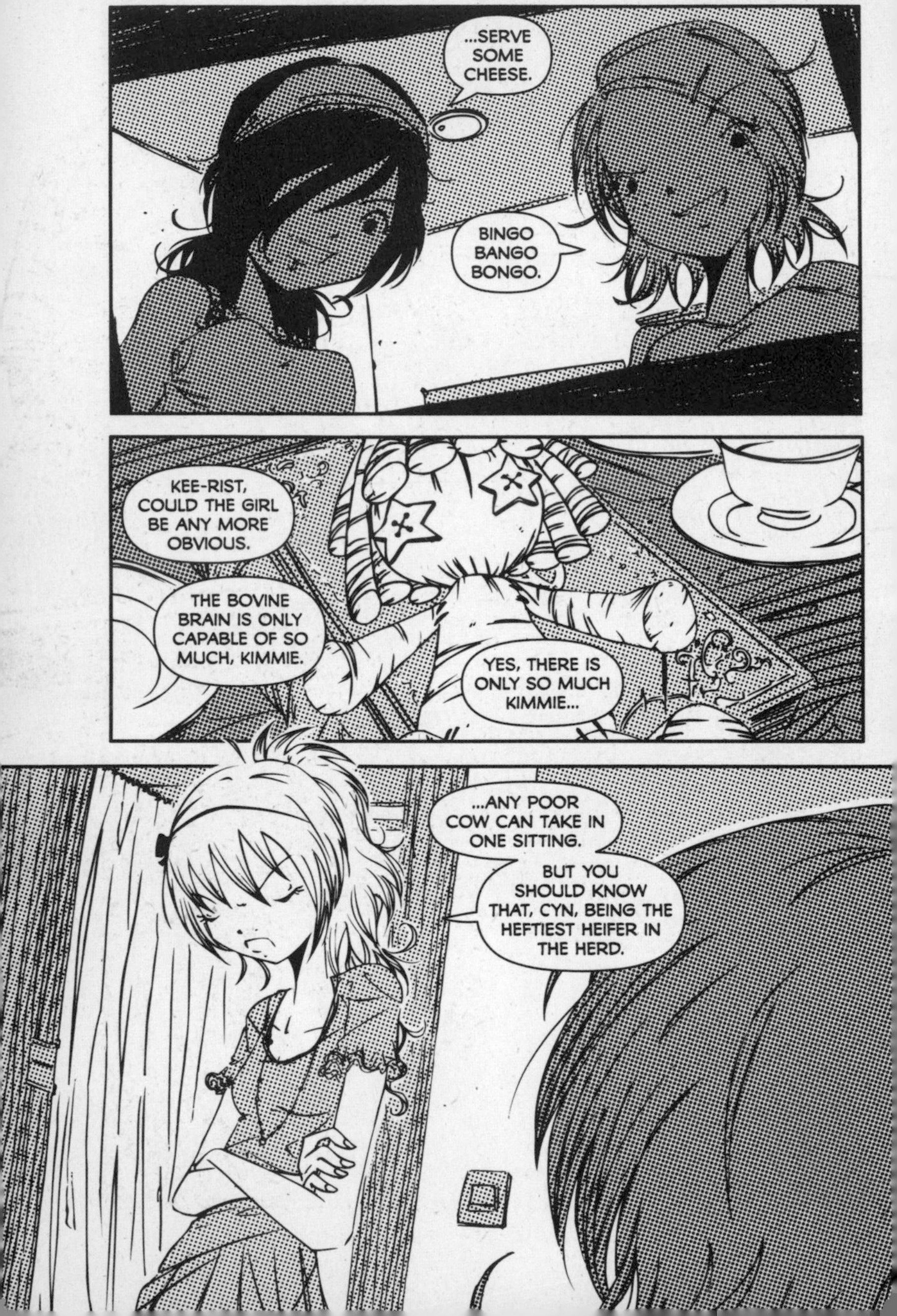
...SERVE SOME CHEESE.
BINGO BANGO BONGO.
KEE-RIST, COULD THE GIRL BE ANY MORE OBVIOUS.
THE BOVINE BRAIN IS ONLY CAPABLE OF SO MUCH, KIMMIE.
YES, THERE IS ONLY SO MUCH KIMMIE...
...ANY POOR COW CAN TAKE IN ONE SITTING.
BUT YOU SHOULD KNOW THAT, CYN, BEING THE HEFTIEST HEIFER IN THE HERD.

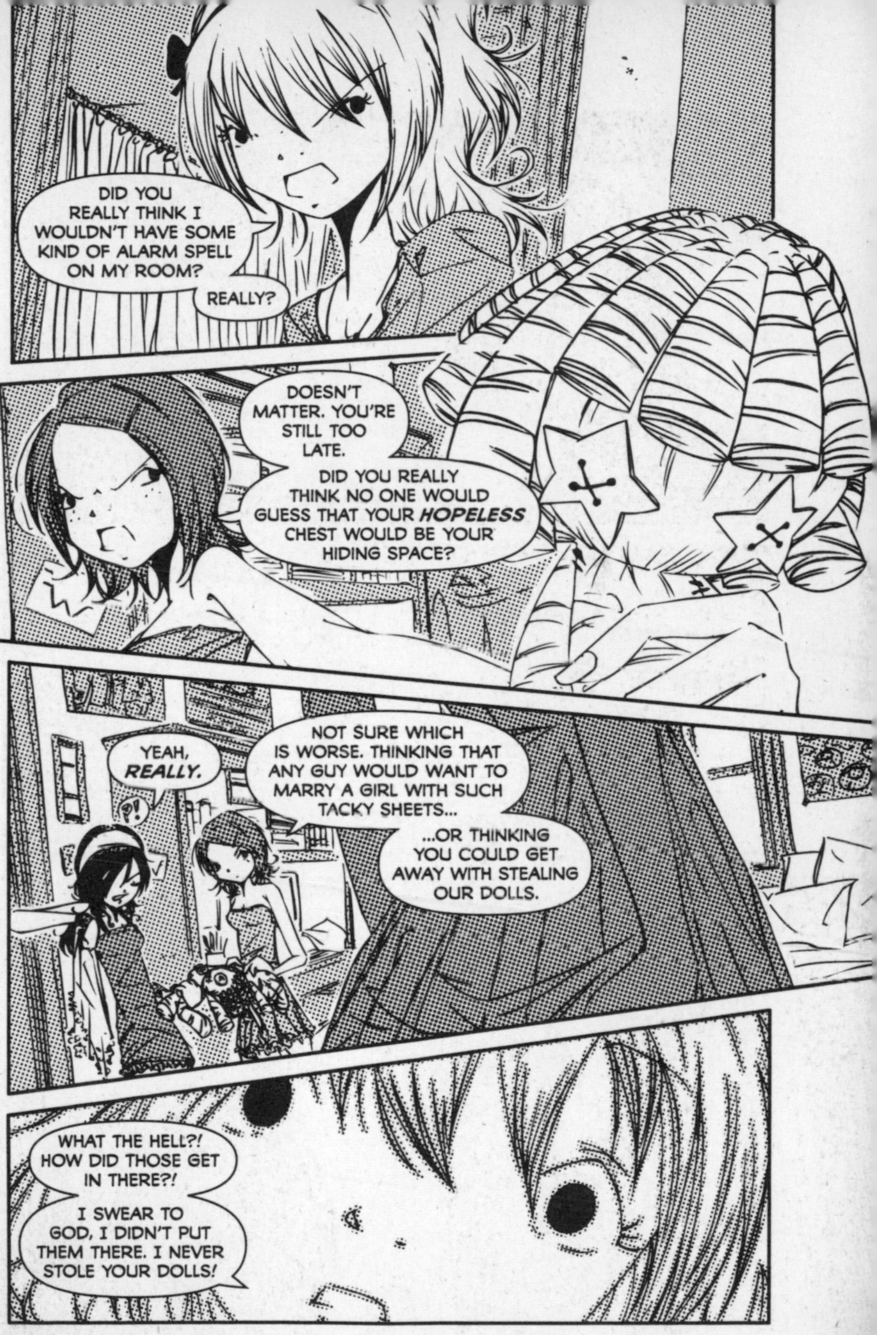

DID YOU REALLY THINK I WOULDN'T HAVE SOME KIND OF ALARM SPELL ON MY ROOM?
REALLY?
DOESN'T MATTER. YOU'RE STILL TOO LATE.
DID YOU REALLY THINK NO ONE WOULD GUESS THAT YOUR *HOPELESS* CHEST WOULD BE YOUR HIDING SPACE?
YEAH, *REALLY.*
NOT SURE WHICH IS WORSE. THINKING THAT ANY GUY WOULD WANT TO MARRY A GIRL WITH SUCH TACKY SHEETS...
...OR THINKING YOU COULD GET AWAY WITH STEALING OUR DOLLS.
WHAT THE HELL?! HOW DID THOSE GET IN THERE?!
I SWEAR TO GOD, I DIDN'T PUT THEM THERE. I NEVER STOLE YOUR DOLLS!

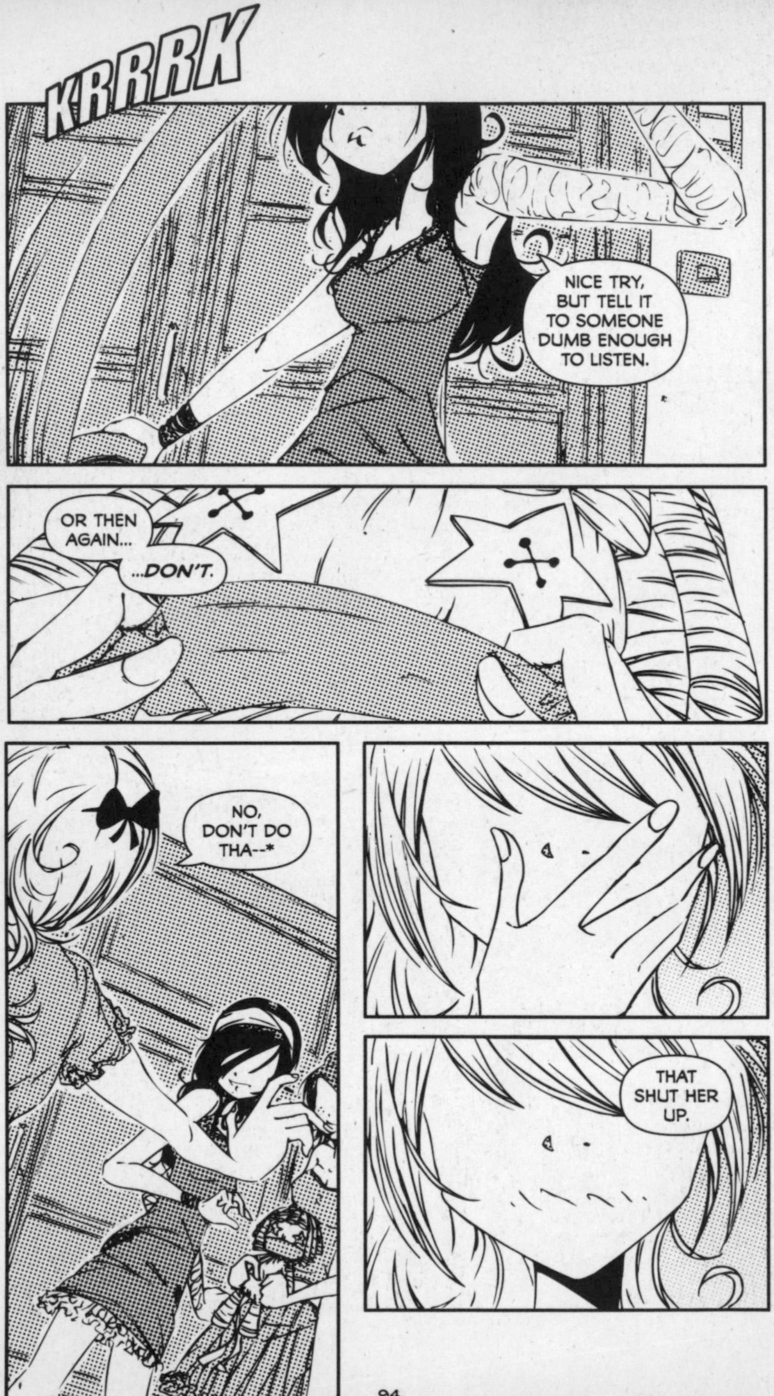
KRRRK
NICE TRY, BUT TELL IT TO SOMEONE DUMB ENOUGH TO LISTEN.
OR THEN AGAIN...
...*DON'T.*
NO, DON'T DO THA--*
THAT SHUT HER UP.

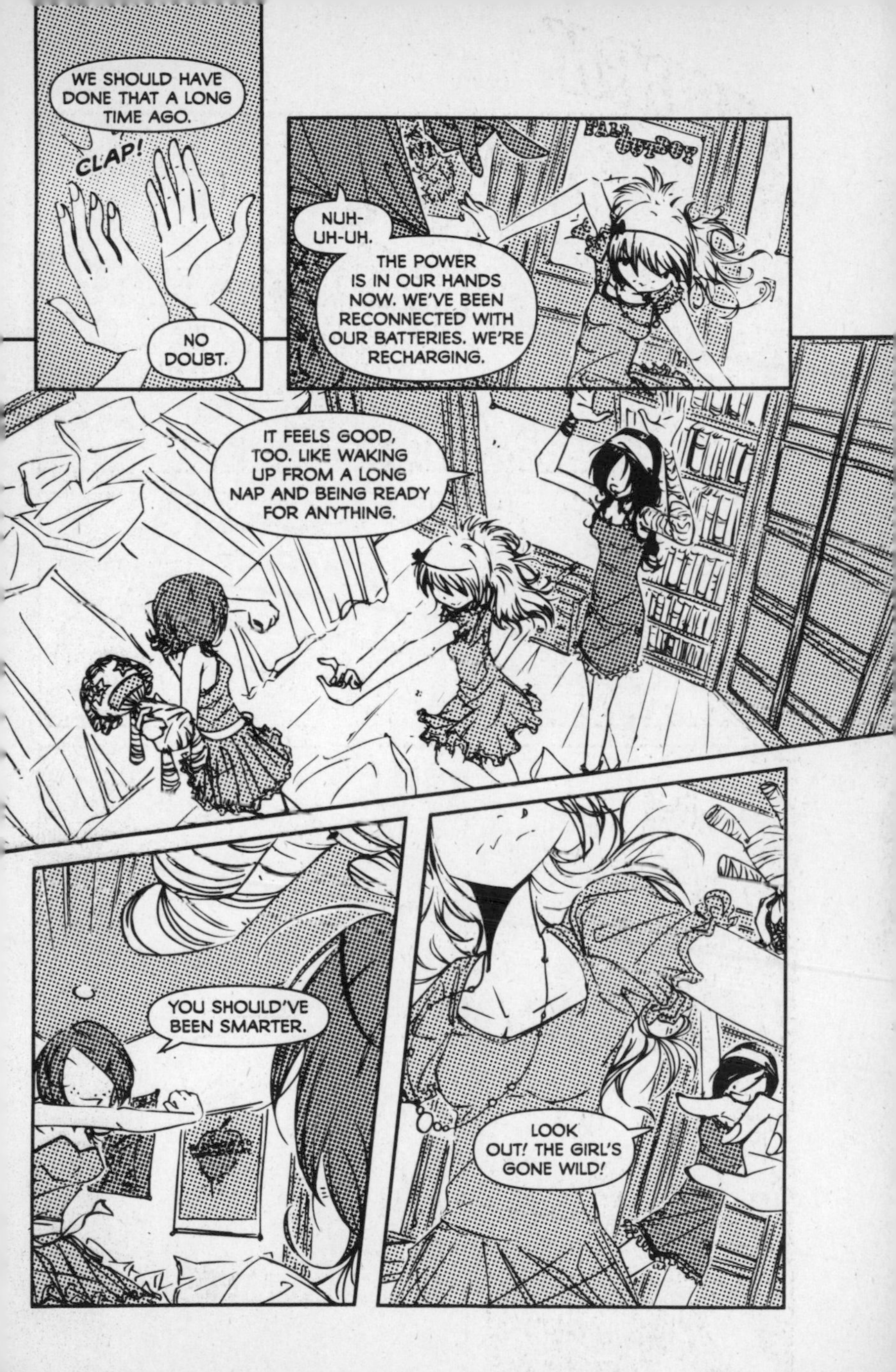
WE SHOULD HAVE DONE THAT A LONG TIME AGO.
CLAP!
NO DOUBT.
NUH-UH-UH.
THE POWER IS IN OUR HANDS NOW. WE'VE BEEN RECONNECTED WITH OUR BATTERIES. WE'RE RECHARGING.
IT FEELS GOOD, TOO. LIKE WAKING UP FROM A LONG NAP AND BEING READY FOR ANYTHING.
YOU SHOULD'VE BEEN SMARTER.
LOOK OUT! THE GIRL'S GONE WILD!

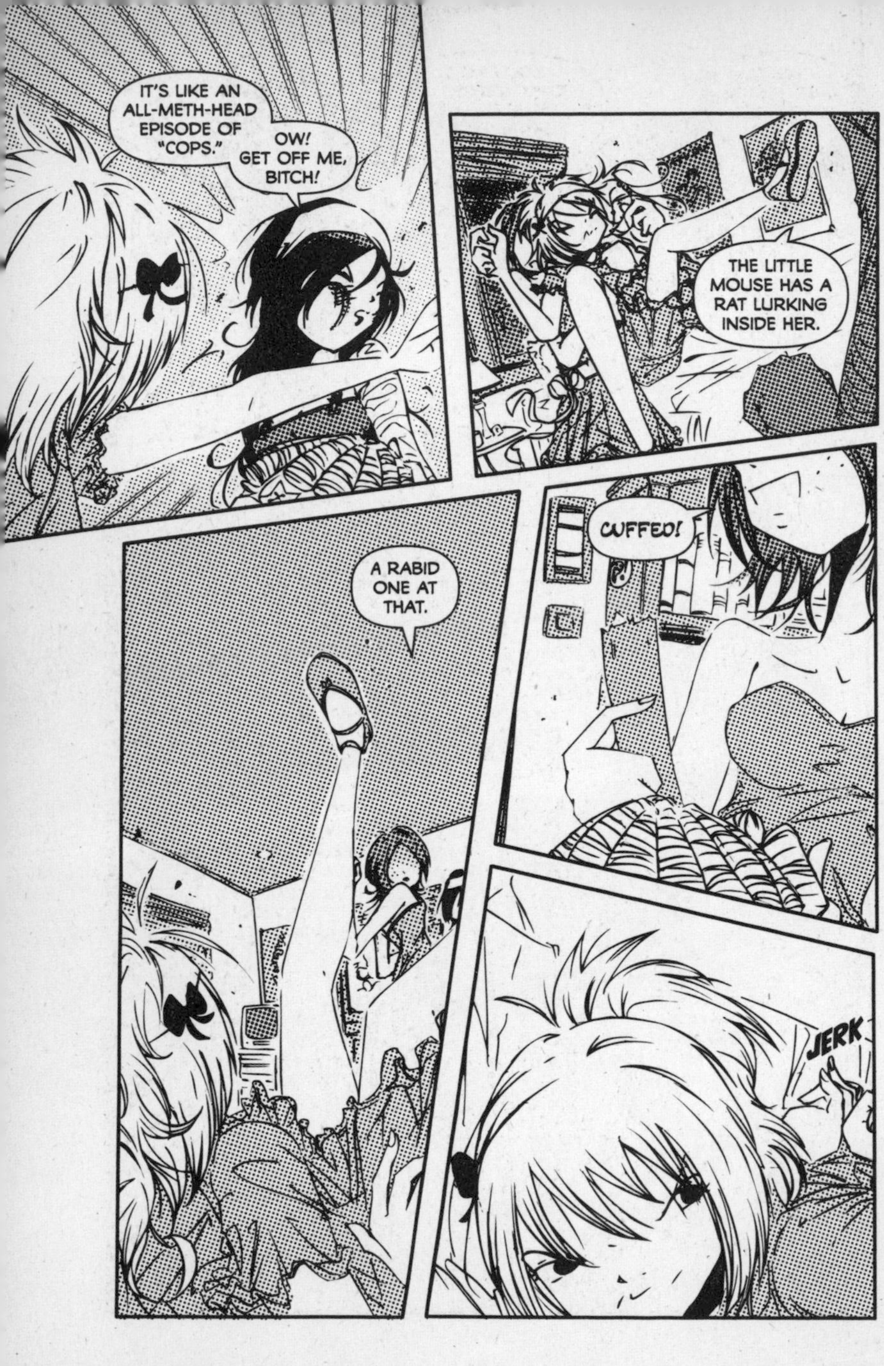
IT'S LIKE AN ALL-METH-HEAD EPISODE OF "COPS."
OW! GET OFF ME, BITCH!
THE LITTLE MOUSE HAS A RAT LURKING INSIDE HER.
A RABID ONE AT THAT.
CUFFED!
JERK

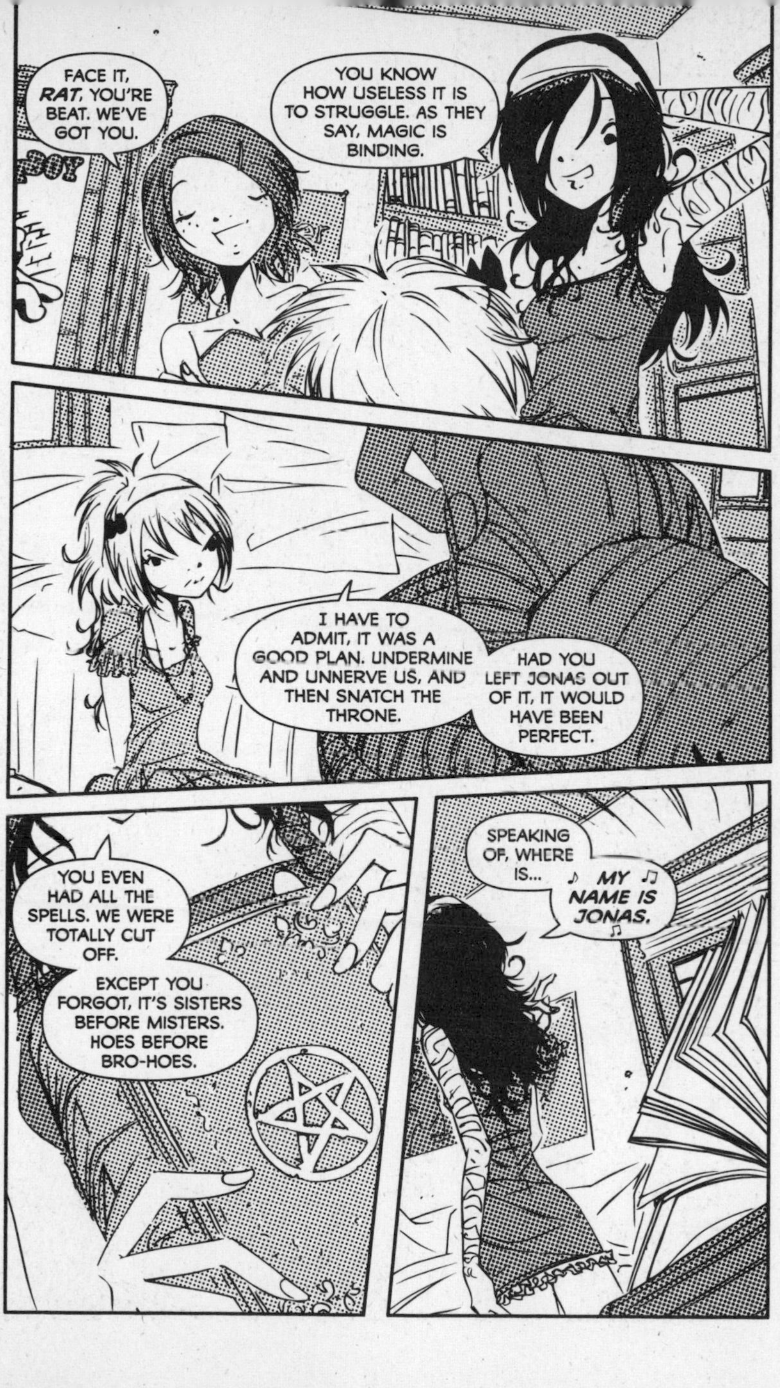
FACE IT, RAT, YOU'RE BEAT. WE'VE GOT YOU.
YOU KNOW HOW USELESS IT IS TO STRUGGLE. AS THEY SAY, MAGIC IS BINDING.
I HAVE TO ADMIT, IT WAS A GOOD PLAN. UNDERMINE AND UNNERVE US, AND THEN SNATCH THE THRONE.
HAD YOU LEFT JONAS OUT OF IT, IT WOULD HAVE BEEN PERFECT.
YOU EVEN HAD ALL THE SPELLS. WE WERE TOTALLY CUT OFF.
EXCEPT YOU FORGOT, IT'S SISTERS BEFORE MISTERS. HOES BEFORE BRO-HOES.
SPEAKING OF, WHERE IS...
♪ MY ♫ NAME IS JONAS. ♫

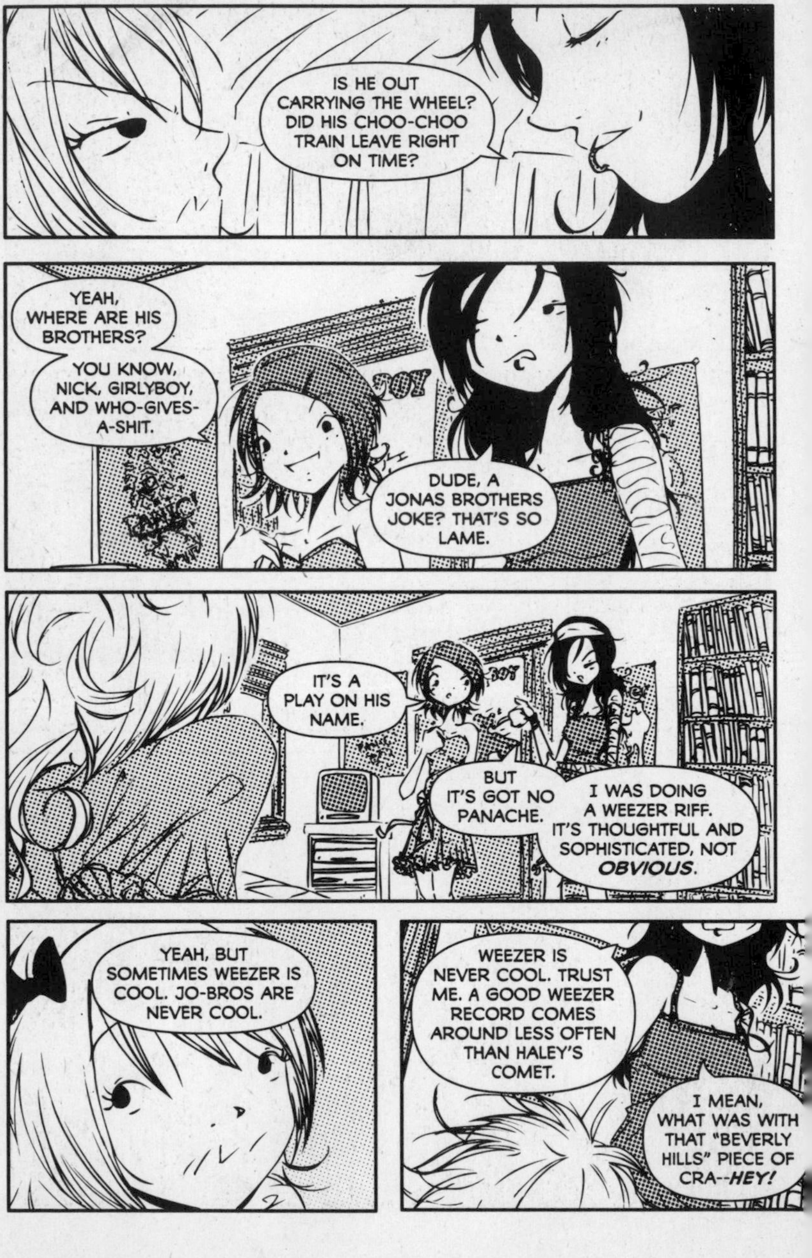
IS HE OUT CARRYING THE WHEEL? DID HIS CHOO-CHOO TRAIN LEAVE RIGHT ON TIME?
YEAH, WHERE ARE HIS BROTHERS?
YOU KNOW, NICK, GIRLYBOY, AND WHO-GIVES-A-SHIT.
DUDE, A JONAS BROTHERS JOKE? THAT'S SO LAME.
IT'S A PLAY ON HIS NAME.
BUT IT'S GOT NO PANACHE.
I WAS DOING A WEEZER RIFF. IT'S THOUGHTFUL AND SOPHISTICATED, NOT *OBVIOUS*.
YEAH, BUT SOMETIMES WEEZER IS COOL. JO-BROS ARE NEVER COOL.
WEEZER IS NEVER COOL. TRUST ME. A GOOD WEEZER RECORD COMES AROUND LESS OFTEN THAN HALEY'S COMET.
I MEAN, WHAT WAS WITH THAT "BEVERLY HILLS" PIECE OF CRA--*HEY!*

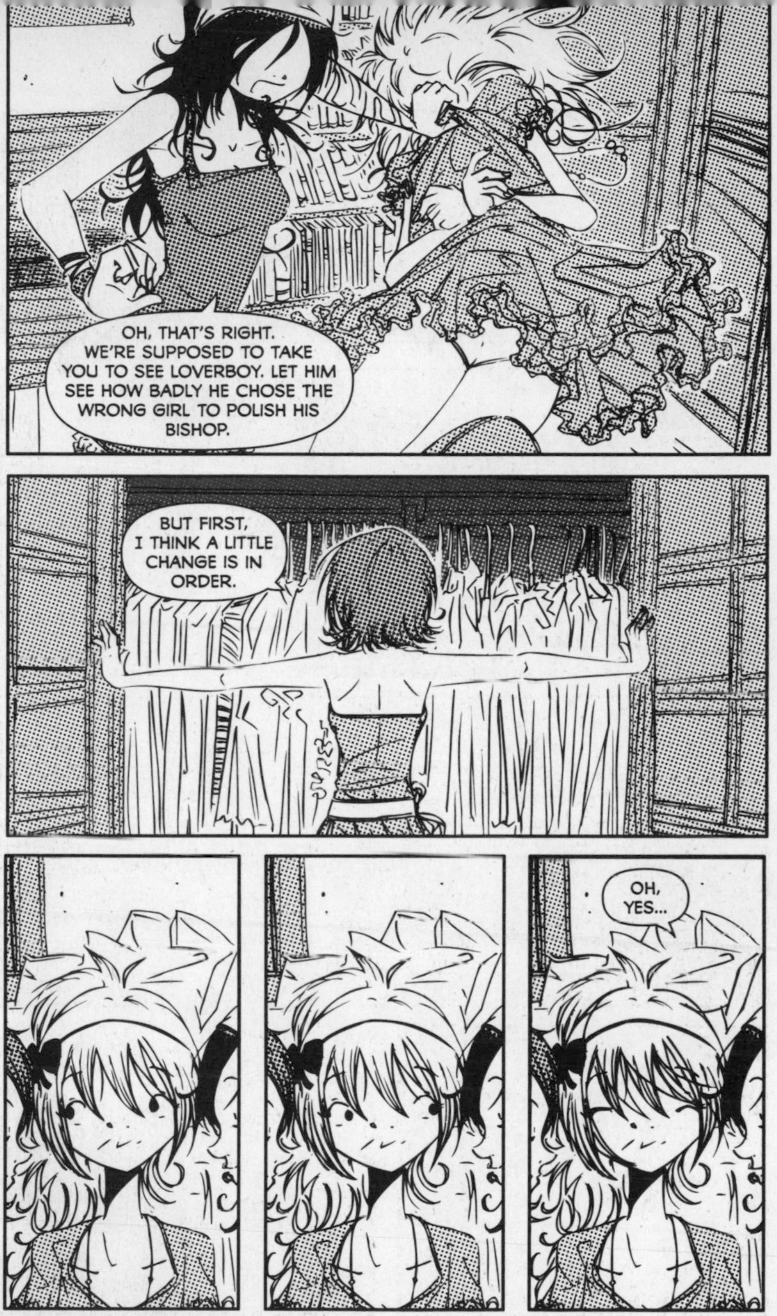
OH, THAT'S RIGHT. WE'RE SUPPOSED TO TAKE YOU TO SEE LOVERBOY. LET HIM SEE HOW BADLY HE CHOSE THE WRONG GIRL TO POLISH HIS BISHOP.
BUT FIRST, I THINK A LITTLE CHANGE IS IN ORDER.
OH, YES...

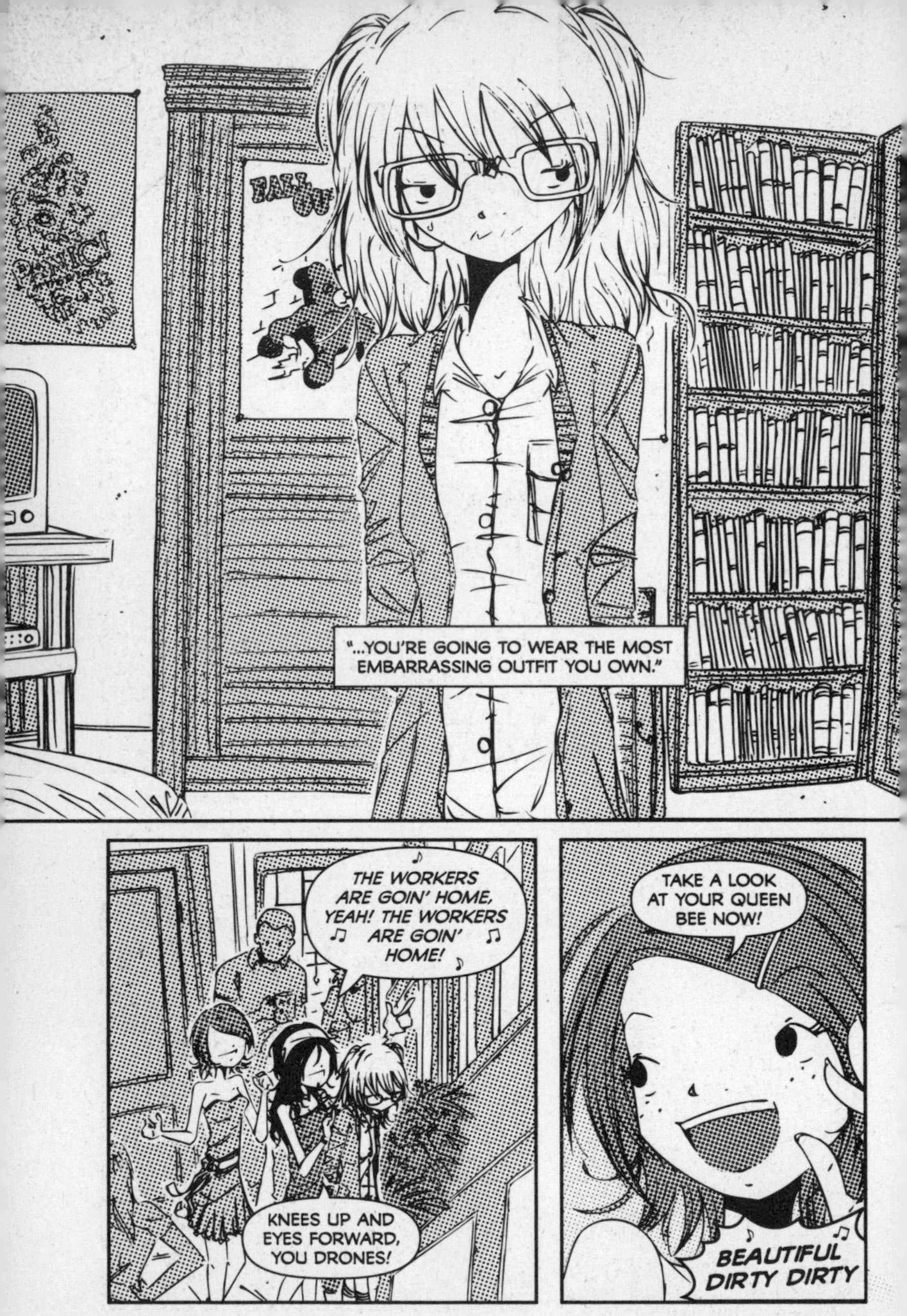
"...YOU'RE GOING TO WEAR THE MOST EMBARRASSING OUTFIT YOU OWN."
THE WORKERS ARE GOIN' HOME, YEAH! THE WORKERS ARE GOIN' HOME!
KNEES UP AND EYES FORWARD, YOU DRONES!
TAKE A LOOK AT YOUR QUEEN BEE NOW!
BEAUTIFUL DIRTY DIRTY

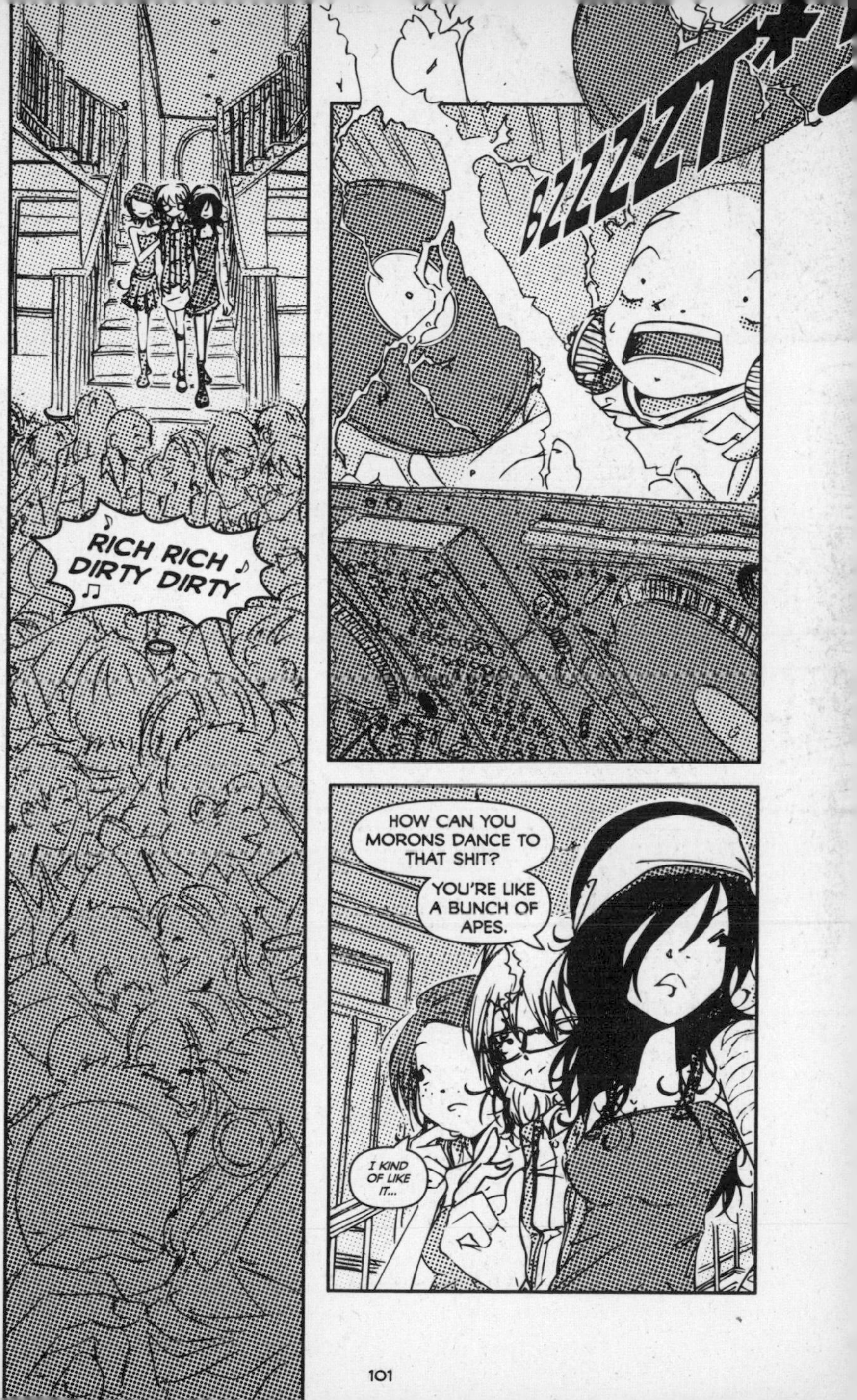
RICH RICH DIRTY DIRTY
BZZZZT
HOW CAN YOU MORONS DANCE TO THAT SHIT?
YOU'RE LIKE A BUNCH OF APES.
I KIND OF LIKE IT...

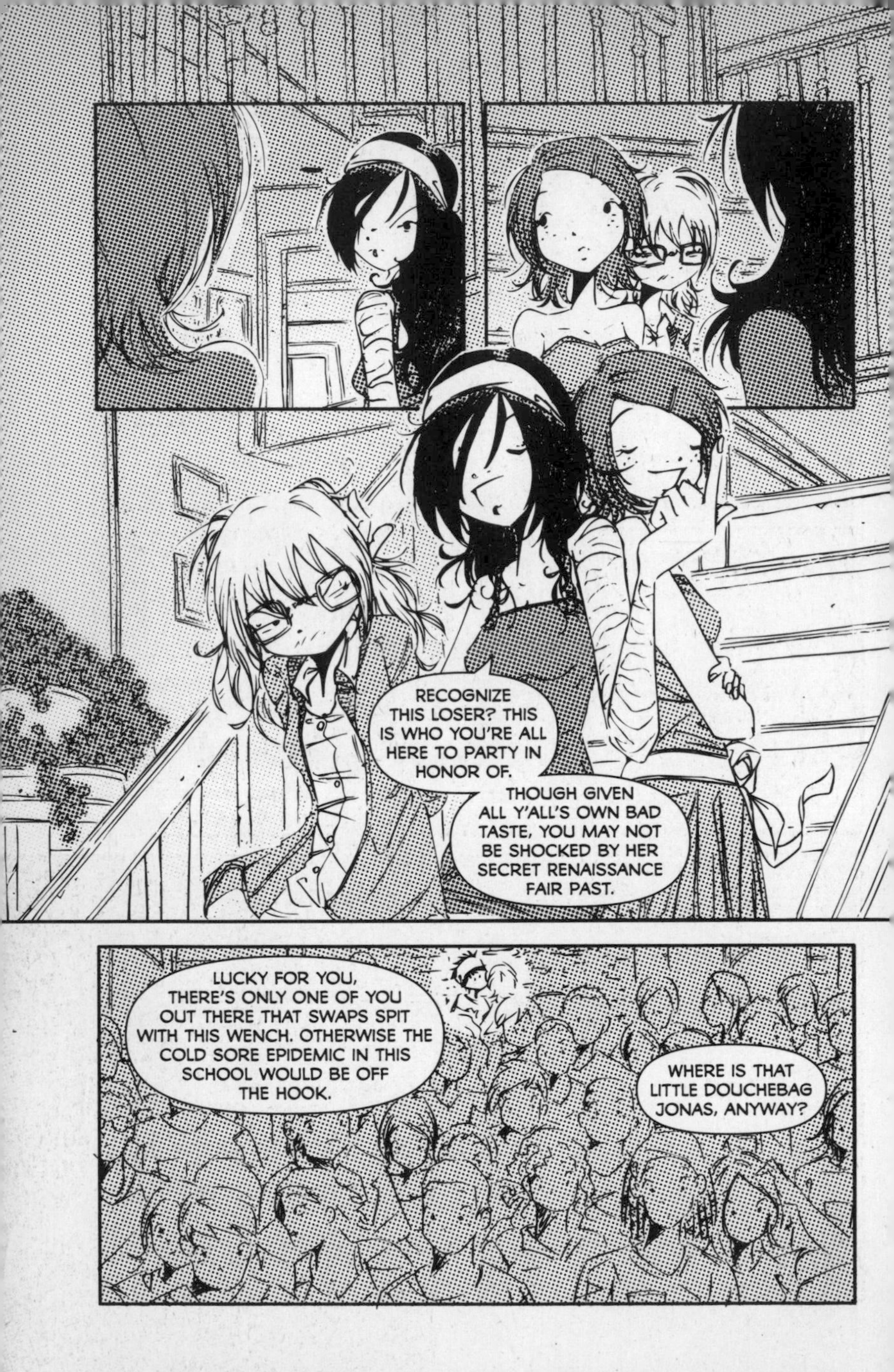
RECOGNIZE THIS LOSER? THIS IS WHO YOU'RE ALL HERE TO PARTY IN HONOR OF.
THOUGH GIVEN ALL Y'ALL'S OWN BAD TASTE, YOU MAY NOT BE SHOCKED BY HER SECRET RENAISSANCE FAIR PAST.
LUCKY FOR YOU, THERE'S ONLY ONE OF YOU OUT THERE THAT SWAPS SPIT WITH THIS WENCH. OTHERWISE THE COLD SORE EPIDEMIC IN THIS SCHOOL WOULD BE OFF THE HOOK.
WHERE IS THAT LITTLE DOUCHEBAG JONAS, ANYWAY?

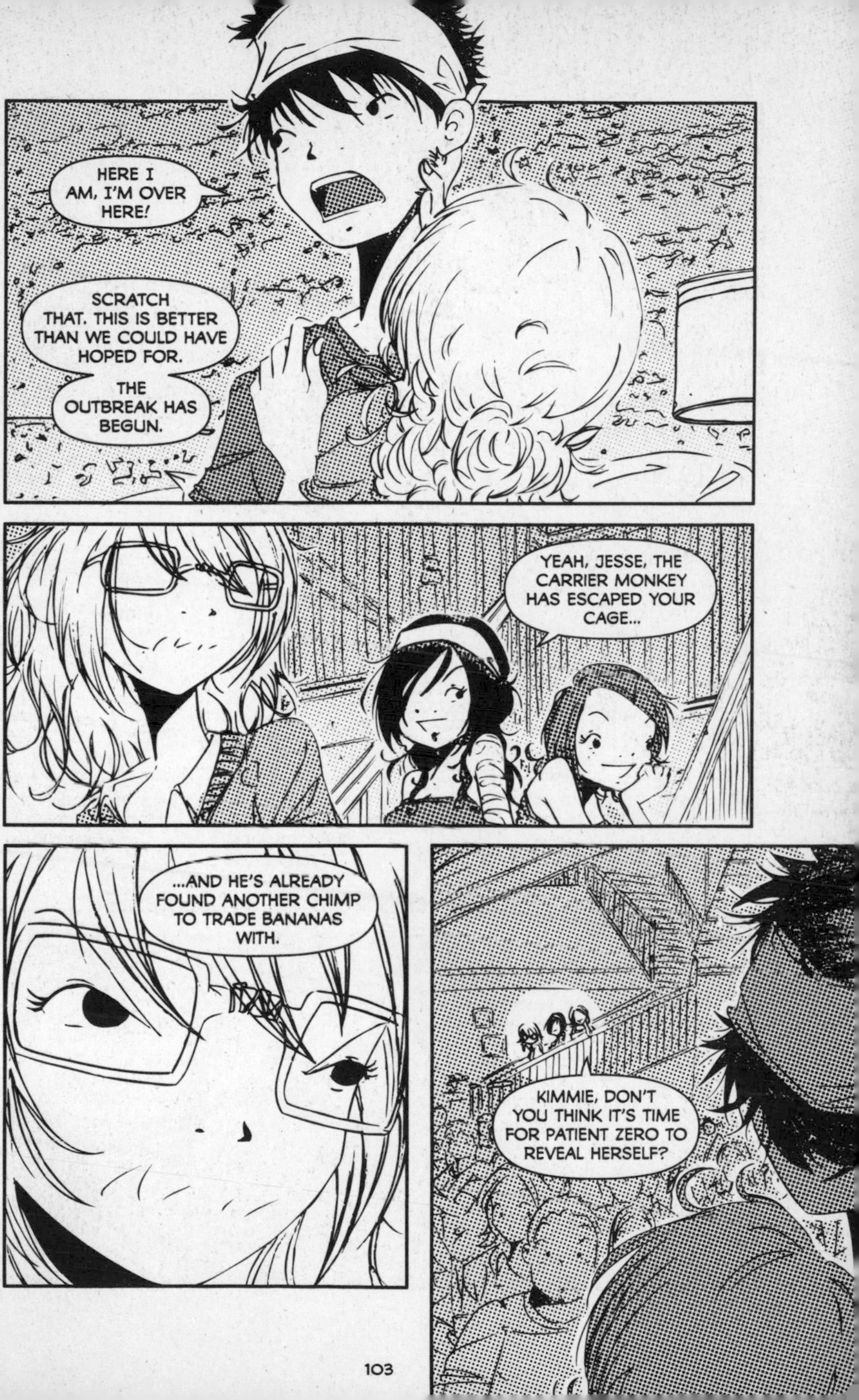
HERE I AM, I'M OVER HERE!
SCRATCH THAT. THIS IS BETTER THAN WE COULD HAVE HOPED FOR.
THE OUTBREAK HAS BEGUN.
YEAH, JESSE, THE CARRIER MONKEY HAS ESCAPED YOUR CAGE...
...AND HE'S ALREADY FOUND ANOTHER CHIMP TO TRADE BANANAS WITH.
KIMMIE, DON'T YOU THINK IT'S TIME FOR PATIENT ZERO TO REVEAL HERSELF?

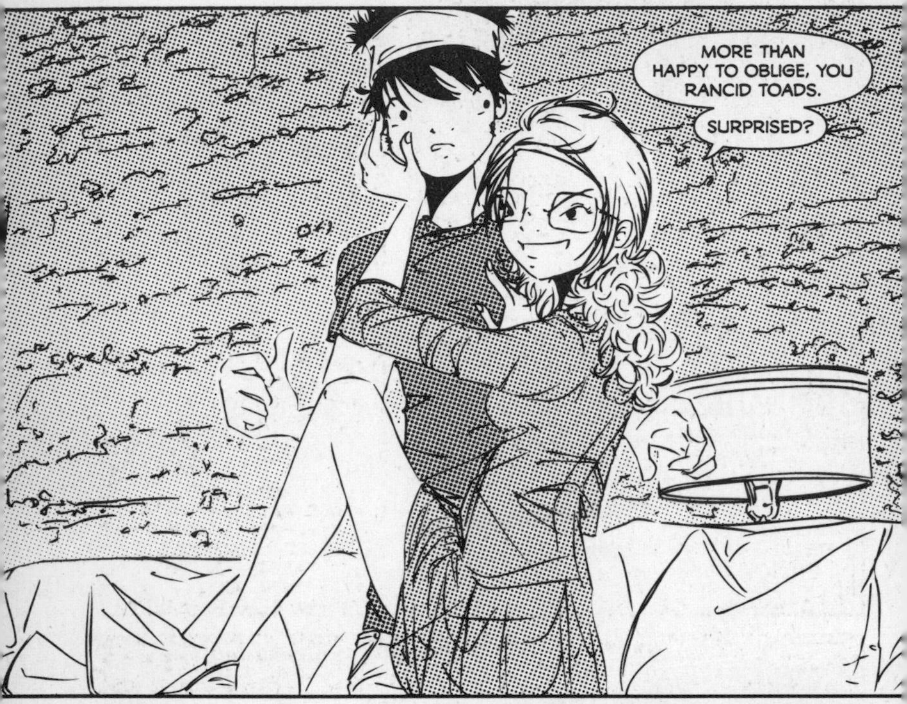
MORE THAN HAPPY TO OBLIGE, YOU RANCID TOADS.
SURPRISED?

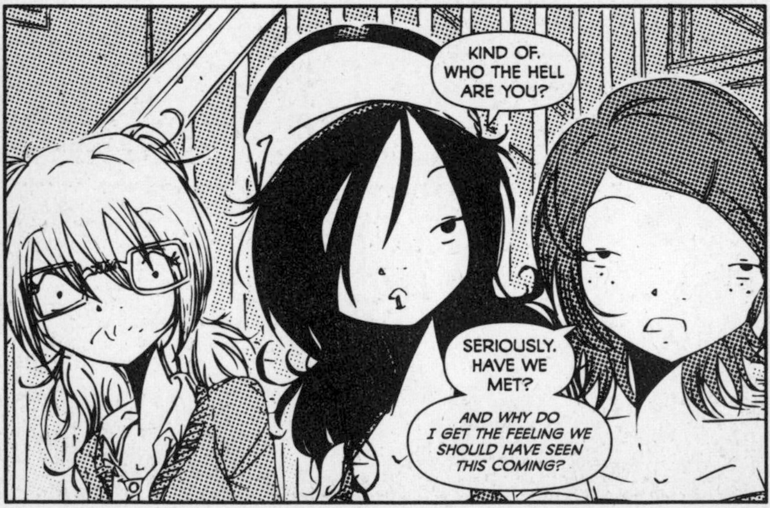
KIND OF. WHO THE HELL ARE YOU?
SERIOUSLY. HAVE WE MET?
AND WHY DO I GET THE FEELING WE SHOULD HAVE SEEN THIS COMING?

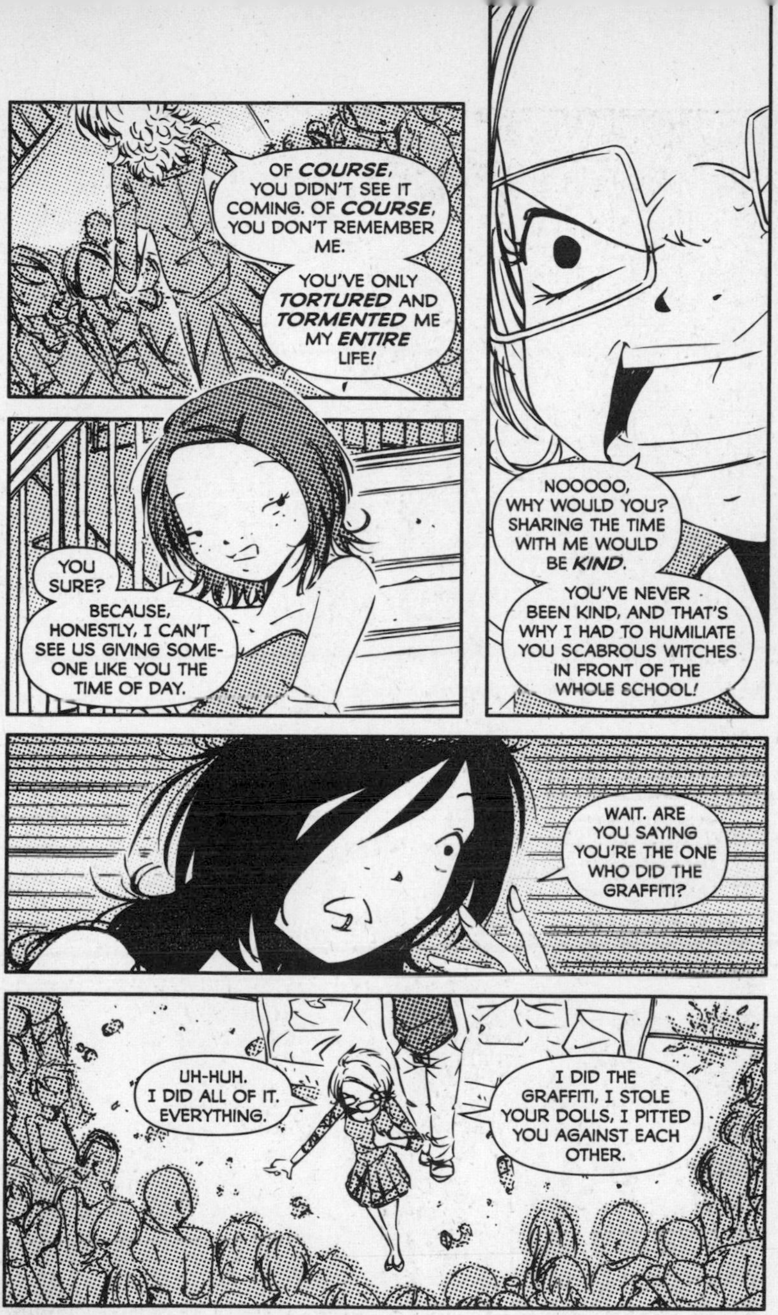
OF *COURSE*, YOU DIDN'T SEE IT COMING. OF *COURSE*, YOU DON'T REMEMBER ME.
YOU'VE ONLY *TORTURED* AND *TORMENTED* ME MY *ENTIRE* LIFE!
YOU SURE?
BECAUSE, HONESTLY, I CAN'T SEE US GIVING SOME-ONE LIKE YOU THE TIME OF DAY.
NOOOOO, WHY WOULD YOU? SHARING THE TIME WITH ME WOULD BE *KIND*.
YOU'VE NEVER BEEN KIND, AND THAT'S WHY I HAD TO HUMILIATE YOU SCABROUS WITCHES IN FRONT OF THE WHOLE SCHOOL!
WAIT. ARE YOU SAYING YOU'RE THE ONE WHO DID THE GRAFFITI?
UH-HUH. I DID ALL OF IT. EVERYTHING.
I DID THE GRAFFITI, I STOLE YOUR DOLLS, I PITTED YOU AGAINST EACH OTHER.

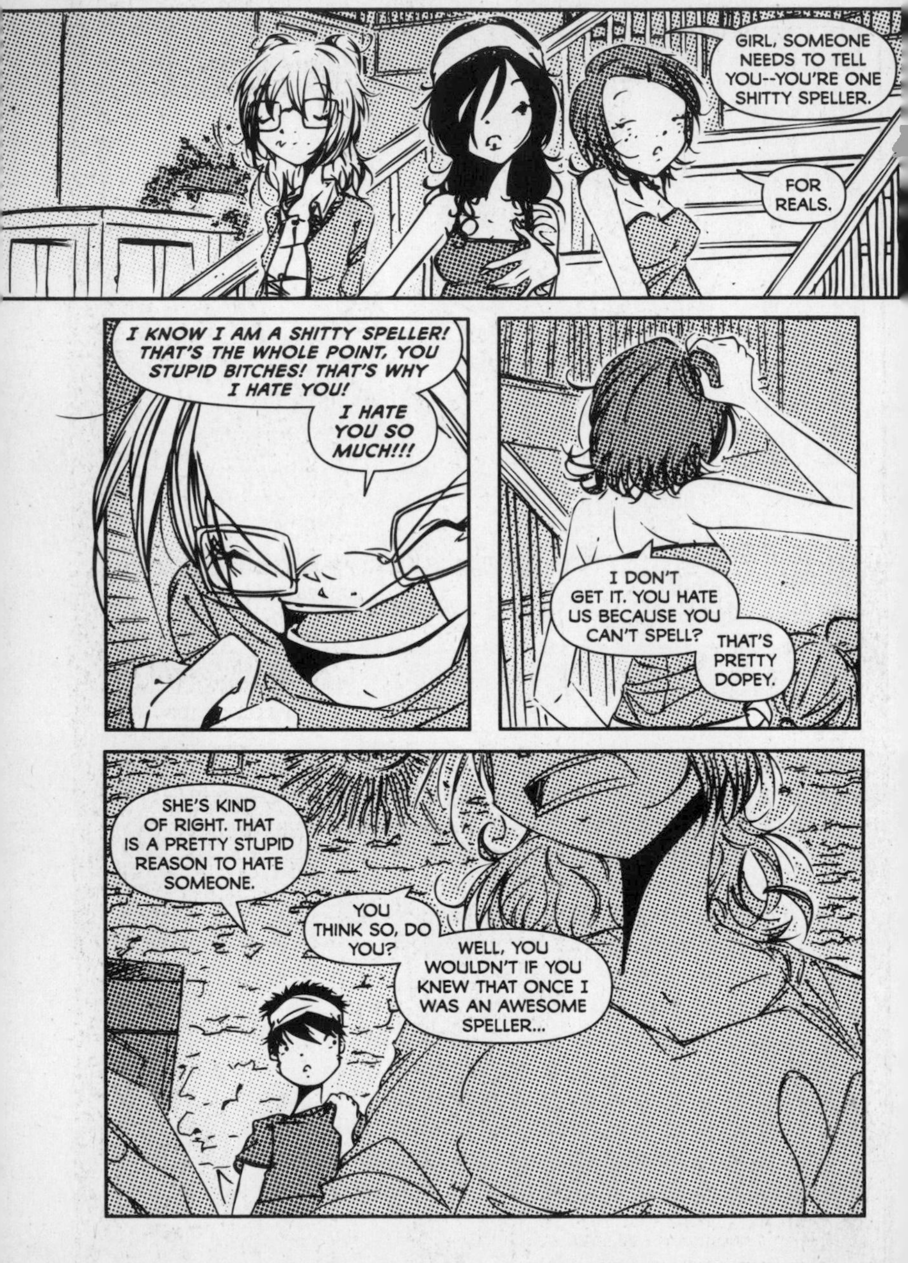
GIRL, SOMEONE NEEDS TO TELL YOU--YOU'RE ONE SHITTY SPELLER.
FOR REALS.
I KNOW I AM A SHITTY SPELLER! THAT'S THE WHOLE POINT, YOU STUPID BITCHES! THAT'S WHY I HATE YOU!
I HATE YOU SO MUCH!!!
I DON'T GET IT. YOU HATE US BECAUSE YOU CAN'T SPELL?
THAT'S PRETTY DOPEY.
SHE'S KIND OF RIGHT. THAT IS A PRETTY STUPID REASON TO HATE SOMEONE.
YOU THINK SO, DO YOU?
WELL, YOU WOULDN'T IF YOU KNEW THAT ONCE I WAS AN AWESOME SPELLER...

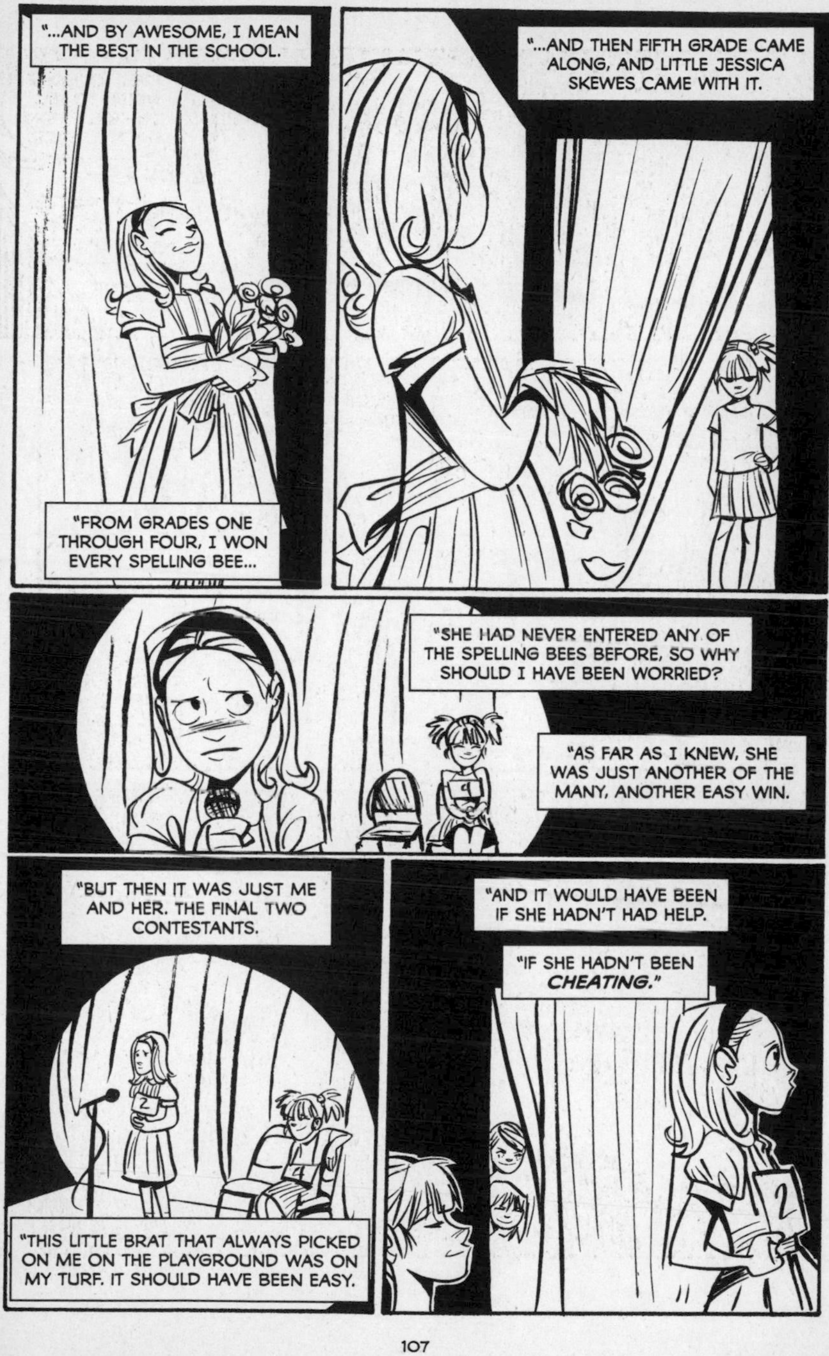
"...AND BY AWESOME, I MEAN THE BEST IN THE SCHOOL.
"FROM GRADES ONE THROUGH FOUR, I WON EVERY SPELLING BEE...
"...AND THEN FIFTH GRADE CAME ALONG, AND LITTLE JESSICA SKEWES CAME WITH IT.
"SHE HAD NEVER ENTERED ANY OF THE SPELLING BEES BEFORE, SO WHY SHOULD I HAVE BEEN WORRIED?
"AS FAR AS I KNEW, SHE WAS JUST ANOTHER OF THE MANY, ANOTHER EASY WIN.
"BUT THEN IT WAS JUST ME AND HER. THE FINAL TWO CONTESTANTS.
2
4
"THIS LITTLE BRAT THAT ALWAYS PICKED ON ME ON THE PLAYGROUND WAS ON MY TURF. IT SHOULD HAVE BEEN EASY.
"AND IT WOULD HAVE BEEN IF SHE HADN'T HAD HELP.
"IF SHE HADN'T BEEN *CHEATING.*"
2

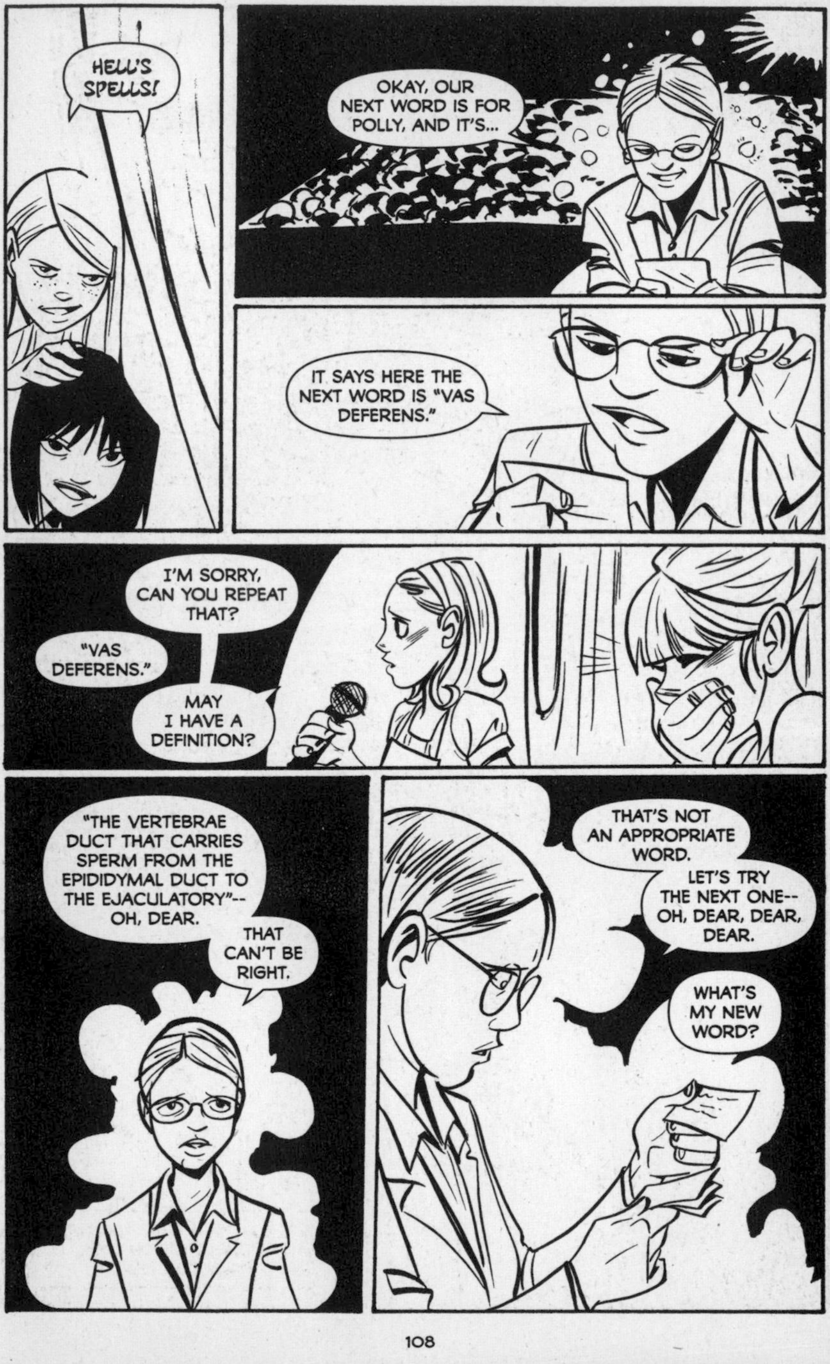
HELL'S SPELLS!
OKAY, OUR NEXT WORD IS FOR POLLY, AND IT'S...
IT SAYS HERE THE NEXT WORD IS "VAS DEFERENS."
I'M SORRY, CAN YOU REPEAT THAT?
"VAS DEFERENS."
MAY I HAVE A DEFINITION?
"THE VERTEBRAE DUCT THAT CARRIES SPERM FROM THE EPIDIDYMAL DUCT TO THE EJACULATORY"-- OH, DEAR.
THAT CAN'T BE RIGHT.
THAT'S NOT AN APPROPRIATE WORD.
LET'S TRY THE NEXT ONE-- OH, DEAR, DEAR, DEAR.
WHAT'S MY NEW WORD?

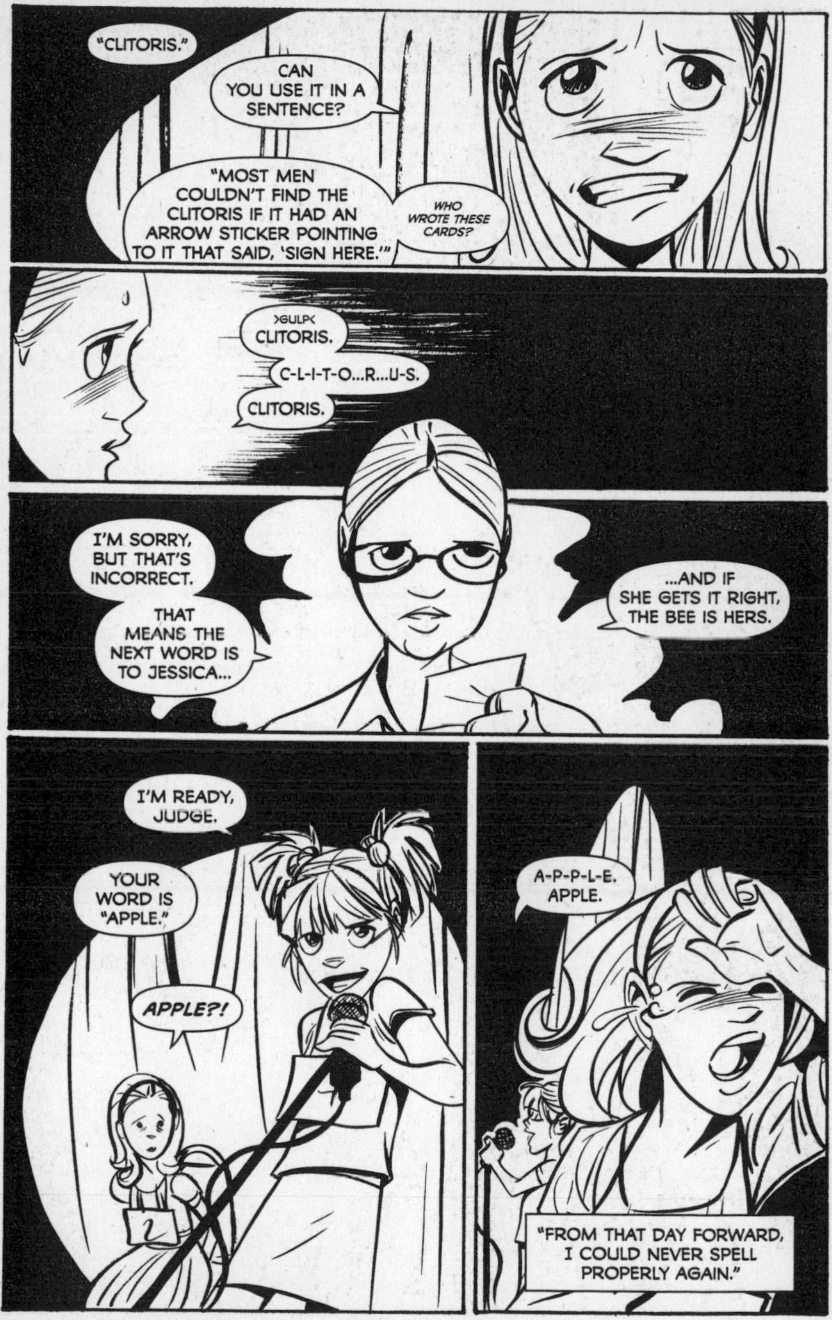
"CLITORIS."
CAN YOU USE IT IN A SENTENCE?
"MOST MEN COULDN'T FIND THE CLITORIS IF IT HAD AN ARROW STICKER POINTING TO IT THAT SAID, 'SIGN HERE.'"
WHO WROTE THESE CARDS?
>GULP< CLITORIS.
C-L-I-T-O...R...U-S.
CLITORIS.
I'M SORRY, BUT THAT'S INCORRECT.
THAT MEANS THE NEXT WORD IS TO JESSICA...
...AND IF SHE GETS IT RIGHT, THE BEE IS HERS.
I'M READY, JUDGE.
YOUR WORD IS "APPLE."
APPLE?!
2
A-P-P-L-E. APPLE.
"FROM THAT DAY FORWARD, I COULD NEVER SPELL PROPERLY AGAIN."

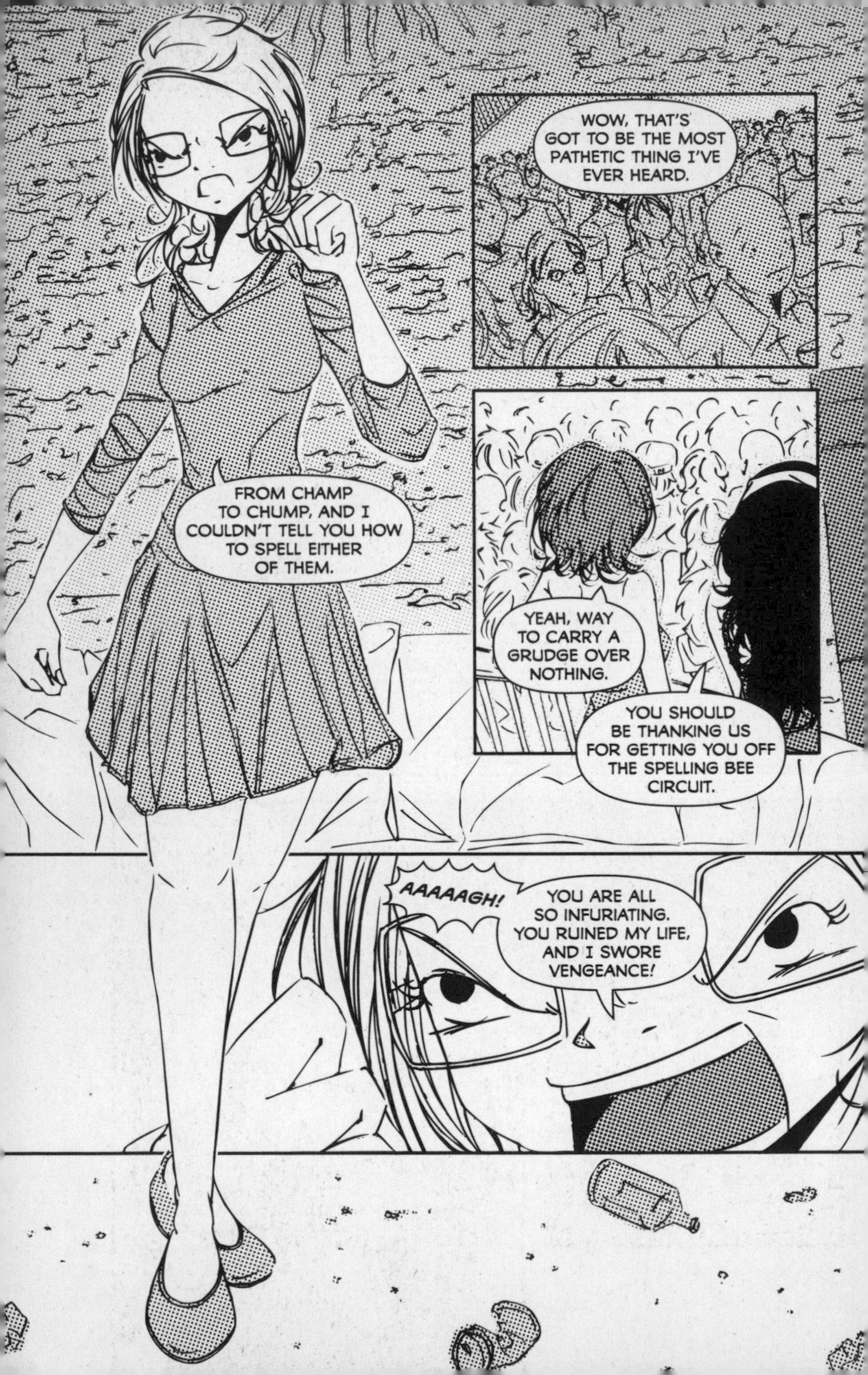
FROM CHAMP TO CHUMP, AND I COULDN'T TELL YOU HOW TO SPELL EITHER OF THEM.
WOW, THAT'S GOT TO BE THE MOST PATHETIC THING I'VE EVER HEARD.
YEAH, WAY TO CARRY A GRUDGE OVER NOTHING.
YOU SHOULD BE THANKING US FOR GETTING YOU OFF THE SPELLING BEE CIRCUIT.
AAAAAGH!
YOU ARE ALL SO INFURIATING. YOU RUINED MY LIFE, AND I SWORE VENGEANCE!

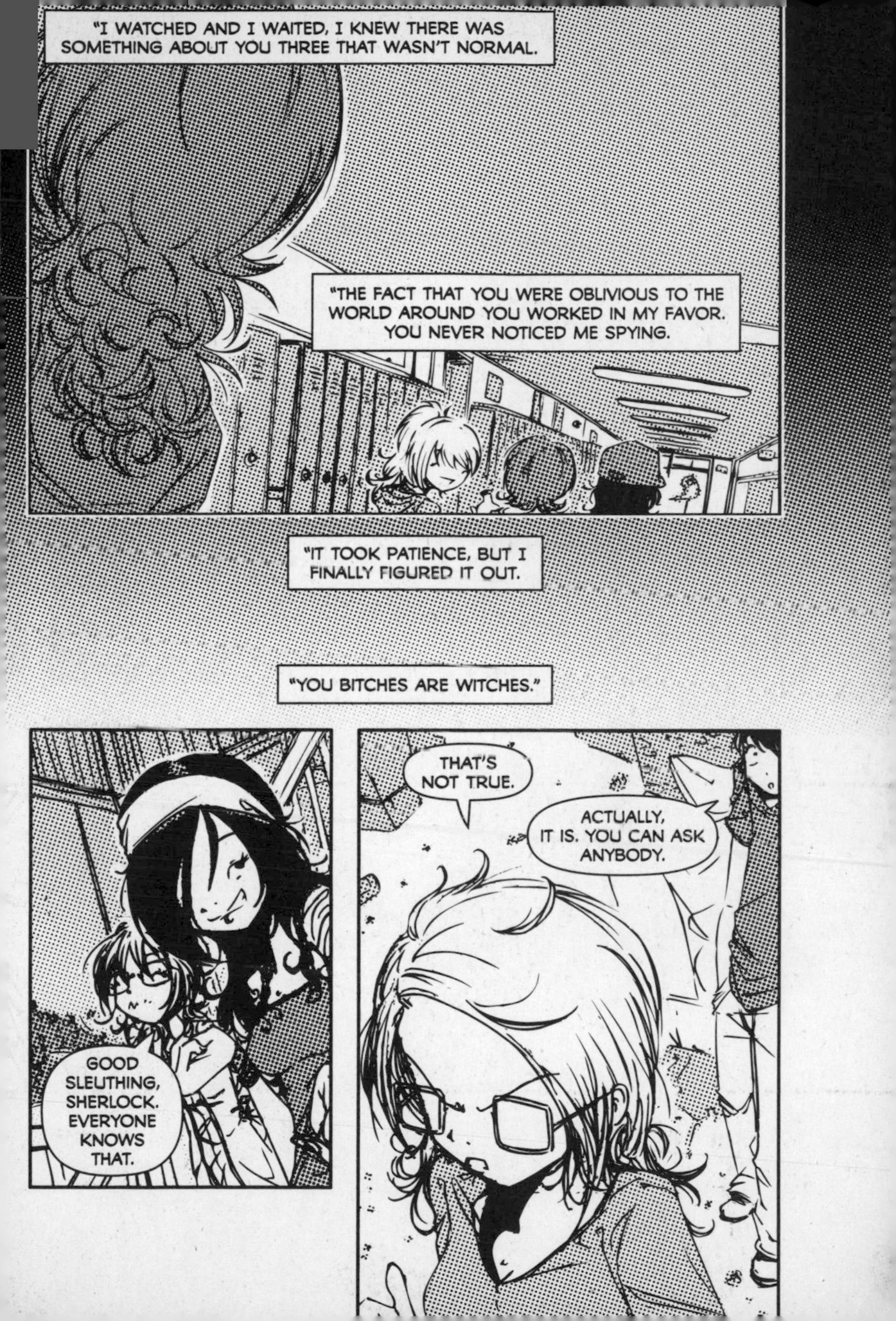
"I WATCHED AND I WAITED, I KNEW THERE WAS SOMETHING ABOUT YOU THREE THAT WASN'T NORMAL.
"THE FACT THAT YOU WERE OBLIVIOUS TO THE WORLD AROUND YOU WORKED IN MY FAVOR. YOU NEVER NOTICED ME SPYING.
"IT TOOK PATIENCE, BUT I FINALLY FIGURED IT OUT.
"YOU BITCHES ARE WITCHES."
GOOD SLEUTHING, SHERLOCK. EVERYONE KNOWS THAT.
THAT'S NOT TRUE.
ACTUALLY, IT IS. YOU CAN ASK ANYBODY.

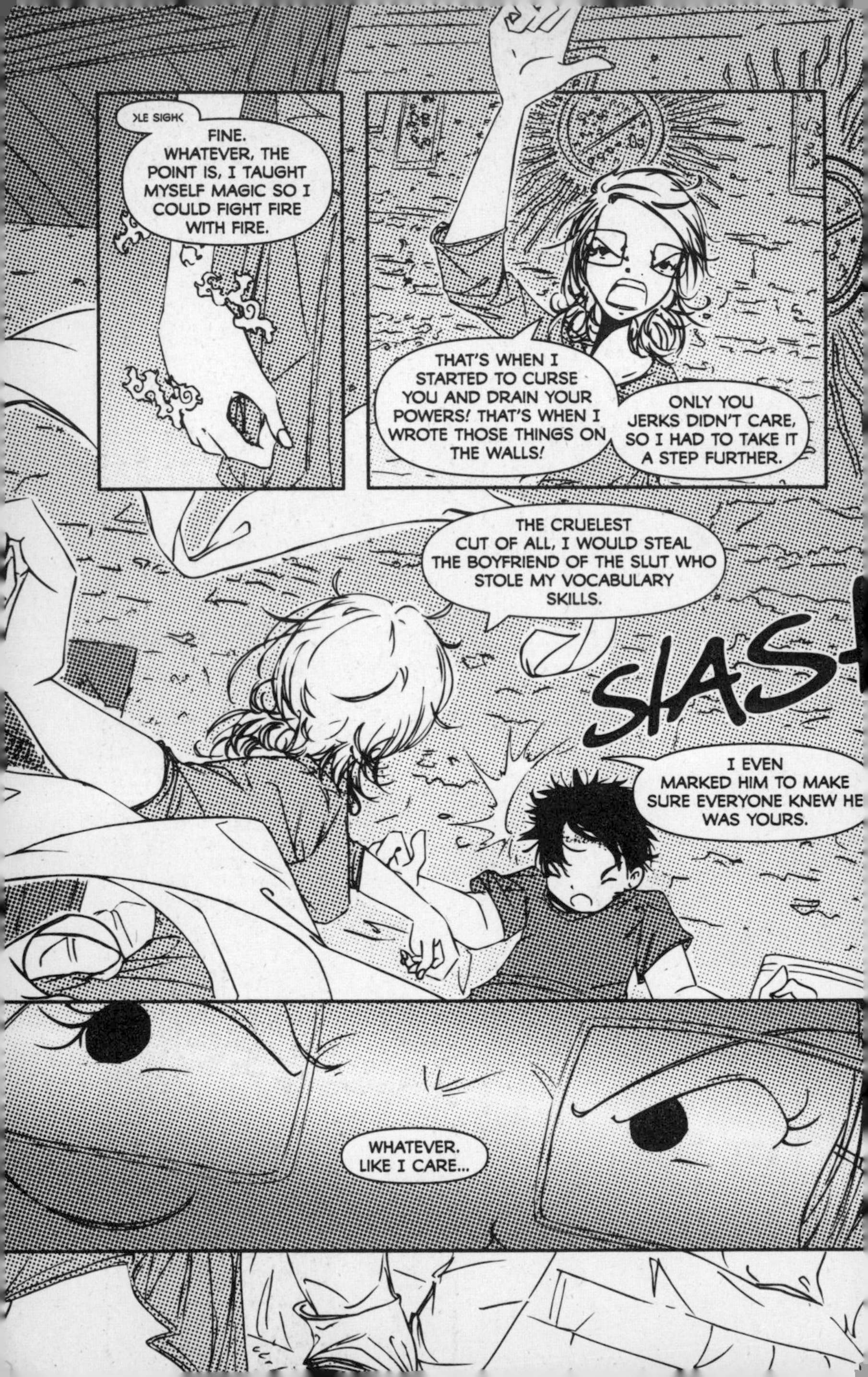

>LE SIGH<
FINE. WHATEVER, THE POINT IS, I TAUGHT MYSELF MAGIC SO I COULD FIGHT FIRE WITH FIRE.
THAT'S WHEN I STARTED TO CURSE YOU AND DRAIN YOUR POWERS! THAT'S WHEN I WROTE THOSE THINGS ON THE WALLS!
ONLY YOU JERKS DIDN'T CARE, SO I HAD TO TAKE IT A STEP FURTHER.
THE CRUELEST CUT OF ALL, I WOULD STEAL THE BOYFRIEND OF THE SLUT WHO STOLE MY VOCABULARY SKILLS.
I EVEN MARKED HIM TO MAKE SURE EVERYONE KNEW HE WAS YOURS.
WHATEVER. LIKE I CARE...

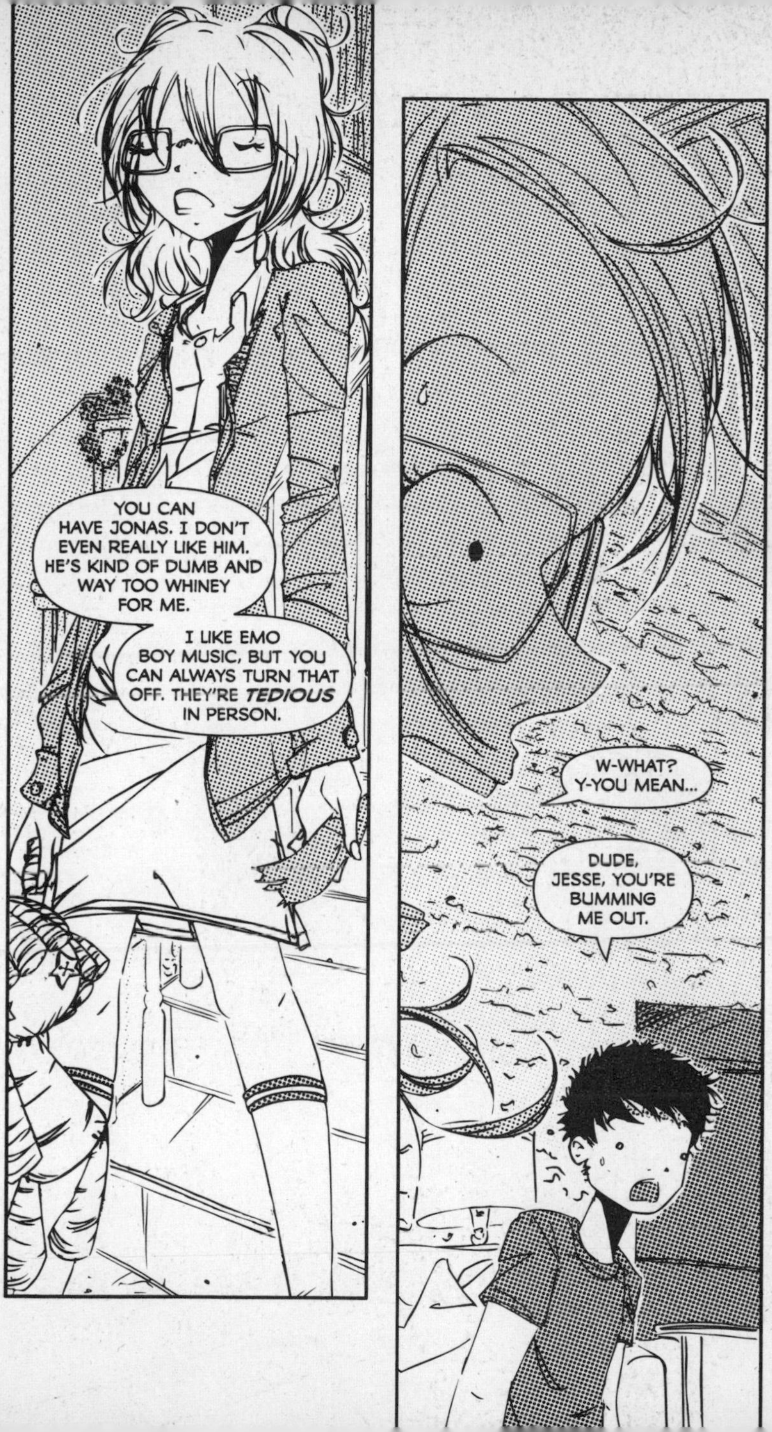
YOU CAN HAVE JONAS. I DON'T EVEN REALLY LIKE HIM. HE'S KIND OF DUMB AND WAY TOO WHINEY FOR ME.
I LIKE EMO BOY MUSIC, BUT YOU CAN ALWAYS TURN THAT OFF. THEY'RE *TEDIOUS* IN PERSON.
W-WHAT? Y-YOU MEAN...
DUDE, JESSE, YOU'RE BUMMING ME OUT.

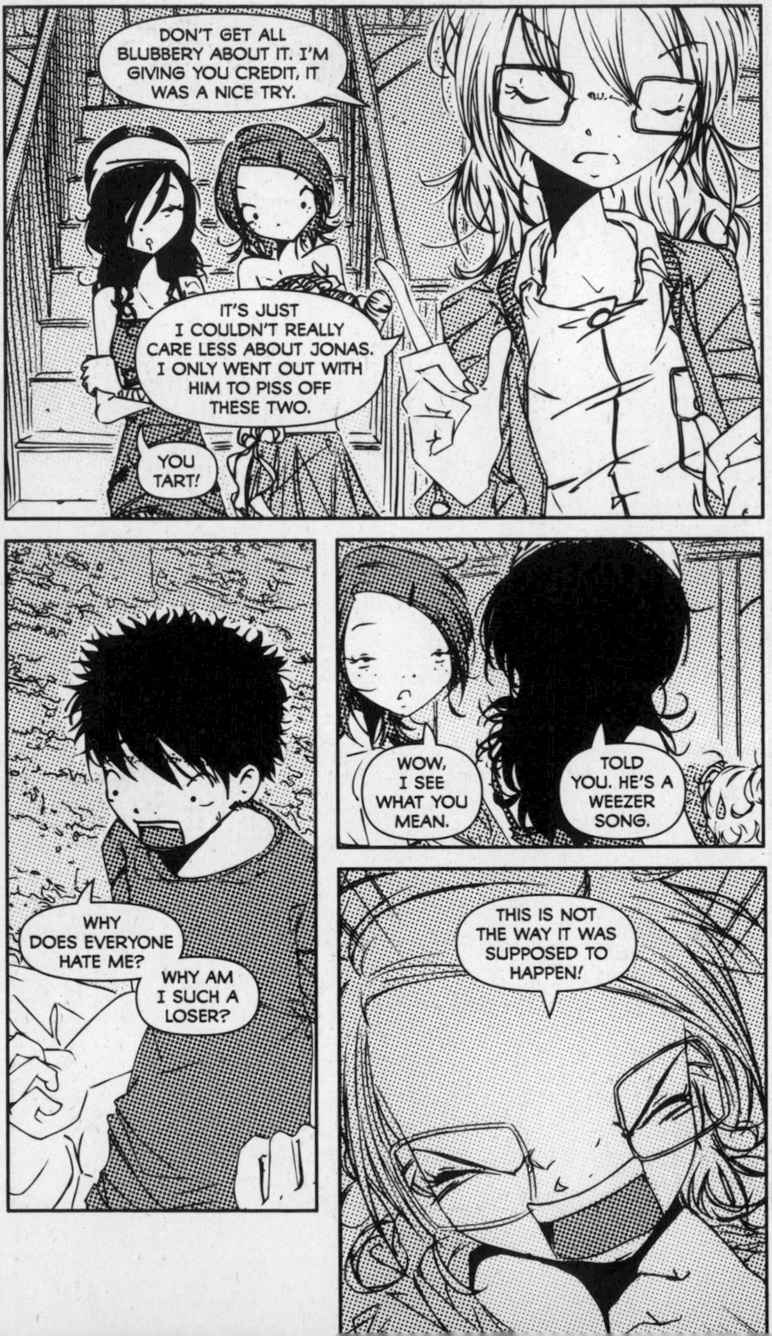
DON'T GET ALL BLUBBERY ABOUT IT. I'M GIVING YOU CREDIT, IT WAS A NICE TRY.
IT'S JUST I COULDN'T REALLY CARE LESS ABOUT JONAS. I ONLY WENT OUT WITH HIM TO PISS OFF THESE TWO.
YOU TART!
WHY DOES EVERYONE HATE ME?
WHY AM I SUCH A LOSER?
WOW, I SEE WHAT YOU MEAN.
TOLD YOU. HE'S A WEEZER SONG.
THIS IS NOT THE WAY IT WAS SUPPOSED TO HAPPEN!

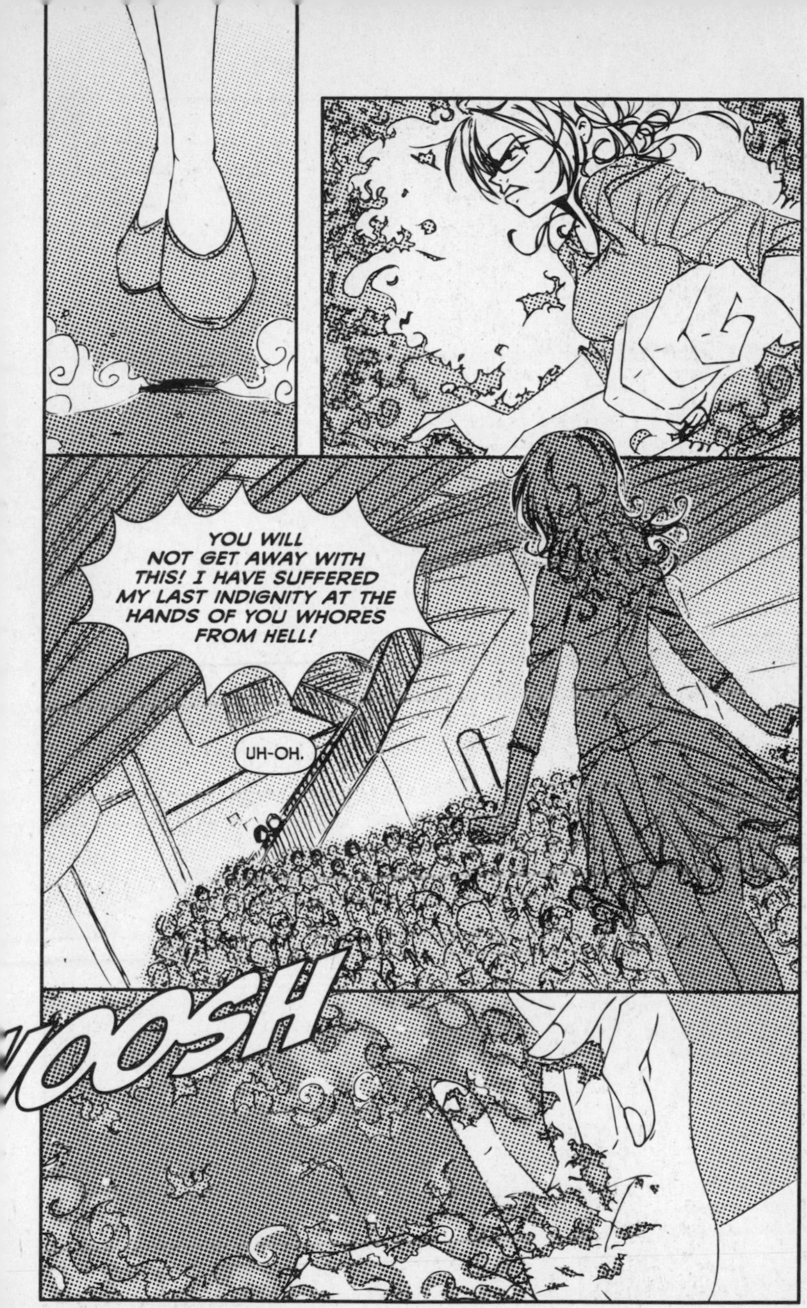
YOU WILL NOT GET AWAY WITH THIS! I HAVE SUFFERED MY LAST INDIGNITY AT THE HANDS OF YOU WHORES FROM HELL!
UH-OH.
WOOSH

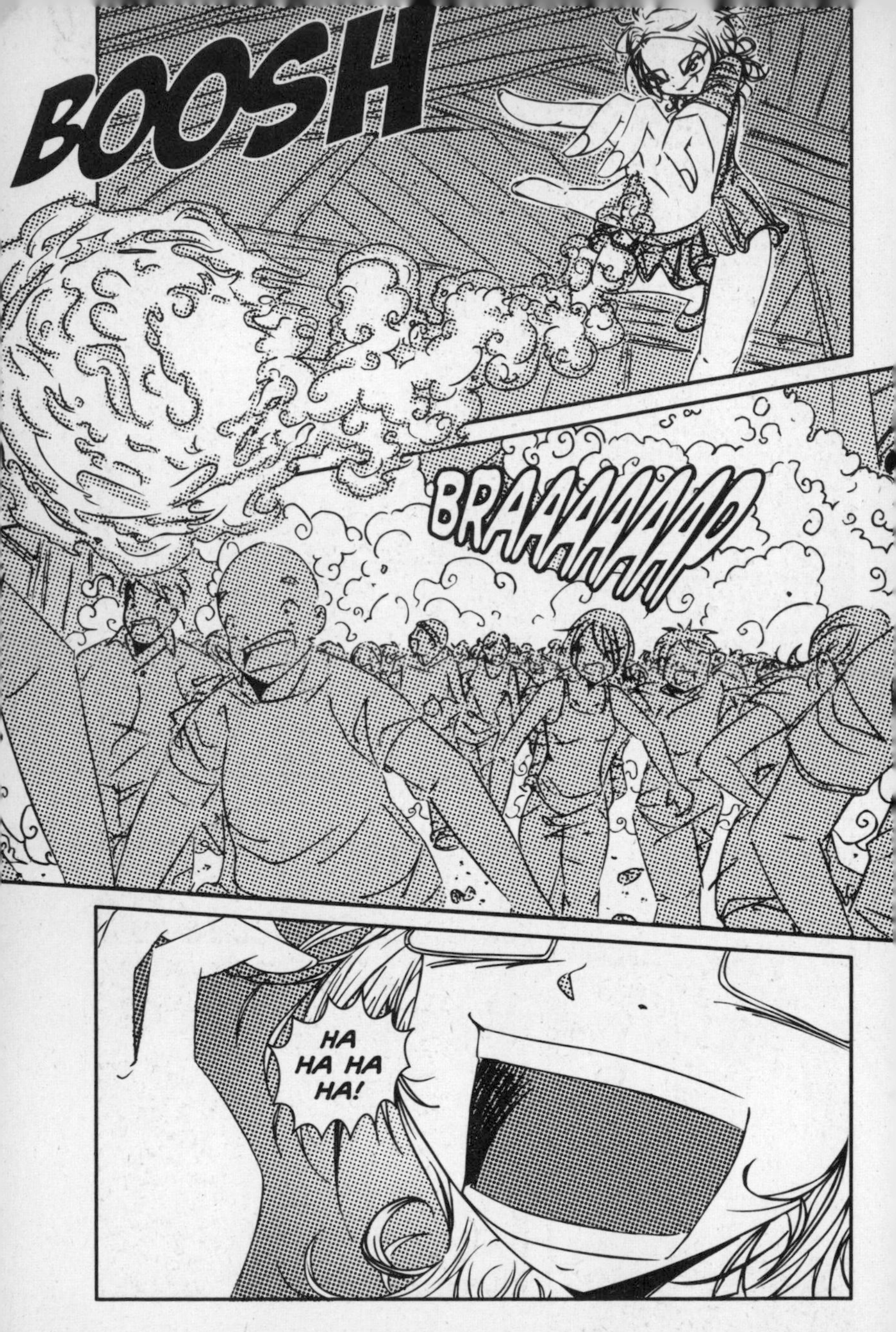
BOOSH
BRAAAAAP
HA HA HA HA!

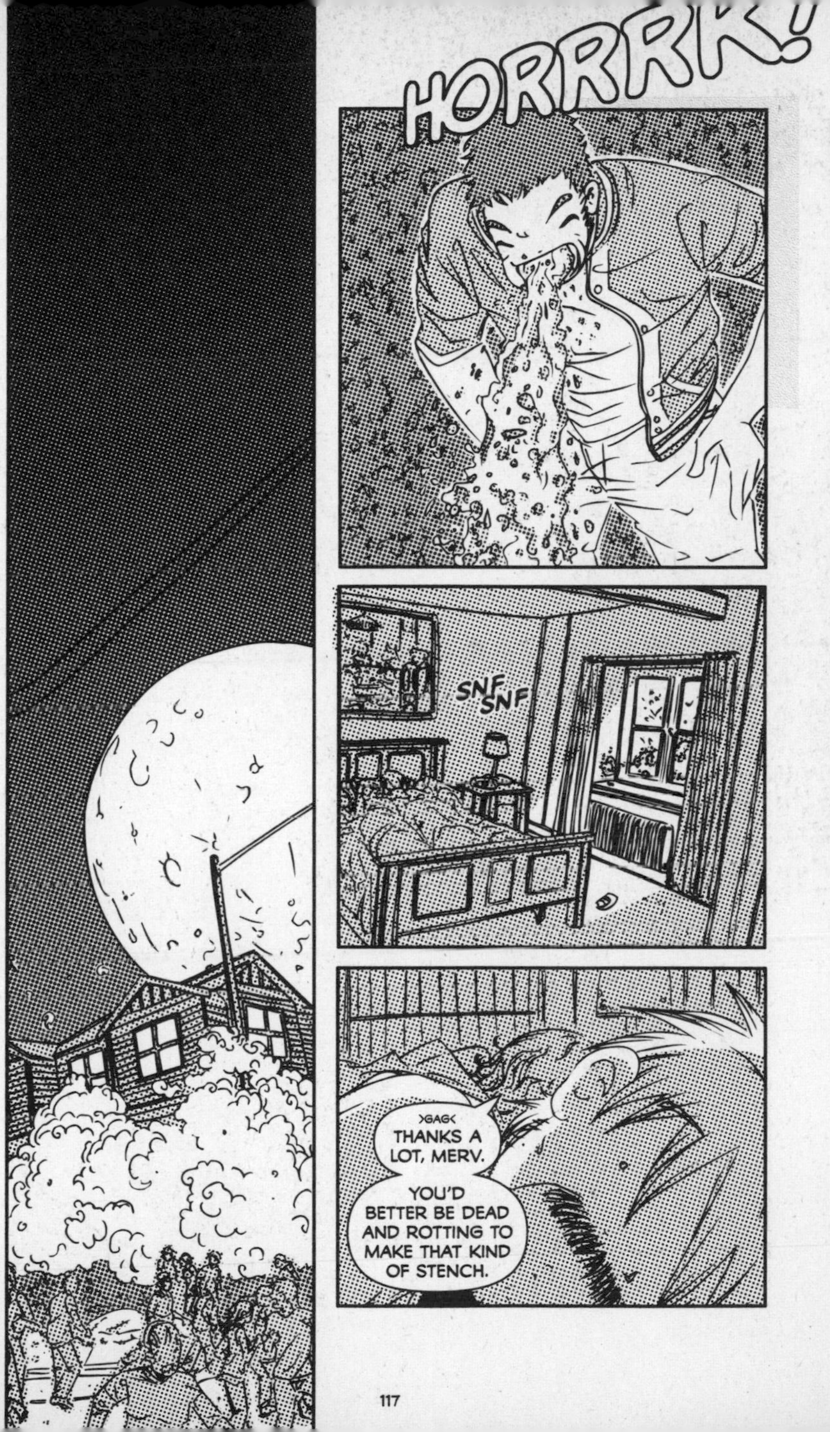

HORRRK!
SNF SNF
›GAG‹
THANKS A LOT, MERV.
YOU'D BETTER BE DEAD AND ROTTING TO MAKE THAT KIND OF STENCH.

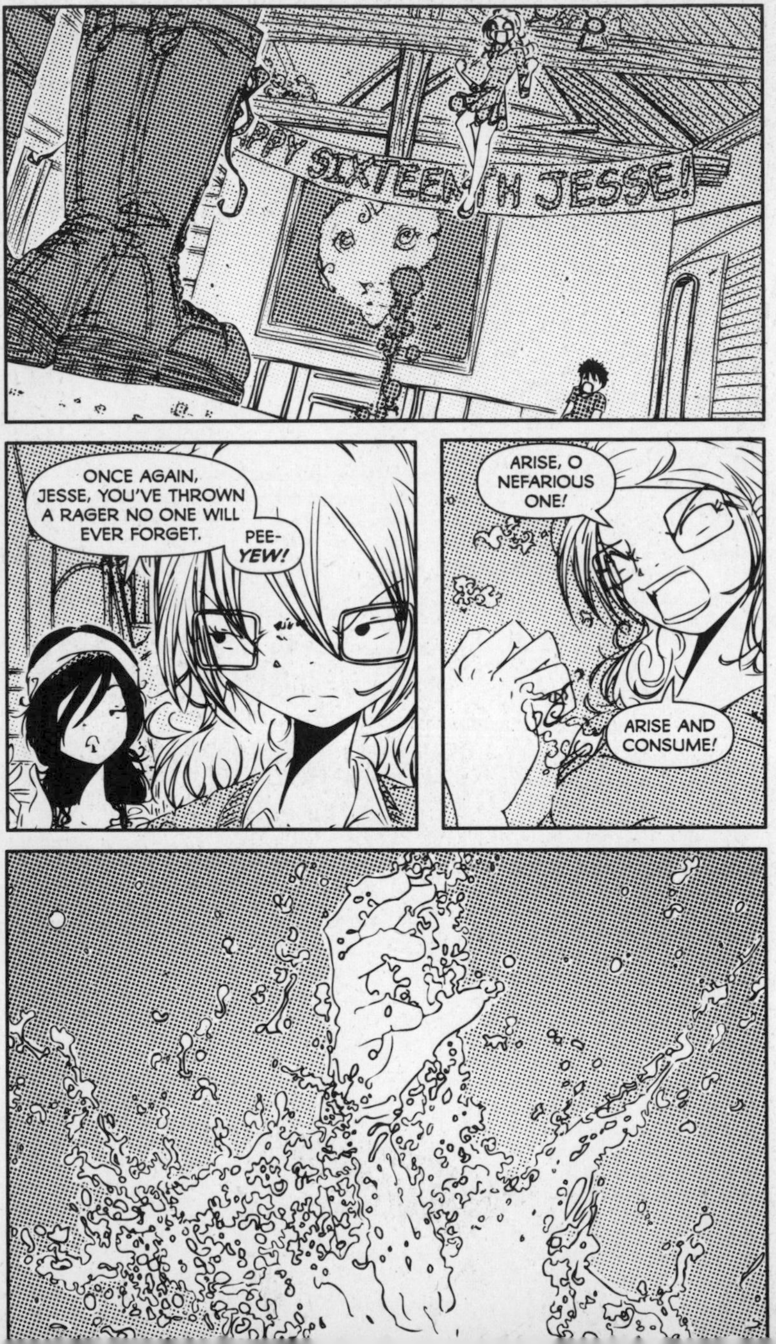
PPY SIXTEEN TH JESSE!
ONCE AGAIN, JESSE, YOU'VE THROWN A RAGER NO ONE WILL EVER FORGET.
PEE-YEW!
ARISE, O NEFARIOUS ONE!
ARISE AND CONSUME!

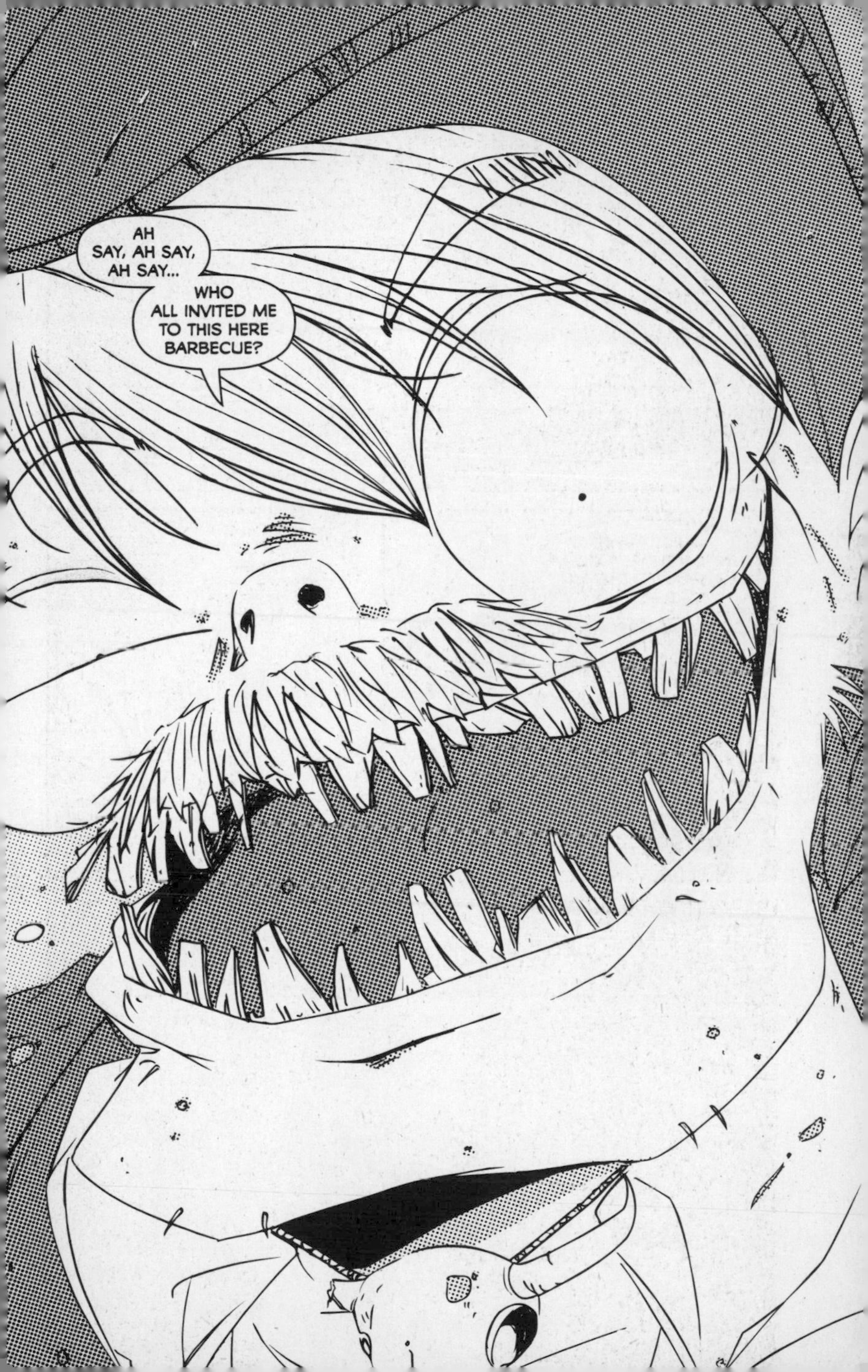
AH SAY, AH SAY, AH SAY...
WHO ALL INVITED ME TO THIS HERE BARBECUE?

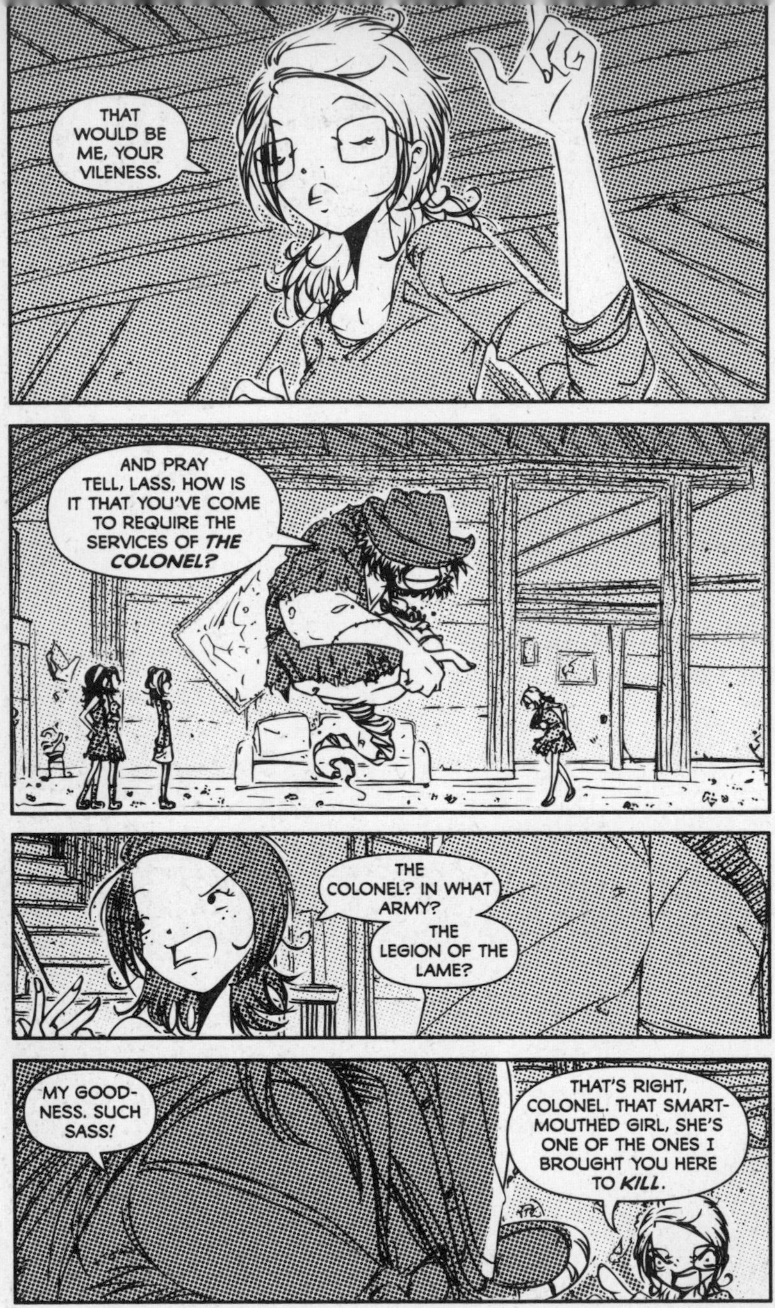
THAT WOULD BE ME, YOUR VILENESS.
AND PRAY TELL, LASS, HOW IS IT THAT YOU'VE COME TO REQUIRE THE SERVICES OF *THE COLONEL?*
THE COLONEL? IN WHAT ARMY?
THE LEGION OF THE LAME?
MY GOOD-NESS. SUCH SASS!
THAT'S RIGHT, COLONEL. THAT SMART-MOUTHED GIRL, SHE'S ONE OF THE ONES I BROUGHT YOU HERE TO *KILL*.

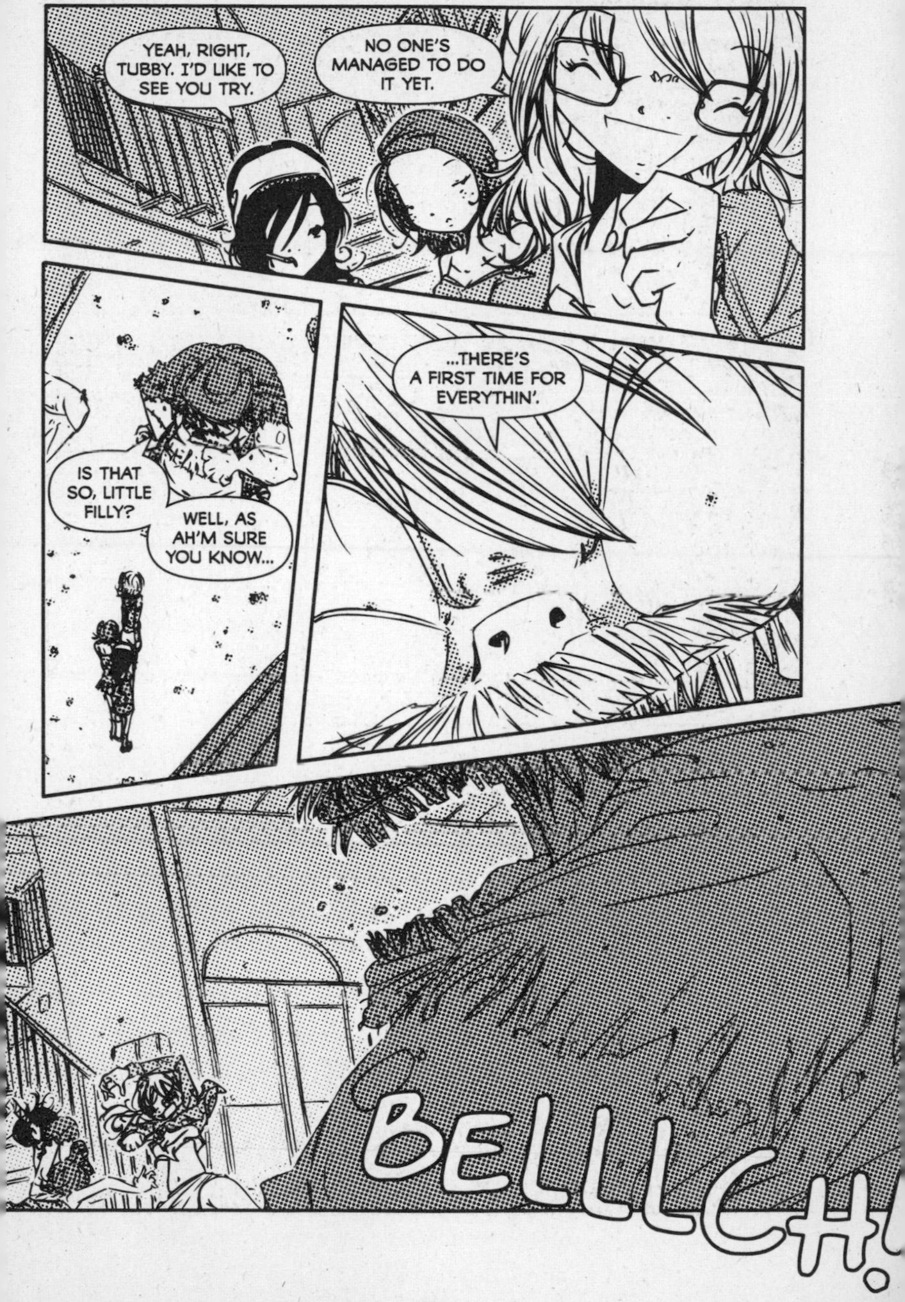
NO ONE'S MANAGED TO DO IT YET.
YEAH, RIGHT, TUBBY. I'D LIKE TO SEE YOU TRY.
IS THAT SO, LITTLE FILLY?
WELL, AS AH'M SURE YOU KNOW...
...THERE'S A FIRST TIME FOR EVERYTHIN'.
BELLLCH!

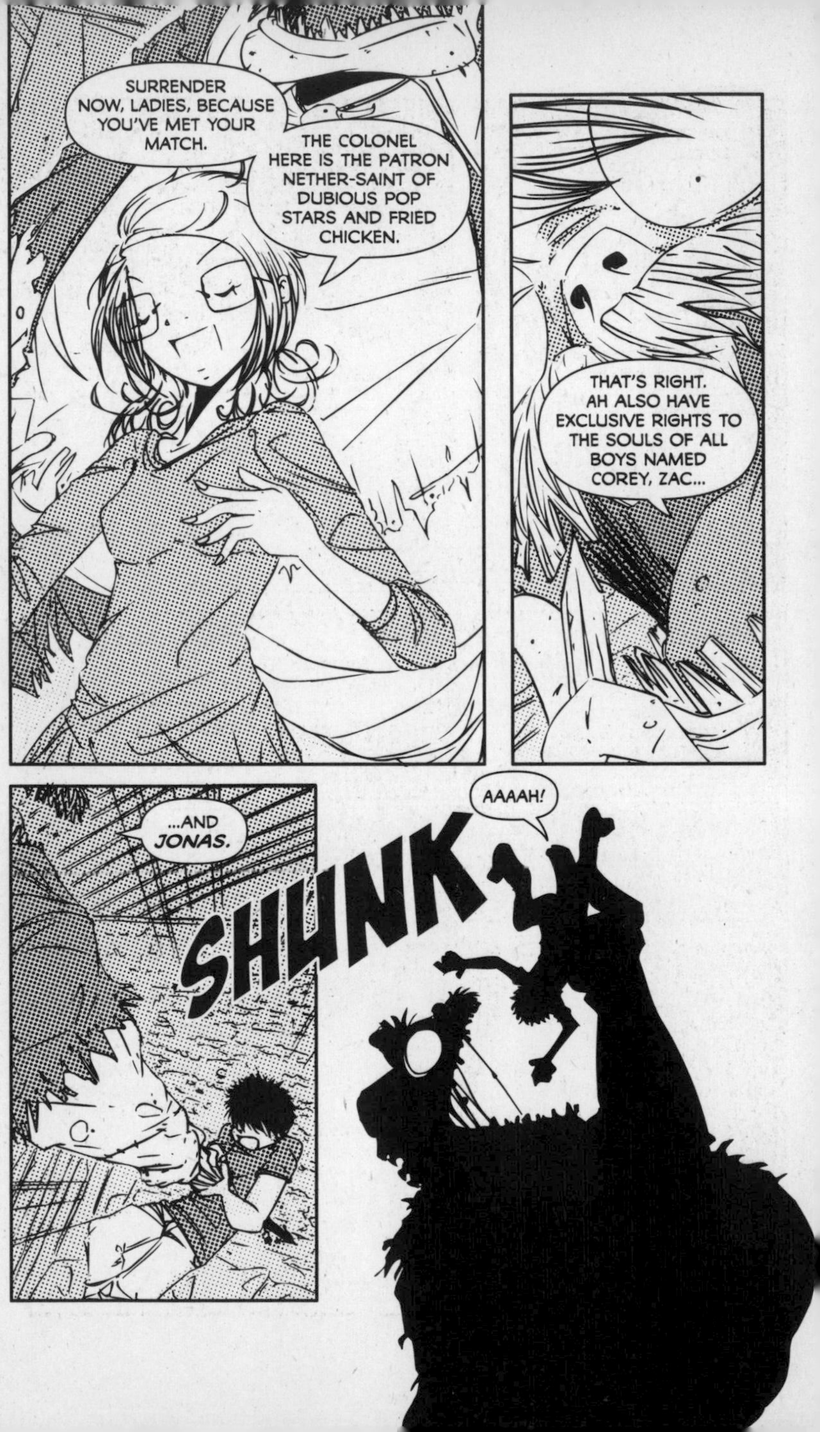
SURRENDER NOW, LADIES, BECAUSE YOU'VE MET YOUR MATCH.
THE COLONEL HERE IS THE PATRON NETHER-SAINT OF DUBIOUS POP STARS AND FRIED CHICKEN.
THAT'S RIGHT. AH ALSO HAVE EXCLUSIVE RIGHTS TO THE SOULS OF ALL BOYS NAMED COREY, ZAC...
...AND JONAS.
SHUNK
AAAAH!

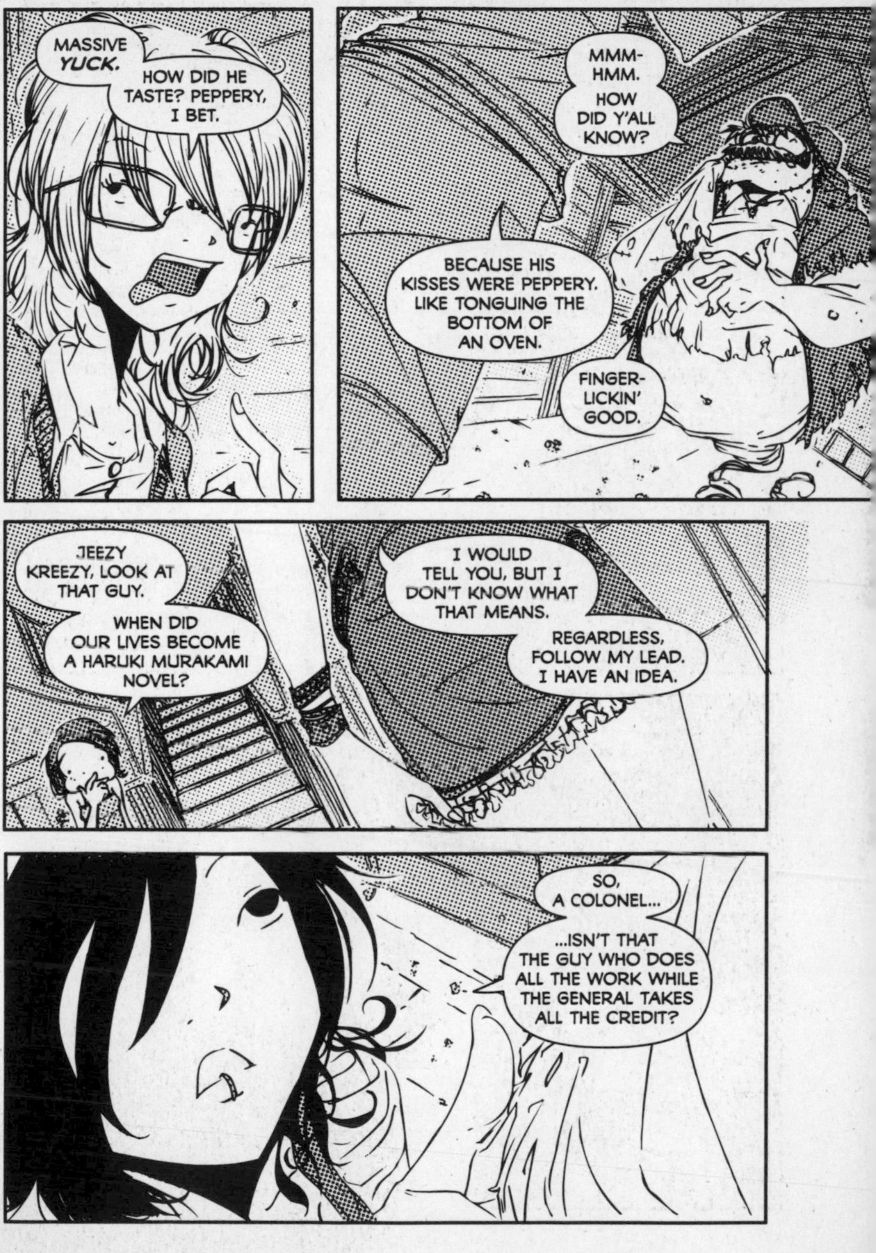
MASSIVE *YUCK.*
HOW DID HE TASTE? PEPPERY, I BET.
MMM-HMM.
HOW DID Y'ALL KNOW?
BECAUSE HIS KISSES WERE PEPPERY. LIKE TONGUING THE BOTTOM OF AN OVEN.
FINGER-LICKIN' GOOD.
JEEZY KREEZY, LOOK AT THAT GUY.
WHEN DID OUR LIVES BECOME A HARUKI MURAKAMI NOVEL?
I WOULD TELL YOU, BUT I DON'T KNOW WHAT THAT MEANS.
REGARDLESS, FOLLOW MY LEAD. I HAVE AN IDEA.
SO, A COLONEL...
...ISN'T THAT THE GUY WHO DOES ALL THE WORK WHILE THE GENERAL TAKES ALL THE CREDIT?

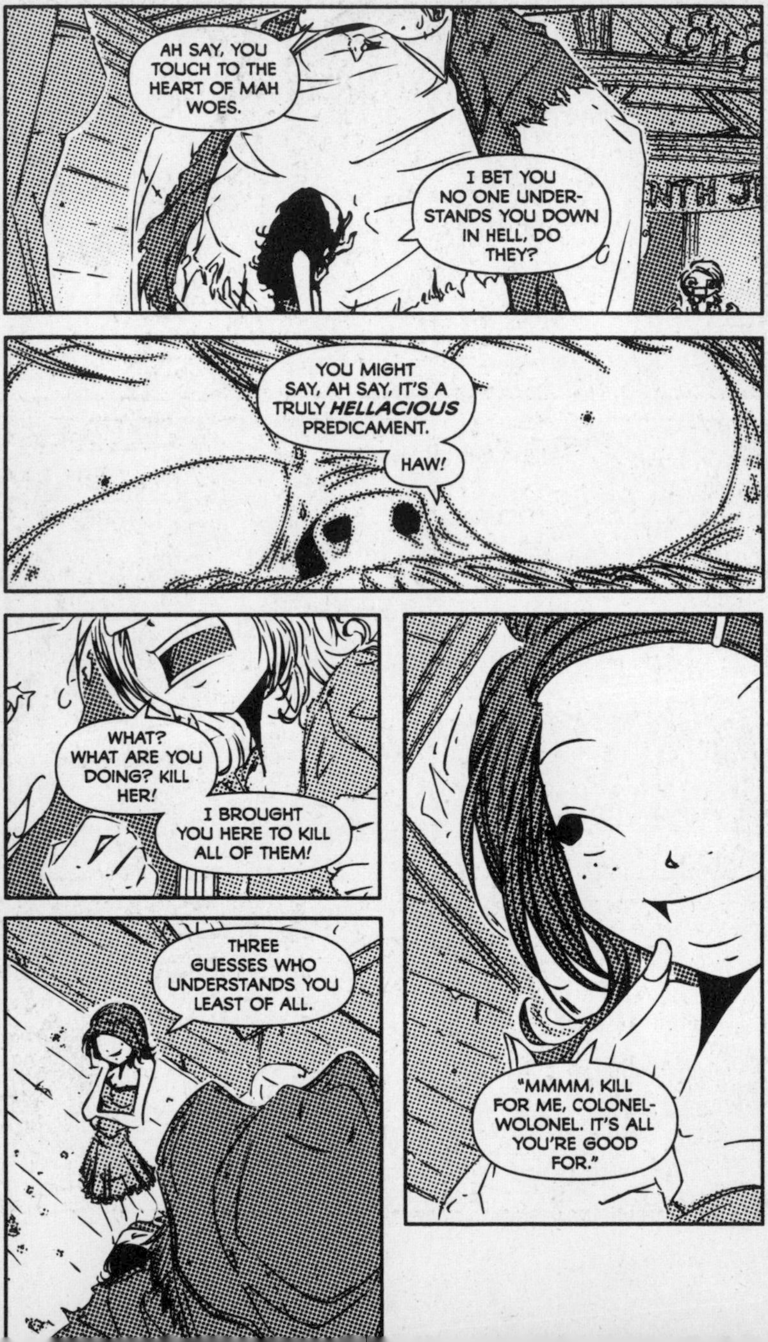
AH SAY, YOU TOUCH TO THE HEART OF MAH WOES.
I BET YOU NO ONE UNDER-STANDS YOU DOWN IN HELL, DO THEY?
YOU MIGHT SAY, AH SAY, IT'S A TRULY *HELLACIOUS* PREDICAMENT.
HAW!
WHAT? WHAT ARE YOU DOING? KILL HER!
I BROUGHT YOU HERE TO KILL ALL OF THEM!
THREE GUESSES WHO UNDERSTANDS YOU LEAST OF ALL.
"MMMM, KILL FOR ME, COLONEL-WOLONEL. IT'S ALL YOU'RE GOOD FOR."

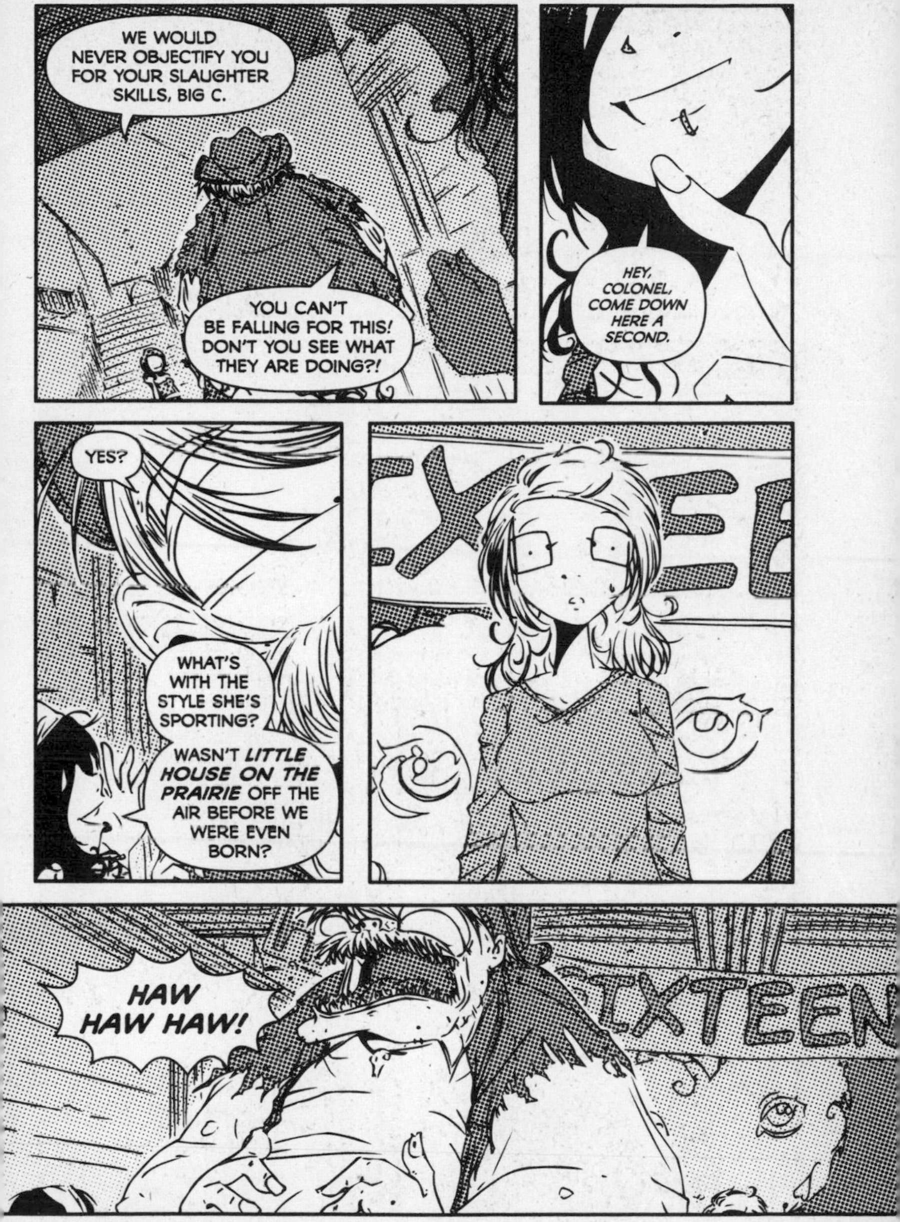
WE WOULD NEVER OBJECTIFY YOU FOR YOUR SLAUGHTER SKILLS, BIG C.
YOU CAN'T BE FALLING FOR THIS! DON'T YOU SEE WHAT THEY ARE DOING?!
HEY, COLONEL, COME DOWN HERE A SECOND.
YES?
WHAT'S WITH THE STYLE SHE'S SPORTING?
WASN'T LITTLE HOUSE ON THE PRAIRIE OFF THE AIR BEFORE WE WERE EVEN BORN?
HAW HAW HAW!
IXTEEN

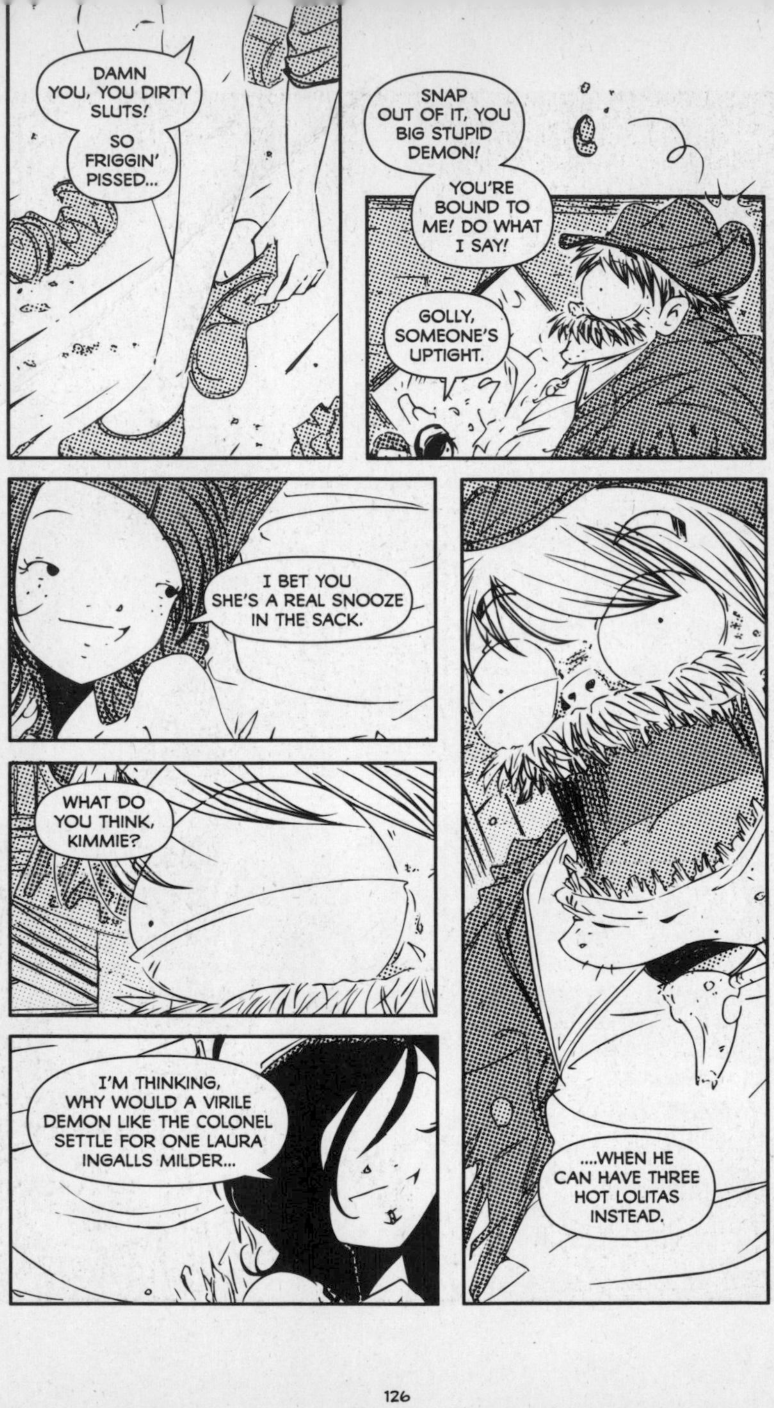
DAMN YOU, YOU DIRTY SLUTS!
SO FRIGGIN' PISSED...
SNAP OUT OF IT, YOU BIG STUPID DEMON!
YOU'RE BOUND TO ME! DO WHAT I SAY!
GOLLY, SOMEONE'S UPTIGHT.
I BET YOU SHE'S A REAL SNOOZE IN THE SACK.
WHAT DO YOU THINK, KIMMIE?
I'M THINKING, WHY WOULD A VIRILE DEMON LIKE THE COLONEL SETTLE FOR ONE LAURA INGALLS MILDER...
....WHEN HE CAN HAVE THREE HOT LOLITAS INSTEAD.

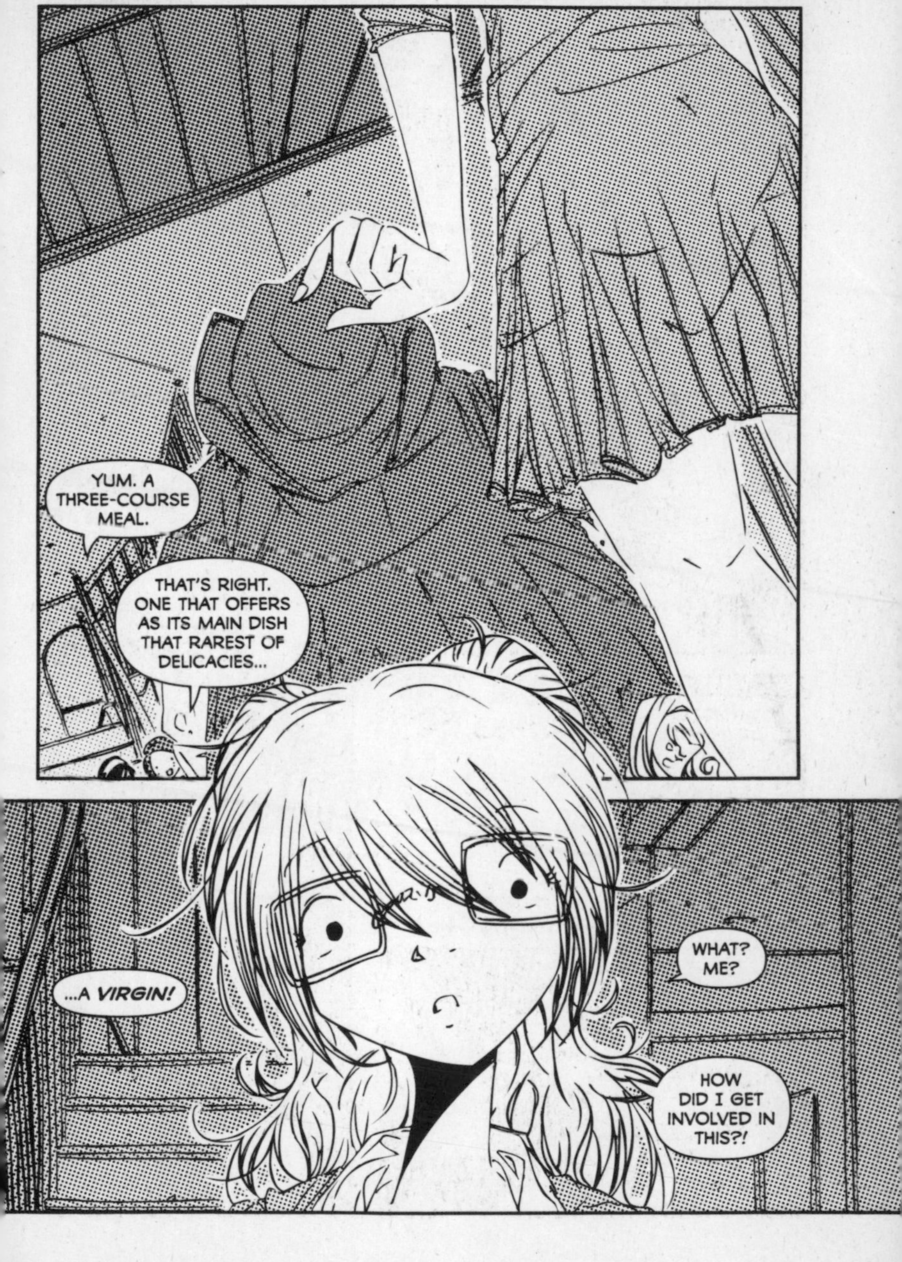
YUM. A THREE-COURSE MEAL.
THAT'S RIGHT. ONE THAT OFFERS AS ITS MAIN DISH THAT RAREST OF DELICACIES...
...A *VIRGIN!*
WHAT? ME?
HOW DID I GET INVOLVED IN THIS?!

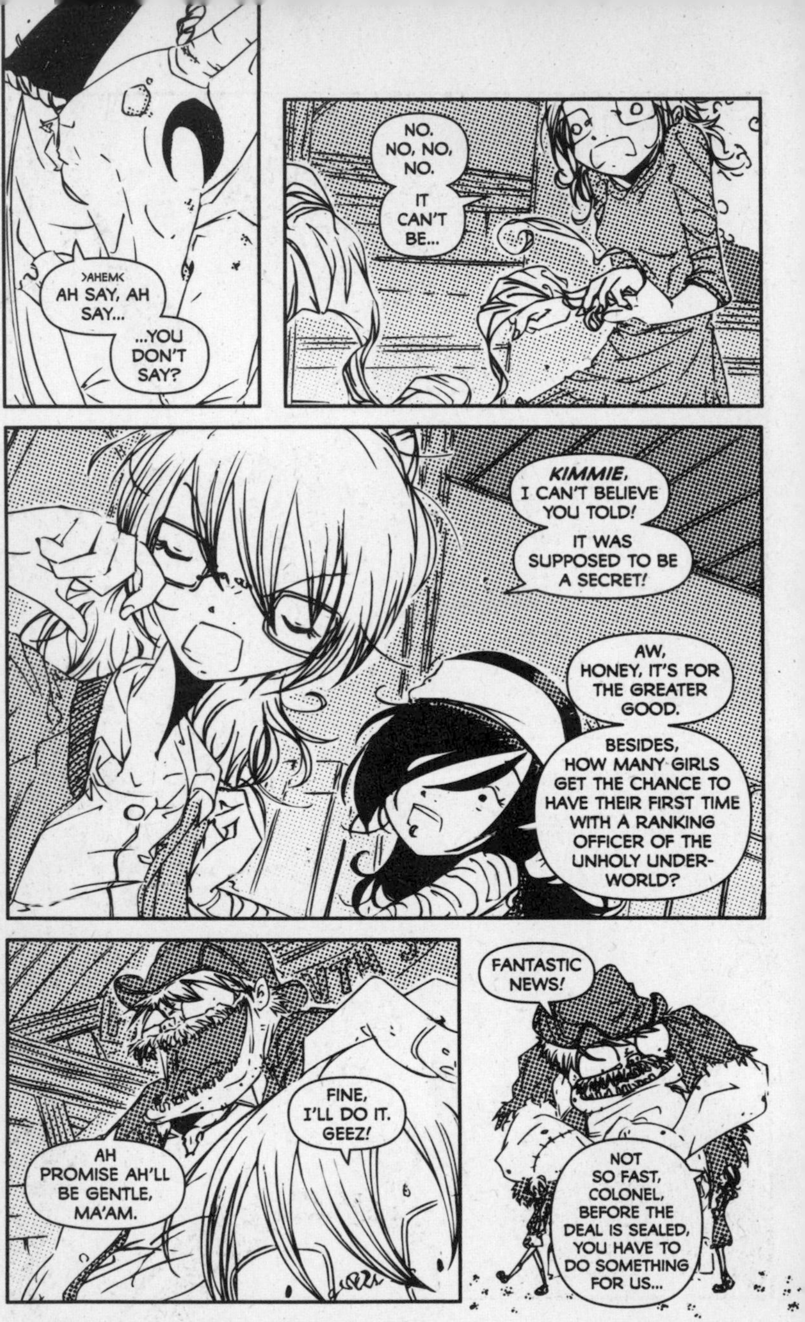
>AHEM<
AH SAY, AH SAY...
...YOU DON'T SAY?
NO. NO, NO, NO.
IT CAN'T BE...
KIMMIE, I CAN'T BELIEVE YOU TOLD!
IT WAS SUPPOSED TO BE A SECRET!
AW, HONEY, IT'S FOR THE GREATER GOOD.
BESIDES, HOW MANY GIRLS GET THE CHANCE TO HAVE THEIR FIRST TIME WITH A RANKING OFFICER OF THE UNHOLY UNDER-WORLD?
FINE, I'LL DO IT. GEEZ!
AH PROMISE AH'LL BE GENTLE, MA'AM.
FANTASTIC NEWS!
NOT SO FAST, COLONEL, BEFORE THE DEAL IS SEALED, YOU HAVE TO DO SOMETHING FOR US...

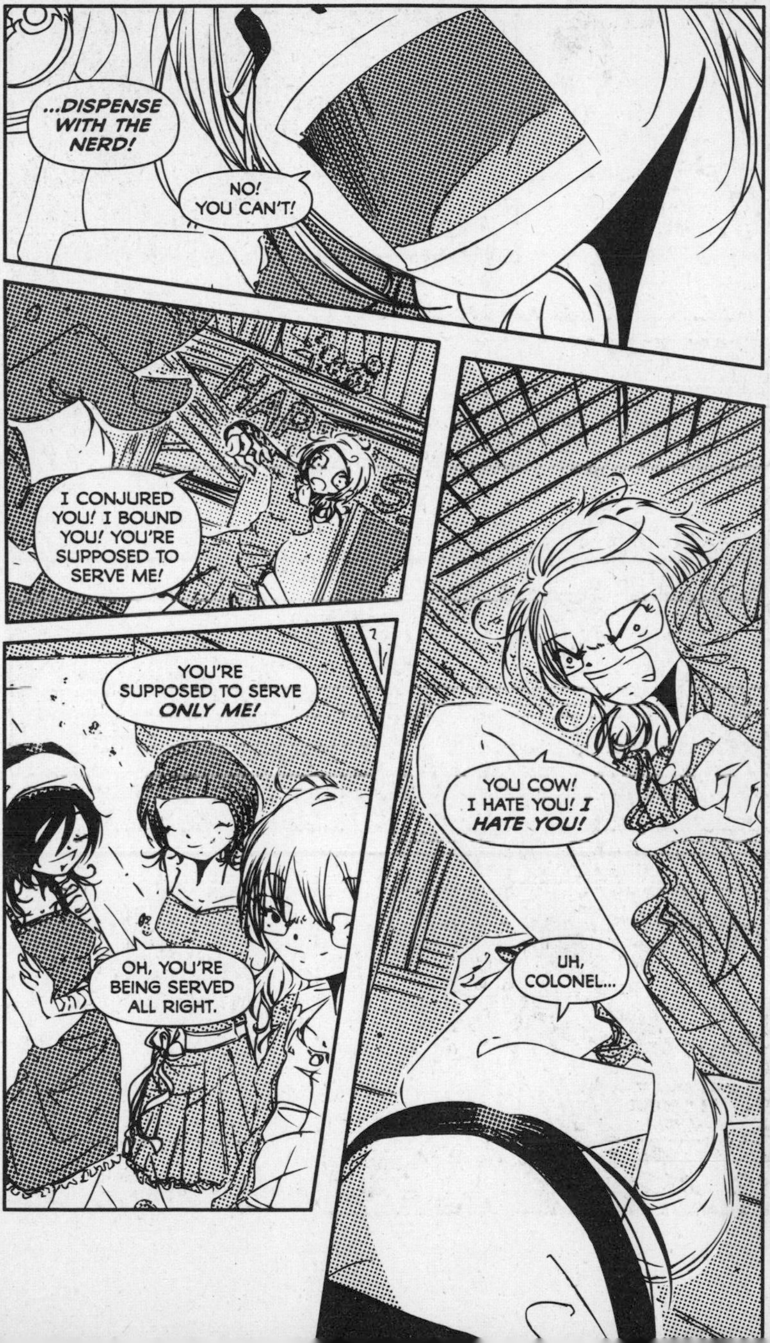
...DISPENSE WITH THE NERD!
NO! YOU CAN'T!
I CONJURED YOU! I BOUND YOU! YOU'RE SUPPOSED TO SERVE ME!
YOU'RE SUPPOSED TO SERVE ONLY ME!
OH, YOU'RE BEING SERVED ALL RIGHT.
YOU COW! I HATE YOU! I HATE YOU!
UH, COLONEL...

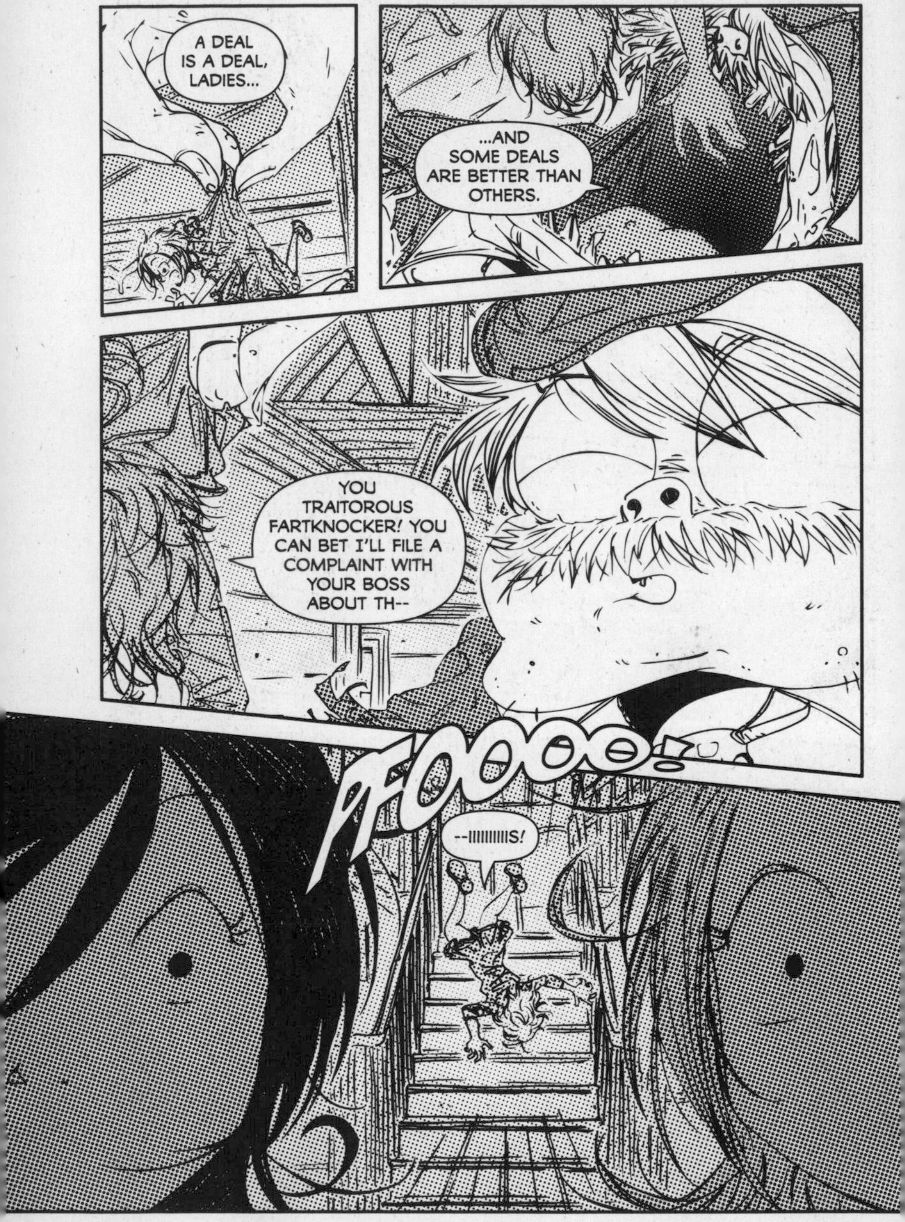
A DEAL IS A DEAL, LADIES...
...AND SOME DEALS ARE BETTER THAN OTHERS.
YOU TRAITOROUS FARTKNOCKER! YOU CAN BET I'LL FILE A COMPLAINT WITH YOUR BOSS ABOUT TH--
FOOOO!
--IIIIIIIIIS!

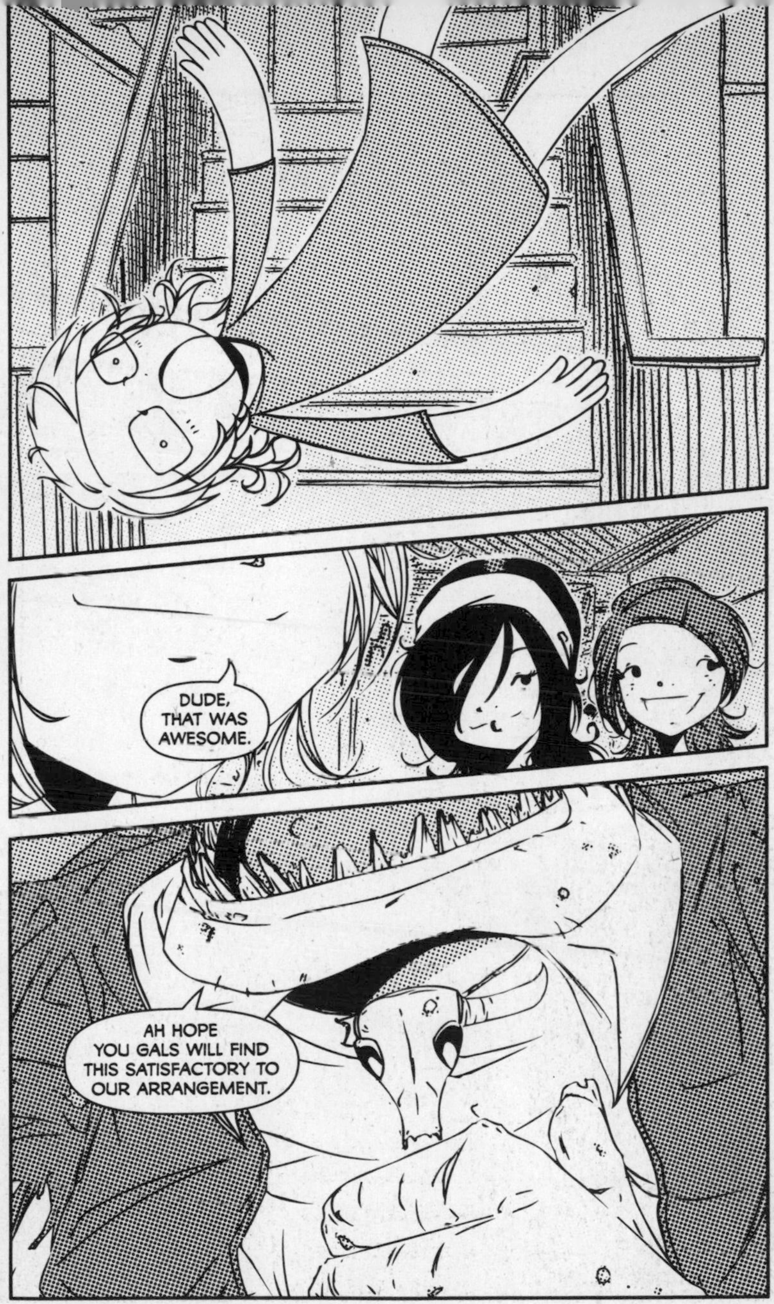

DUDE, THAT WAS AWESOME.
AH HOPE YOU GALS WILL FIND THIS SATISFACTORY TO OUR ARRANGEMENT.

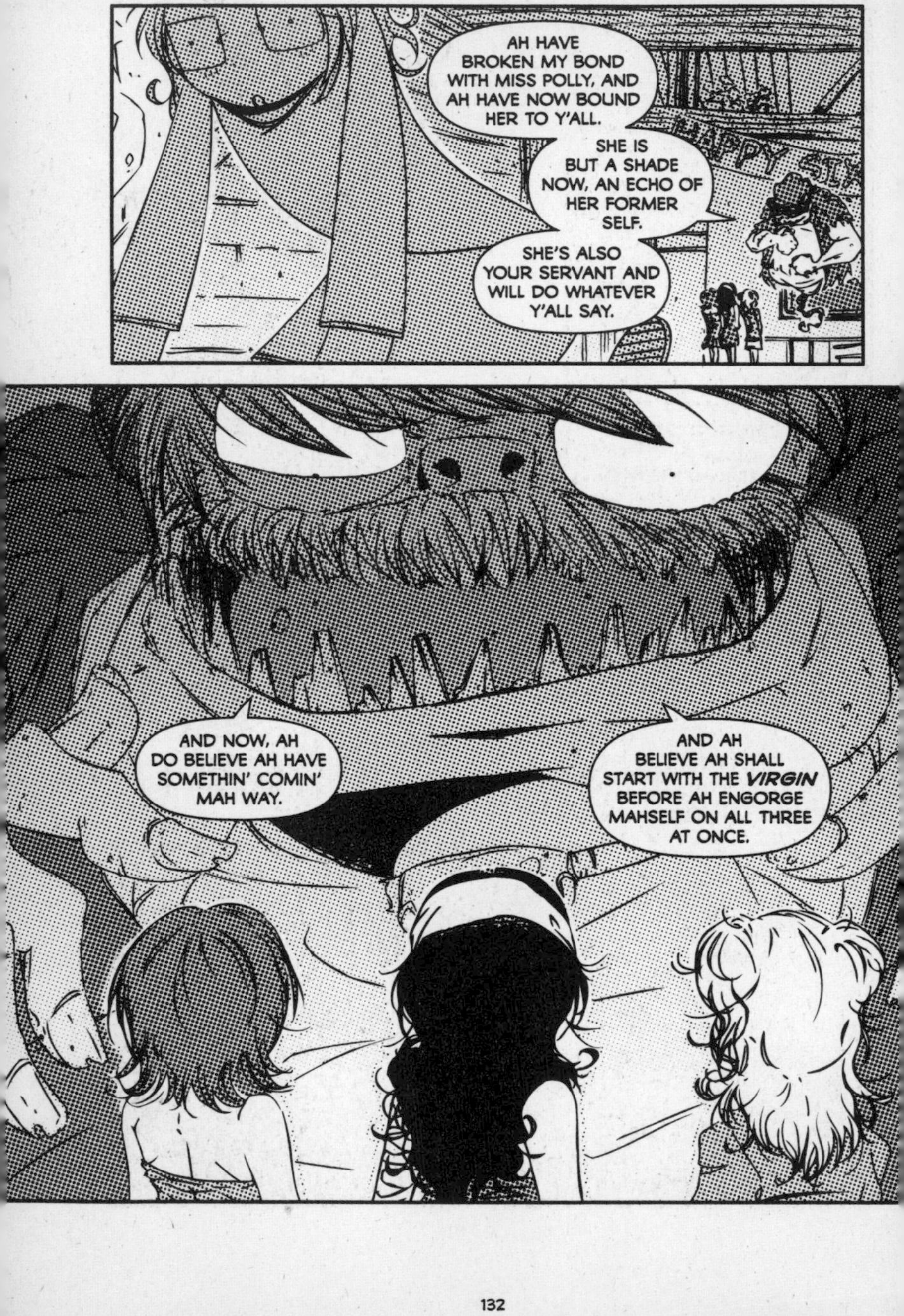
AH HAVE BROKEN MY BOND WITH MISS POLLY, AND AH HAVE NOW BOUND HER TO Y'ALL.
SHE IS BUT A SHADE NOW, AN ECHO OF HER FORMER SELF.
SHE'S ALSO YOUR SERVANT AND WILL DO WHATEVER Y'ALL SAY.
AND NOW, AH DO BELIEVE AH HAVE SOMETHIN' COMIN' MAH WAY.
AND AH BELIEVE AH SHALL START WITH THE *VIRGIN* BEFORE AH ENGORGE MAHSELF ON ALL THREE AT ONCE.

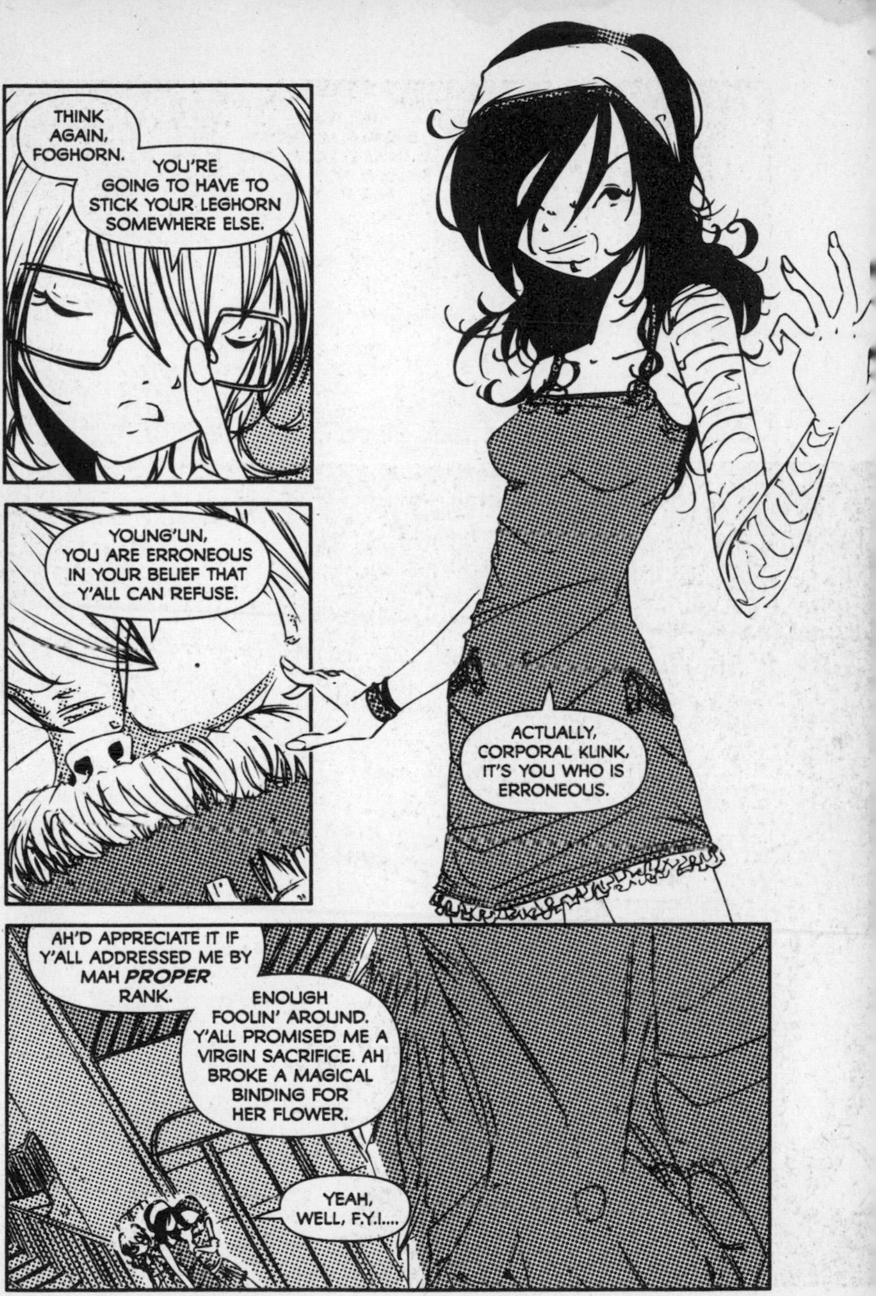
THINK AGAIN, FOGHORN.
YOU'RE GOING TO HAVE TO STICK YOUR LEGHORN SOMEWHERE ELSE.
YOUNG'UN, YOU ARE ERRONEOUS IN YOUR BELIEF THAT Y'ALL CAN REFUSE.
ACTUALLY, CORPORAL KLINK, IT'S YOU WHO IS ERRONEOUS.
AH'D APPRECIATE IT IF Y'ALL ADDRESSED ME BY MAH *PROPER* RANK.
ENOUGH FOOLIN' AROUND. Y'ALL PROMISED ME A VIRGIN SACRIFICE. AH BROKE A MAGICAL BINDING FOR HER FLOWER.
YEAH, WELL, F.Y.I....

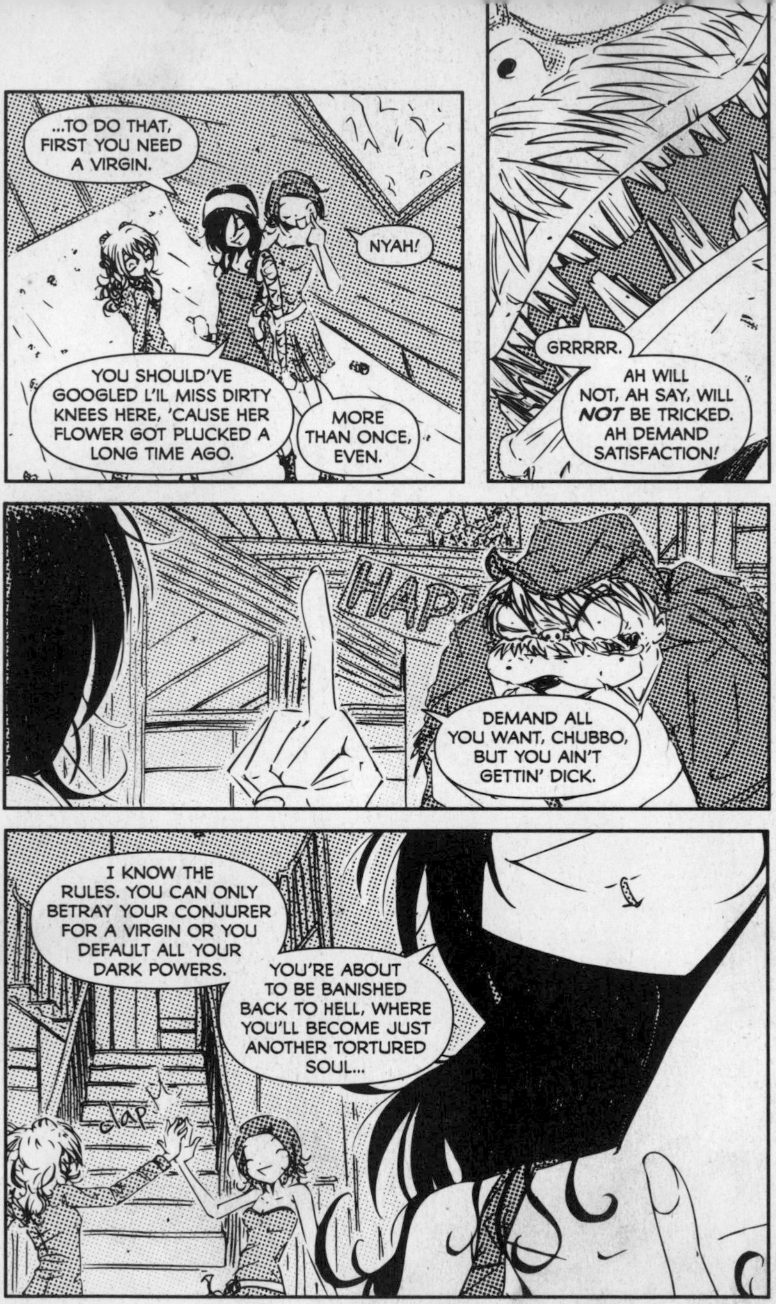
...TO DO THAT, FIRST YOU NEED A VIRGIN.
NYAH!
YOU SHOULD'VE GOOGLED L'IL MISS DIRTY KNEES HERE, 'CAUSE HER FLOWER GOT PLUCKED A LONG TIME AGO.
MORE THAN ONCE, EVEN.
GRRRRR.
AH WILL NOT, AH SAY, WILL NOT BE TRICKED. AH DEMAND SATISFACTION!
HAP
DEMAND ALL YOU WANT, CHUBBO, BUT YOU AIN'T GETTIN' DICK.
I KNOW THE RULES. YOU CAN ONLY BETRAY YOUR CONJURER FOR A VIRGIN OR YOU DEFAULT ALL YOUR DARK POWERS.
YOU'RE ABOUT TO BE BANISHED BACK TO HELL, WHERE YOU'LL BECOME JUST ANOTHER TORTURED SOUL...
clap

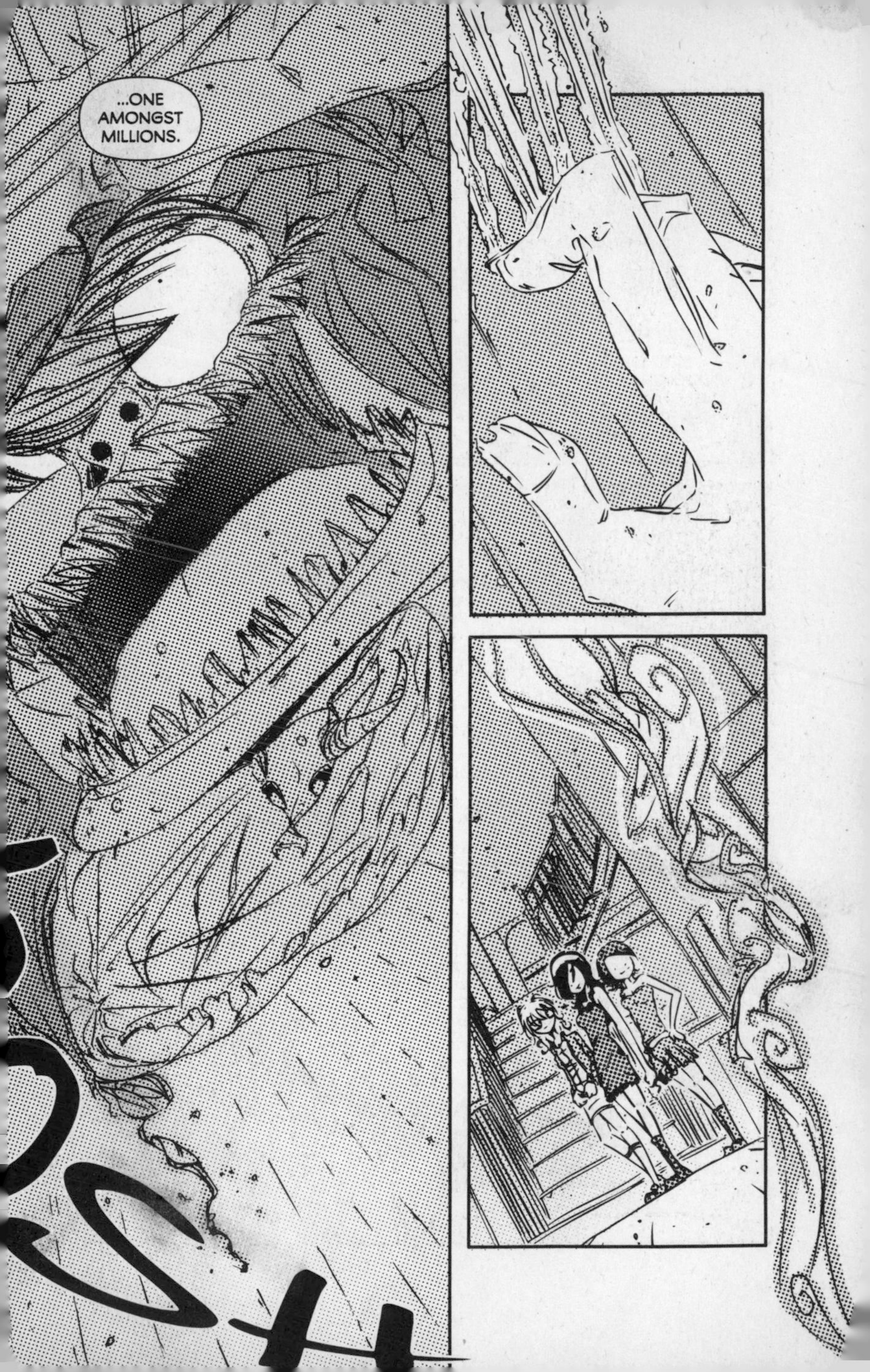
...ONE
AMONGST
MILLIONS.

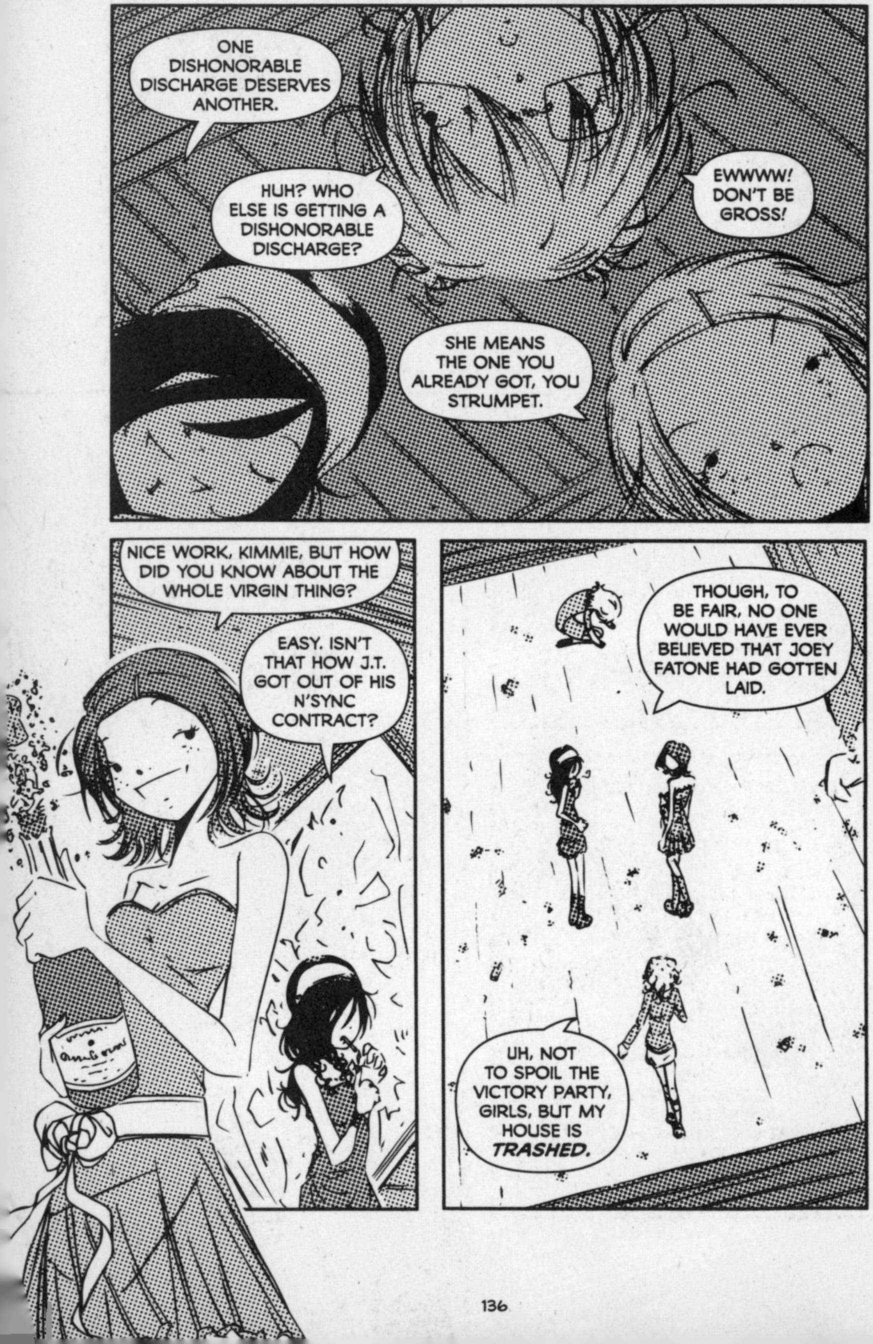
ONE DISHONORABLE DISCHARGE DESERVES ANOTHER.
HUH? WHO ELSE IS GETTING A DISHONORABLE DISCHARGE?
EWWWW! DON'T BE GROSS!
SHE MEANS THE ONE YOU ALREADY GOT, YOU STRUMPET.
NICE WORK, KIMMIE, BUT HOW DID YOU KNOW ABOUT THE WHOLE VIRGIN THING?
EASY. ISN'T THAT HOW J.T. GOT OUT OF HIS N'SYNC CONTRACT?
THOUGH, TO BE FAIR, NO ONE WOULD HAVE EVER BELIEVED THAT JOEY FATONE HAD GOTTEN LAID.
UH, NOT TO SPOIL THE VICTORY PARTY, GIRLS, BUT MY HOUSE IS *TRASHED.*

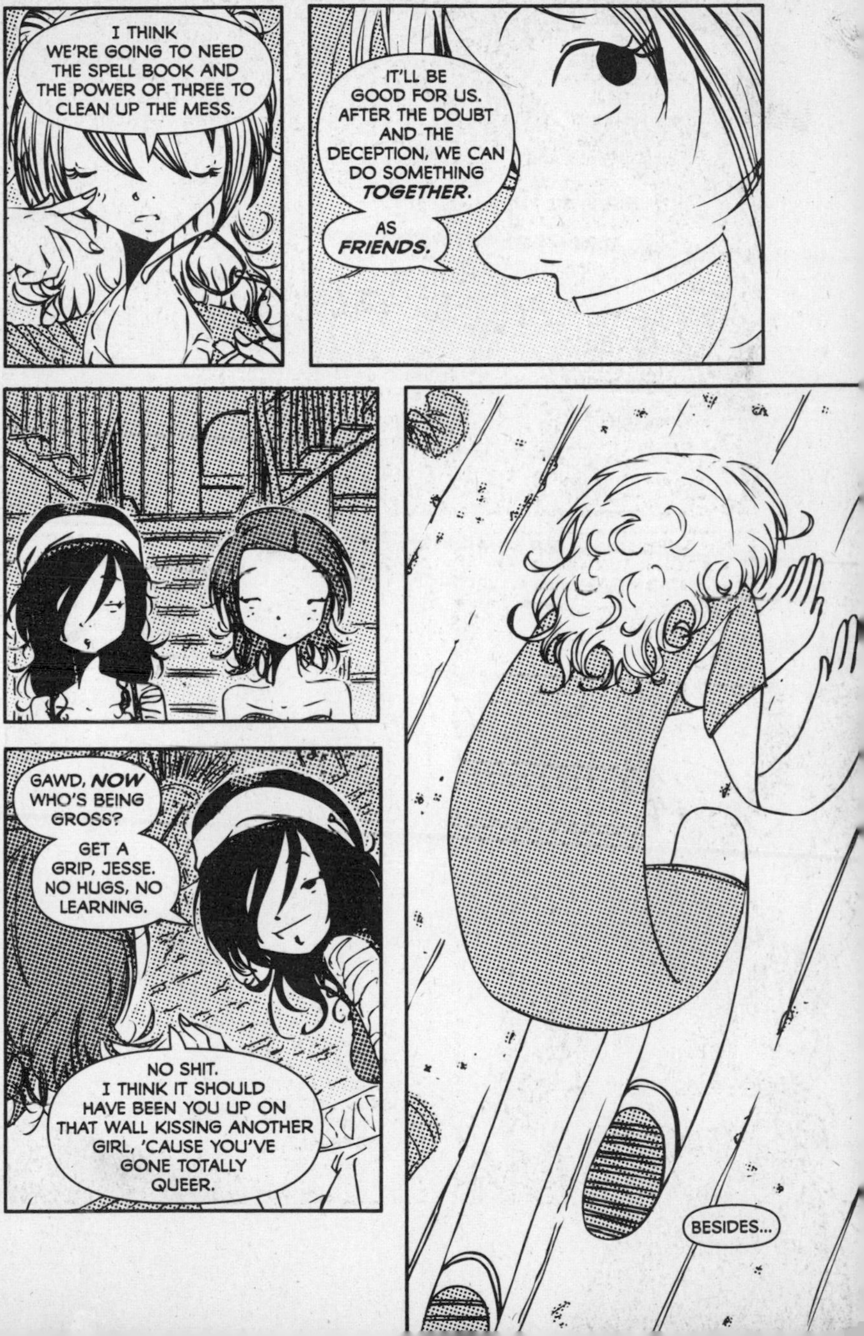

I THINK WE'RE GOING TO NEED THE SPELL BOOK AND THE POWER OF THREE TO CLEAN UP THE MESS.
IT'LL BE GOOD FOR US. AFTER THE DOUBT AND THE DECEPTION, WE CAN DO SOMETHING *TOGETHER*.
AS *FRIENDS.*
GAWD, *NOW* WHO'S BEING GROSS?
GET A GRIP, JESSE. NO HUGS, NO LEARNING.
NO SHIT. I THINK IT SHOULD HAVE BEEN YOU UP ON THAT WALL KISSING ANOTHER GIRL, 'CAUSE YOU'VE GONE TOTALLY QUEER.
BESIDES...

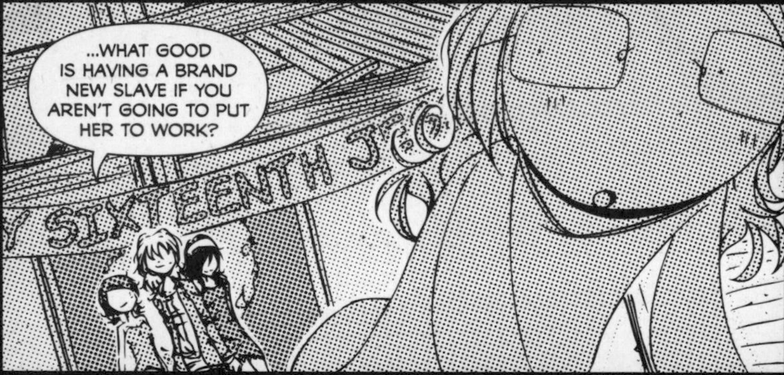
...WHAT GOOD IS HAVING A BRAND NEW SLAVE IF YOU AREN'T GOING TO PUT HER TO WORK?
SIXTEENTH

Chapter 5
"F*&k You Very Much"

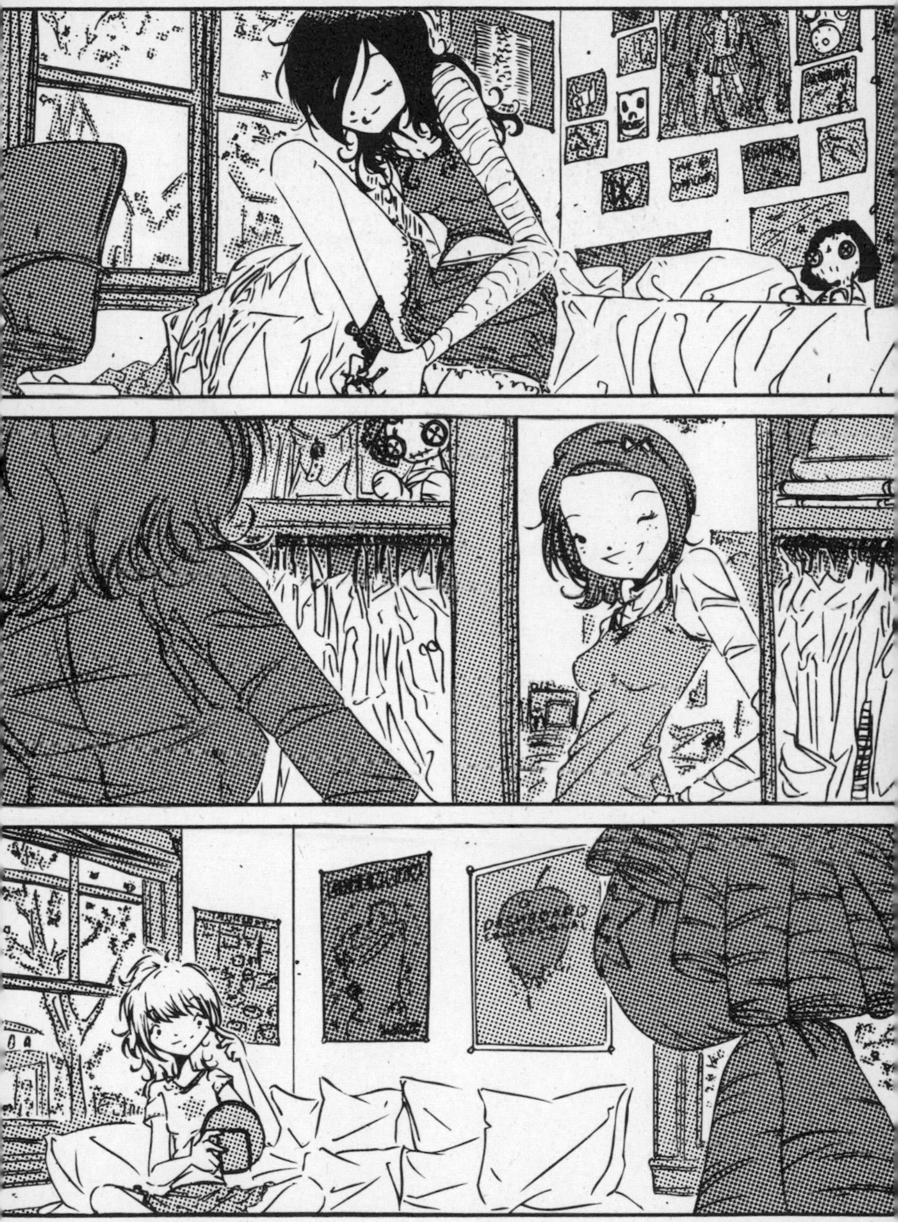

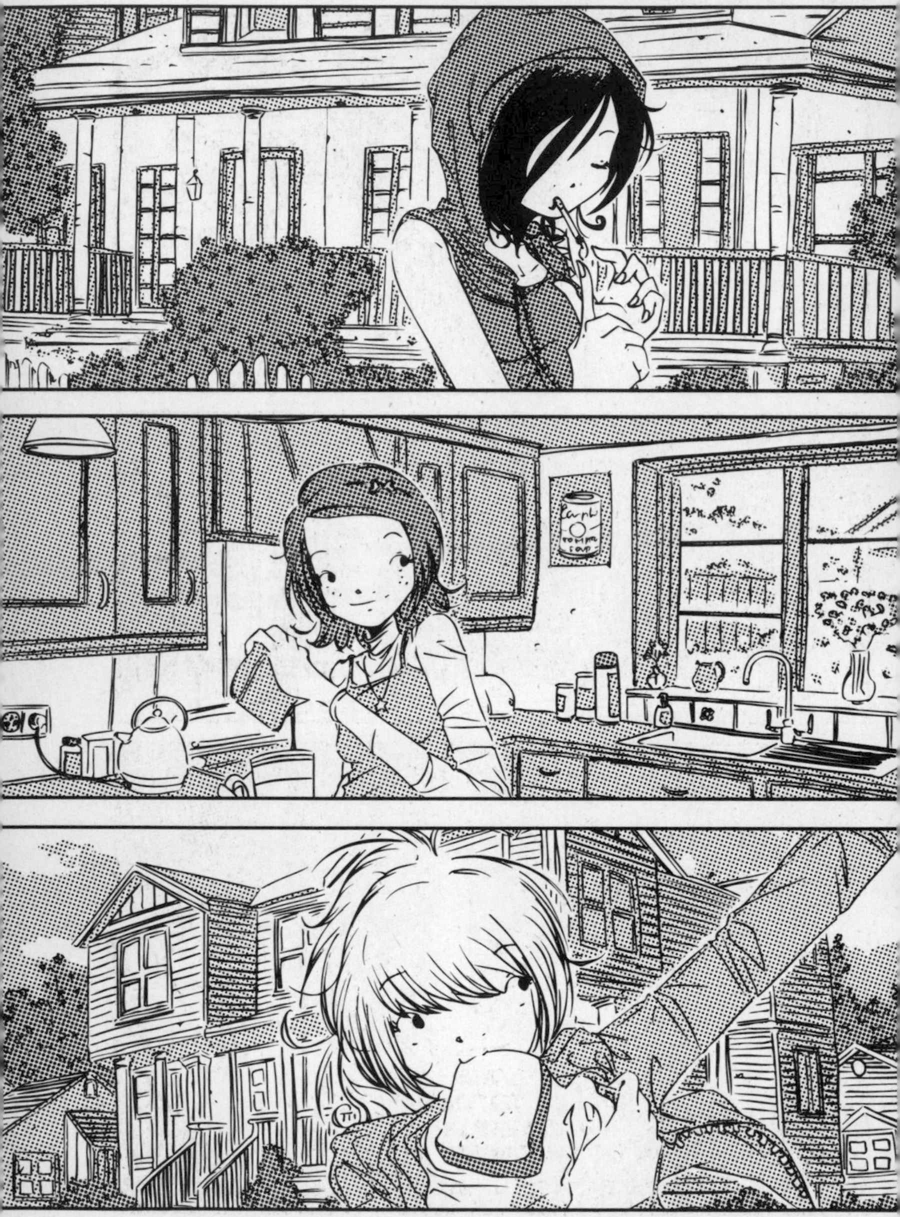

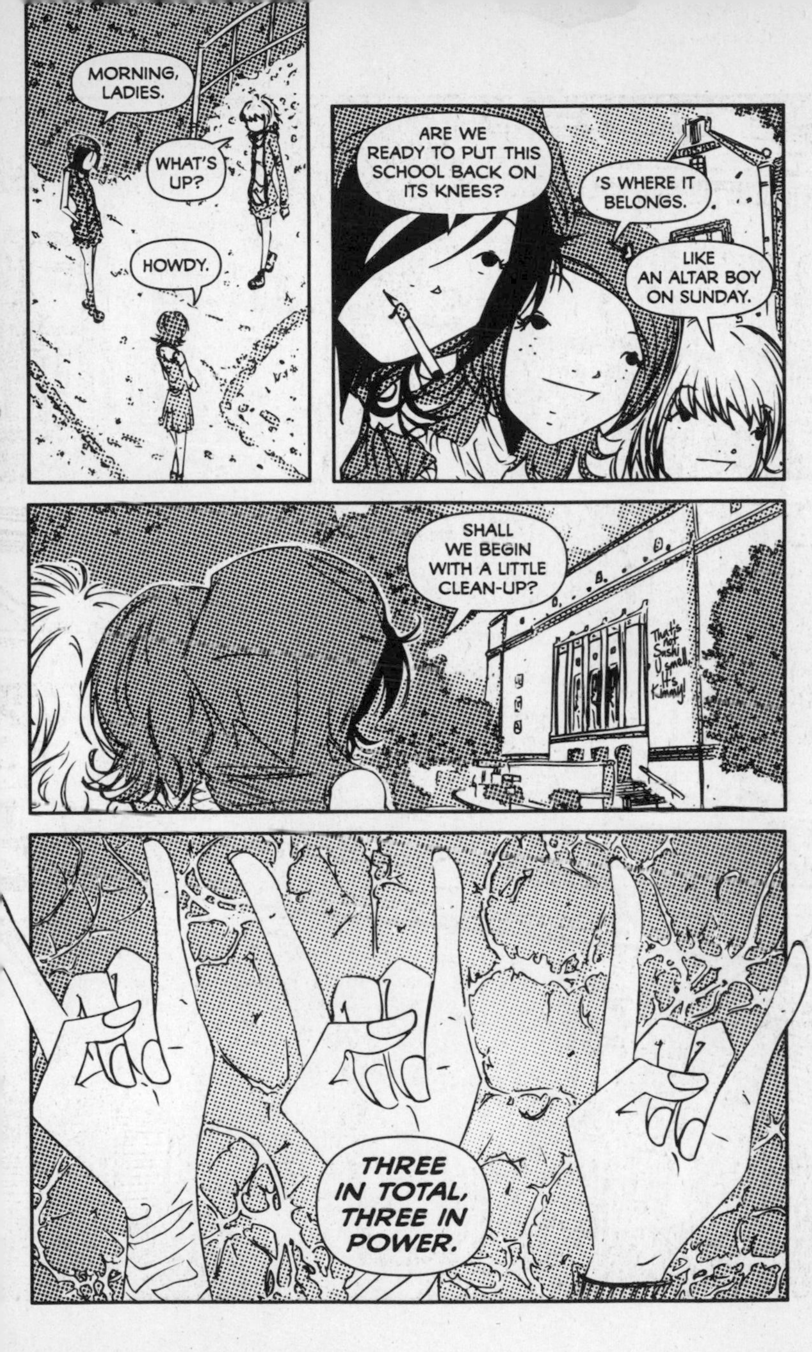
MORNING, LADIES.
WHAT'S UP?
HOWDY.
ARE WE READY TO PUT THIS SCHOOL BACK ON ITS KNEES?
'S WHERE IT BELONGS.
LIKE AN ALTAR BOY ON SUNDAY.
SHALL WE BEGIN WITH A LITTLE CLEAN-UP?
That's not Sushi U smell. It's Kimmy!
THREE IN TOTAL, THREE IN POWER.

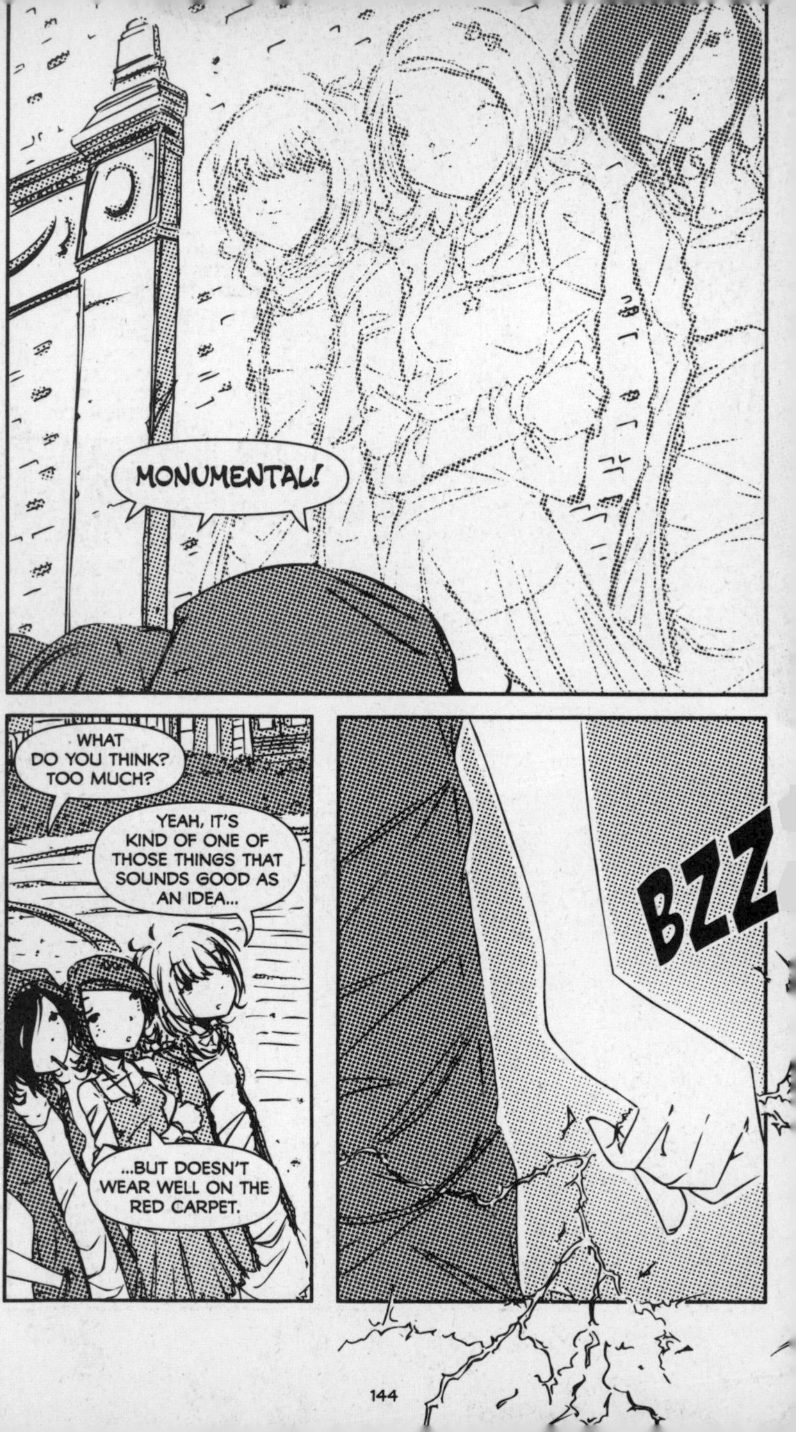
MONUMENTAL!
WHAT DO YOU THINK? TOO MUCH?
YEAH, IT'S KIND OF ONE OF THOSE THINGS THAT SOUNDS GOOD AS AN IDEA...
...BUT DOESN'T WEAR WELL ON THE RED CARPET.
BZZ

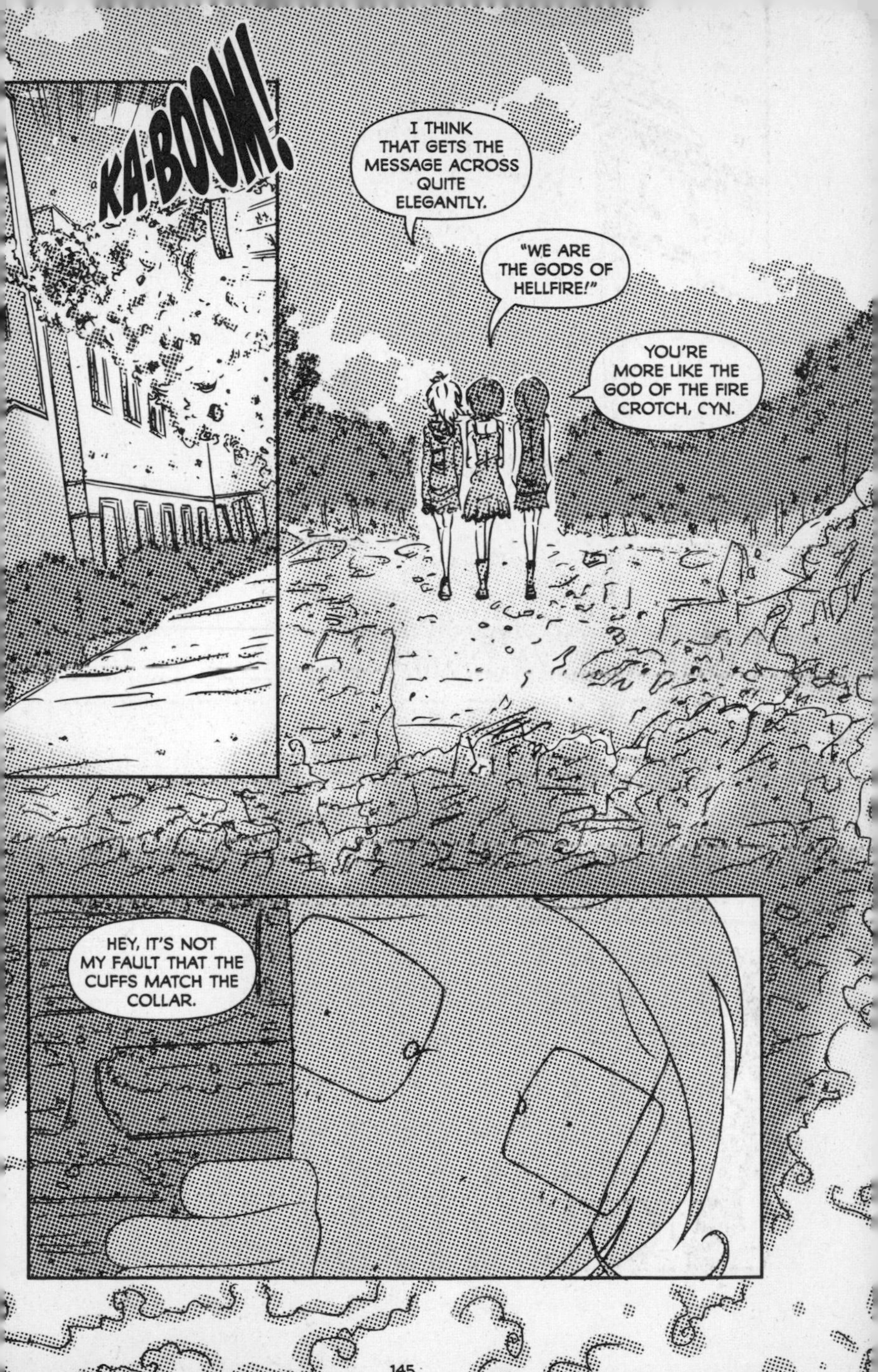
KA-BOOM!
I THINK THAT GETS THE MESSAGE ACROSS QUITE ELEGANTLY.
"WE ARE THE GODS OF HELLFIRE!"
YOU'RE MORE LIKE THE GOD OF THE FIRE CROTCH, CYN.
HEY, IT'S NOT MY FAULT THAT THE CUFFS MATCH THE COLLAR.

ABOUT THE AUTHORS

JAMIE S. RICH is the author of four prose novels, including *Cut My Hair, I Was Someone Dead*, and *The Everlasting*. He wrote the comics series *Love the Way You Love*, which was illustrated by Marc Ellerby. Additionally, he has had short stories in *Four-Letter Worlds*, *Buffy the Vampire Slayer: Food Chain*, *Put the Book Back on the Shelf*, *The Dark Horse Book of the Dead*, and *This is a Souvenir*, teaming him with artists as diverse as Andi Watson, Chynna Clugston, Guy Davis, Natalie Nourigat, and Kelley Seda. He spends a lot of his time watching movies, which he reviews for DVDTalk.com.

Rich first collaborated with JOËLLE JONES on the acclaimed comic book *12 Reasons Why I Love Her*, and they have since shown up as a team in the pages of *Popgun*, *Portland Noir*, and *Madman Atomic Comics*. Joëlle also did the cover and interior illustrations for Jamie's novel *Have You Seen the Horizon Lately?*, and their most recent full-length effort was the acclaimed crime graphic novel, *You Have Killed Me*.

On her own, Jones has contributed to the long-running comics series *Fables* at DC/Vertigo, the Dark Horse anthologies *Noir* and *Sexy Chix*, and she drew the Minx young adult graphic novel *Token*, written by Alisa Kwitney. She has drawn two issues of the Eisner-nominated series *Madame Xanadu*, written by Matt Wagner, and worked with writer Zack Whedon on a comic book spin-off of the popular *Dr. Horrible* web series. She is currently working on a long-form comic for Vertigo called *The Starving Artist*, as well as *Troublemaker*, a collaboration with best-selling author Janet Evanovich that continues the writer's series of *Alexandra Barnaby* novels.

NICOLAS HITORI DE is a comic artist and illustrator living in Amiens, France. Having studied at les ateliers des beaux arts of Paris and Disney Accademia in Milan, he has created works in print (Disney, Milan), publicity, tv (M6, Nolife) and music (Virgin Princesse). After collaborating on Josh Howard's *Dead@17* series, he met Jamie S. Rich on Myspace and has now realized his dream to be published by Oni Press.

www.confessions123.com • www.joellejones.com • nicohitoride.com

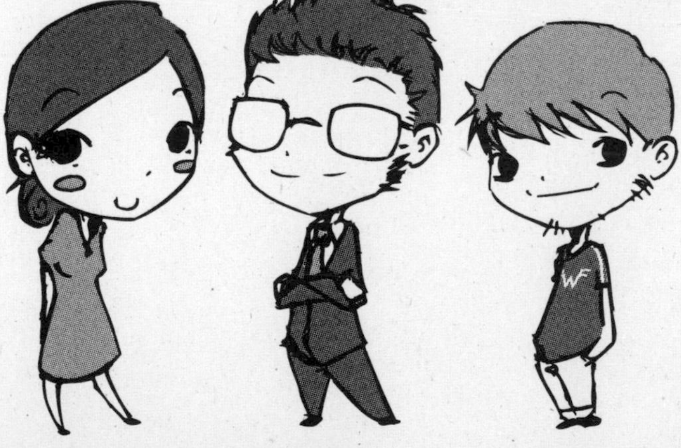

WF

OTHER TITLES FROM JAMIE S. RICH AND JOËLLE JONES

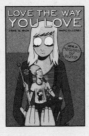

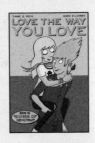

LOVE THE WAY YOU LOVE

JAMIE S. RICH
MARC ELLERBY
LOVE THE WAY YOU LOVE

LOVE THE WAY YOU LOVE: SIDE A
By Jamie S. Rich & Marc Ellerby
200 Pages • Digest • B&W interiors
$11.95 US • ISBN 978-1-932664-66-9

LOVE THE WAY YOU LOVE: SIDE B
By Jamie S. Rich & Marc Ellerby
200 Pages • Digest • B&W interiors
$11.95 US • ISBN 978-1-932664-95-9

Jamie S. Rich
& Joëlle Jones
12 Reasons Why I Love Her

YOU HAVE KILLED ME
JAMIE S. RICH
&
JOËLLE JONES

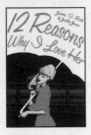

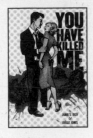

12 REASONS WHY I LOVE HER
By Jamie S. Rich & Joëlle Jones
144 pages • 6"x9" trade paperback • B&W interiors
$14.95 US • ISBN 978-1-932664-51-5

YOU HAVE KILLED ME
By Jamie S. Rich & Joëlle Jones
192 Pages • hardcover • B&W interiors
$19.95 US • ISBN 978-1-932664-88-1

CUT MY HAIR

I WAS SOMEONE DEAD

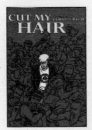

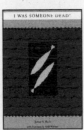

CUT MY HAIR
By Jamie S. Rich
236 pages • 6"x9" trade paperback • Illustrated prose
$15.95 US • ISBN 978-0-9700387-0-8

I WAS SOMEONE DEAD
By Jamie S. Rich with Andi Watson
136 pages • Digest • Illustrated prose
$9.95 US • ISBN 978-1-932664-26-3

The EVERLASTING
A novel by
JAMIE S. RICH

HAVE YOU SEEN THE HORIZON LATELY
JAMIE S. RICH

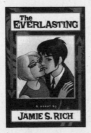

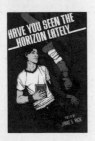

THE EVERLASTING
By Jamie S. Rich
496 pages • 6"x9" trade paperback • Novel
$19.95 US • ISBN 978-932664-54-6

HAVE YOU SEEN THE HORIZON LATELY?
By Jamie S. Rich
380 pages • 6"x9" trade paperback • Novel
$19.95 US • ISBN 978-1-932664-73-7

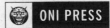

OTHER BOOKS FROM ONI PRESS...

THE BIG BOOK OF
BARRY
WEEN
BOY GENIUS
JUDD WINICK

RICK SPEARS CHUCK BB
BLACK METAL

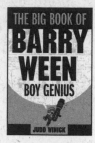

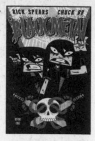

BIG BOOK OF BARRY WEEN,
BOY GENIUS
By Judd Winick
360 Pages • 6"x9" trade paperback • B&W interiors
$19.95 US • ISBN 978-1-934964-03-3

BLACK METAL
By Rick Spears & Chuck BB
160 pages • Digest • B&W interiors
$11.95 US • ISBN 978-1-932664-72-0

blue monday
THE KIDS ARE ALRIGHT

COURTNEY CRUMRIN AND THE NIGHT THINGS

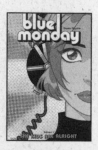

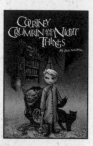

BLUE MONDAY, VOL. 1:
THE KIDS ARE ALRIGHT
By Chynna Clugston
136 pages • Digest • B&W interiors
$11.95 US • ISBN 978-1-929998-62-3

COURTNEY CRUMRIN, VOL. 1:
THE NIGHT THINGS
By Ted Naifeh
128 Pages • Digest • B&W interiors
$11.95 US • ISBN 978-1-929998-60-9

LABOR DAYS

NORTH WORLD

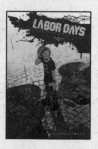

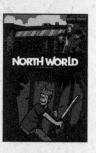

LABOR DAYS, VOL. 1
By Philip Gelatt & Rick Lacy
144 pages, 6"x9" trade paperback • B&W interiors
$11.95 US • ISBN 978-1-932664-92-8

NORTH WORLD , VOL. 1:
THE EPIC OF CONRAD
By Lars Brown
152 pages • Digest • B&W interiors
$11.95 US • ISBN 978-1-932664-91-1

SCOTT PILGRIM'S
PRECIOUS LITTLE LIFE
VOL. 1
BRYAN LEE O'MALLEY

SIDESCROLLERS
MATTHEW LOUX

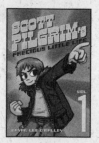

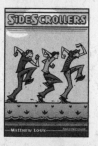

SCOTT PILGRIM, VOL. 1:
SCOTT PILGRIM'S PRECIOUS LITTLE LIFE
By Bryan Lee O'Malley
168 pages • Digest • B&W interiors
$11.99 US • ISBN 978-1-932664-08-9

SIDESCROLLERS
By Matthew Loux
216 pages • Digest • B&W interiors
$11.95 US • ISBN 978-1-932664-50-8

For more information on these and other fine Oni Press comic books and graphic novels, visit www.onipress.com. To find a comic specialty store in your area, call 1-888-COMICBOOK or visit www.comicshops.us.

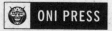

ONI PRESS

www.onipress.com